The title-essay, with its incisive analysis of Christianity, is followed by a major statement of Russell's own beliefs, discussions of immortality, the misery caused by religion, and the danger of looking to it for help.

'He is the most robust, as well as the most witty, infidel since Voltaire and he cannot fail to sharpen men's sense of what is entailed both in belief and in unbelief.'

*The Spectator*

'What makes the book valuable, as everything from Lord Russell's pen must be, is precisely his life-long uncompromising intellectual honesty.'

*Times Literary Supplement*

## BY BERTRAND RUSSELL

# Why I am not
# a Christian

## and other essays on religion and related subjects

BERTRAND RUSSELL

London
**UNWIN PAPERBACKS**
Boston          Sydney

First published in Great Britain by
George Allen & Unwin 1957
Reprinted three times
First published in paperback 1967
Reprinted three times
First published in Unwin Paperbacks 1975
Re-issued 1979
Reprinted 1982, 1983, 1985, 1987

**UNWIN® PAPERBACKS**
**40 Museum Street, London WC1A 1LU, UK**

Unwin Paperbacks,
Park Lane, Hemel Hempstead, Herts, HP2 4TE, UK

Allen & Unwin Inc.,
Fifty Cross Street, Winchester, Mass 01890, USA

George Allen & Unwin Australia Pty Ltd,
8 Napier Street, North Sydney, NSW 2060, Australia

© George Allen & Unwin (Publishers) Ltd 1957, 1967, 1975


ISBN 0 04 200028 9

Printed in Great Britain by
Cox & Wyman Ltd, Reading
Typeset in 9 on 10 point Plantin

## Editor's Introduction

Bertrand Russell has been a prolific writer all his life and some of his best work is contained in little pamphlets and in articles contributed to various periodicals. This is especially true of his discussions of religion, many of which are little known outside certain rationalist circles. In the present volume I have collected a number of these essays on religion as well as some other pieces like the articles on 'Freedom and the Colleges' and 'Our Sexual Ethics' which are still of great topical interest.

Although he is most honoured for his contributions to such purely abstract subjects as logic and the theory of knowledge, it is a fair guess that Russell will be equally remembered in years to come as one of the great heretics in morals and religion. He has never been a purely technical philosopher. He has always been deeply concerned with the fundamental questions to which religions have given their respective answers – questions about man's place in the universe and the nature of the good life. He has brought to his treatment of these questions the same incisiveness, wit and eloquence and he has expressed himself in the same sparkling prose for which his other works are famous. These qualities make the essays included in this book perhaps the most moving and the most graceful presentation of the Freethinker's position since the days of Hume and Voltaire.

A book by Bertrand Russell on religion would be worth publishing at any time. At present, when we are witnessing a campaign for the revival of religion which is carried on with all the slickness of modern advertising techniques, a restatement of the unbeliever's case seems particularly desirable. From every corner and on every level, high, low, and middle-brow, we have for several years been bombarded with theological propaganda. *Life* magazine assures us editorially that 'except for dogmatic materialists and fundamentalists', the war between evolution and Christian belief 'has been over for many years' and that 'science itself . . . discourages the notion that the universe, or life, or man could have evolved by pure chance'. Professor Toynbee, one of the more dignified apologists, tells us that we 'cannot meet the Communist challenge on a secular ground'. Norman Vincent Peale, Monsignor Sheen and other professors of religious psychiatry extol the blessings of faith in columns read by millions, in best-selling books and over nation-wide weekly radio and television programmes. Politicians of all parties, many of whom were not at all noted for piety before they began to compete for public office, make sure that they are known as dutiful churchgoers and never fail to bring God into their learned discourses. Outside the classrooms of the better colleges the negative side to this question is hardly ever presented.

A book such as this, with its uncompromising affirmation of the secularist viewpoint, is all the more called for today because the religious offensive has not been restricted to propaganda on a grand scale. In the United States it has also assumed the shape of numerous attempts, many of them successful, to undermine the separation of Church and State as provided in the Constitution. These attempts are too many to be detailed here; but perhaps two or three illustrations will sufficiently indicate this disturbing trend which if it remains unchecked will make those who are opposed to traditional religion into second-class citizens. A few months ago, for instance, a sub-committee of the House of Representatives included in a Concurrent Resolution the amazing proposition that 'loyalty to God' is an essential qualification for the best government service. 'Service of *any* person in *any* capacity in or under the government,' the legislators officially asserted, 'should be characterised by devotion to God.' This resolution is not yet law but may soon become so if it is not vigorously opposed. Another resolution making 'In God We Trust' the national motto of the United States has been passed by both Houses and is now the law of the land. Professor George Axtelle, of New York University, one of the few outspoken critics of these and similar moves, appropriately referred to them, in testimony before a Senate committee, as 'tiny but significant erosions' of the principle of church-state separation.

The attempts to inject religion, where the Constitution expressly prohibits it, are by no means confined to Federal legislation. Thus in New York City, to take just one particularly glaring example, the Board of Superintendents of the Board of Education prepared in 1955 a 'Guiding Statement for Supervisors and Teachers' which bluntly stated that 'the public schools encouraged the belief in God, recognising the simple fact that ours is a religious nation', and furthermore that the public schools 'identify God as the ultimate source of natural and moral law'. If this statement had been adopted hardly a subject in the New York City school curriculum would have remained free from theological intrusion. Even such apparently secular studies as science and mathematics were to be taught with religious overtones. 'Scientists and mathematicians,' the statement declared, 'conceive of the universe as a logical, orderly, predictable place. Their consideration of the vastness and the splendour of the heavens, the marvels of the human body and mind, the beauty of nature, the mystery of photosynthesis, the mathematical structure of the universe or the notion of infinity cannot do other than lead to humbleness before God's handiwork. One can only say "When I consider the Heavens the work of Thy Hands".' So innocent a subject as 'Industrial Arts' was not left alone. 'In industrial arts,' the philosophers of the Board of Superintendents asserted, 'the observation of the wonders of the composition of metals, the grain and the beauty of woods, the ways of electricity and the characteristic properties of the materials used invariably gives rise to speculation about the planning and the orderliness of the natural world and the marvellous working of a Supreme Power.' This report was greeted with such an outburst of indignation from civic and several of the more liberal religious groups that adoption of it by the Board of Education became impossible. A modified version, with the most objectionable passages struck out, was subsequently adopted. Even the revised version, however, contains enough theological language to make a secularist wince, and it is to be hoped that its constitutionality will be challenged in the courts.

There has been amazingly little opposition to most of the encroachments of ecclesiastical interests. One reason for this seems to be the widespread belief that religion is nowadays mild and tolerant and that persecutions are a thing of the past. This is a dangerous illusion. While many religious leaders are undoubtedly genuine friends of freedom and toleration and are furthermore confirmed believers in the separation of Church and State, there are unfortunately many others who would still persecute if they could and who do persecute when they can.

In Great Britain the situation is somewhat different. There are established churches and religious instruction is legally sanctioned in all state schools. Nevertheless, the temper of the country is much more tolerant and men in public life have less hesitation to be openly known as unbelievers. In Great Britain, too, however, vulgar pro-religious propaganda is rampant and the more aggressive religious groups are doing their best to prevent Freethinkers from stating their case. The recent Beveridge Report for instance, recommended that the B.B.C. should give a hearing to representatives of Rationalist opinion. The B.B.C. officially accepted this recommendation but has done next to nothing to implement it. The talks by Margaret Knight on 'Morals without Religion' were one of the very few attempts to present the position of unbelievers on an important topic. Mrs Knight's talks provoked furious outbursts of indignation on the part of assorted bigots which appear to have frightened the B.B.C. into its former subservience to religious interests.

To help dispel complacency on this subject I have added, as an appendix to this book, a very full account of how Bertrand Russell was prevented from becoming Professor of Philosophy at the College of the City of New York. The facts of this case deserve to be more widely known, if only to show the incredible distortions and abuses of power which fanatics are willing to employ when they are out to vanquish an enemy. Those people who succeeded in nullifying Russell's appointment are the same who now would destroy the secular character of the United States. They and their British counterparts are on the whole more powerful today than they were in 1940.

The City College case should be written up in detail also in simple fairness to Bertrand Russell himself, who was viciously maligned at the time both by the judge who heard the petition and in large sections of the press. Russell's views and actions were the subject of unbridled misrepresentation and people unfamiliar with his books must have received a completely erroneous impression of what he stood for. I hope that the story as here recounted, together with the reproduction of some of Russell's actual discussions of the 'offending' topics, will help to set the record straight.

Several of the essays included in this volume are reprinted with the kind permission of their original publishers. In this connection I should like to thank Messrs Watts and Co. who are the publishers of *Why I am not a Christian* and *Has Religion Made Useful Contributions to Civilisation?*, Messrs Routledge and Kegan Paul who published *What I Believe*, Messrs Hutchinson and Co. who published *Do we Survive Death?*, Messrs Nicholson and Watson who are the original publishers of *The Fate of Thomas Paine*, and the *American Mercury* in whose pages 'Our Sexual Ethics' and 'Freedom and the Colleges' first appeared. I also wish to thank my friends Professor Antony Flew, Ruth Hoffman, Sheila Meyer, and my students Marilyn Charney, Sara Kilian, and John Viscide, who helped me in many ways in the preparation of this book.

Finally, I wish to express my gratitude to Bertrand Russell himself who blessed this project from the beginning and whose keen interest all the way was a major source of inspiration.

*New York City, October* 1956                    PAUL EDWARDS

# Preface

Professor Edwards's republication of various essays of mine concerned with theological subjects is a cause of gratitude to me, especially in view of his admirable prefatory observations. I am particularly glad that this opportunity has occurred for reaffirming my convictions on the subjects with which the various essays deal.

There has been a rumour in recent years to the effect that I have become less opposed to religious orthodoxy than I formerly was. This rumour is totally without foundation. I think all the great religions of the world – Buddhism, Hinduism, Christianity, Islam, and Communism – both untrue and harmful. It is evident as a matter of logic that, since they disagree, not more than one of them can be true. With very few exceptions, the religion which a man accepts is that of the community in which he lives, which makes it obvious that the influence of environment is what has led him to accept the religion in question. It is true that Scholastics invented what professed to be logical arguments proving the existence of God, and that these arguments, or others of a similar tenor, have been accepted by many eminent philosophers, but the logic to which these traditional arguments appealed is of an antiquated Aristotelian sort which is now rejected by practically all logicians except such as are Catholics. There is one of these arguments which is not purely logical. I mean the argument from design. This argument, however, was destroyed by Darwin; and, in any case could only be made logically respectable at the cost of abandoning God's omnipotence. Apart from logical cogency, there is to me something a little odd about the ethical valuations of those who think that an omnipotent, omniscient, and benevolent Deity, after preparing the ground by many millions of years of lifeless nebulae, would consider Himself adequately rewarded by the final emergence of Hitler and Stalin and the H-bomb.

The question of the truth of a religion is one thing, but the question of its usefulness is another. I am as firmly convinced that religions do harm as I am that they are untrue.

The harm that is done by a religion is of two sorts, the one depending on the kind of belief which it is thought ought to be given to it, and the other upon the particular tenets believed. As regards the kind of belief: it is thought virtuous to have faith – that is to say, to have a conviction which cannot be shaken by contrary evidence. Or, if contrary evidence might induce doubt, it is held that contrary evidence must be suppressed. On such grounds the young are not allowed to hear arguments, in Russia, in favour of Capitalism, or, in America, in favour of Communism. This keeps the faith of both intact and ready for internecine war. The conviction that it is important to believe this or that, even if a free inquiry would not support the belief, is one which is common to almost all religions and which inspires all systems of State education. The consequence is that the minds of the young are stunted and are filled with fanatical hostility both to those who have other fanaticisms, and, even more virulently, to those who object to all fanaticisms. A habit of basing convictions upon evidence, and of giving to them only that degree of certainty which the evidence warrants, would, if it became general, cure most of the ills from which the world is suffering. But at present, in most countries, education aims at preventing the growth of such a habit, and men who refuse to profess belief in some system of unfounded dogmas are not considered suitable as teachers of the young.

The above evils are independent of the particular creed in question and exist equally in all creeds which are held dogmatically. But there are also, in most religions, specific ethical tenets which do definite harm. The Catholic condemnation of birth-control, if it could prevail, would make the mitigation of poverty and the abolition of war impossible. The Hindu beliefs that the cow is a sacred animal and that it is wicked for widows to remarry cause quite needless suffering. The Communist belief in the dictatorship of a minority of True Believers has produced a whole crop of abominations.

We are sometimes told that only fanaticism can make a social group effective. I think this is totally contrary to the lessons of history. But, in any case, only those who slavishly worship success can think that effectiveness is admirable without regard to what is effected. For my part, I think it better to do a little good than to do much harm. The world that I should wish to see would be one freed from the virulence of group hostilities and capable of realising that happiness for all is to be derived rather from co-operation than from strife. I should wish to see a world in which education aimed at mental freedom rather than at imprisoning the minds of the young in a rigid armour of dogma calculated to protect them through life against the shafts of impartial evidence. The world needs open hearts and open minds, and it is not through rigid systems, whether old or new, that these can be derived.

BERTRAND RUSSELL

# Contents

## Chapter 1

# Why I am not a Christian

*This lecture was delivered on March 6, 1927, at Battersea Town Hall, under the auspices of the South London Branch of the National Secular Society.*

As your Chairman has told you, the subject about which I am going to speak to you tonight is 'Why I am not a Christian'. Perhaps it would be as well, first of all, to try to make out what one means by the word 'Christian'. It is used these days in a very loose sense by a great many people. Some people mean no more by it than a person who attempts to live a good life. In that sense I suppose there would be Christians in all sects and creeds; but I do not think that that is the proper sense of the world, if only because it would imply that all the people who are not Christians – all the Buddhists, Confucians, Mohammedans, and so on – are not trying to live a good life. I do not mean by a Christian any person who tries to live decently according to his lights. I think that you must have a certain amount of definite belief before you have a right to call yourself a Christian. The word does not have quite such a full-blooded meaning now as it had in the times of St Augustine and St Thomas Aquinas. In those days, if a man said that he was a Christian it was known what he meant. You accepted a whole collection of creeds which were set out with great precision, and every single syllable of those creeds you believed with the whole strength of your convictions.

## WHAT IS A CHRISTIAN?

Nowadays it is not quite that. We have to be a little more vague in our meaning of Christianity. I think, however, that there are two different items which are quite essential to anybody calling himself a Christian. The first is one of a dogmatic nature – namely, that you must believe in God and immortality. If you do not believe in those two things, I do not think that you can properly call yourself a Christian. Then, further than that, as the name implies, you must have some kind of belief about Christ. The Mohammedans, for instance, also believe in God and in immortality, and yet they would not call themselves Christians. I think you must have at the very lowest the belief that Christ was, if not divine, at least the best and wisest of men. If you are not going to believe that much about Christ, I do not think you have any right to call yourself a Christian. Of course there is another sense which you find in *Whitaker's Almanack* and in geography books, where the population of the world is said to be divided into Christians, Mohammedans, Buddhists, fetish worshippers, and so on; and in that sense we are all Christians. The geography books count us all in, but that is a purely geographical sense, which I suppose we can ignore. Therefore I take it that when I tell you why I am not a Christian I have to tell you two different things; first, why I do not believe in God and in immortality; and, secondly, why I do not think that Christ was the best and wisest of men, although I grant Him a very high degree of moral goodness.

But for the successful efforts of unbelievers in the past, I could not take so elastic a definition of Christianity as that. As I said before, in olden days it had a much more full-blooded sense. For instance, it concluded the belief in hell. Belief in eternal hell fire was an essential item of Christian belief until pretty recent times. In this country, as you know, it ceased to be an essential item because of a decision of the Privy Council, and from that decision the Archbishop of Canterbury and the Archbishop of York dissented; but in this country our religion is settled by Act of Parliament, and therefore the Privy Council was able to override Their Graces and hell was no longer necessary to a Christian. Consequently I shall not insist that a Christian must believe in hell.

### THE EXISTENCE OF GOD

To come to this question of the existence of God, it is a large and serious question, and if I were to attempt to deal with it in any adequate manner I should have to keep you here until Kingdom Come, so that you will have to excuse me if I deal with it in a somewhat summary fashion. You know, of course, that the Catholic Church has laid it down as a dogma that the existence of God can be proved by the unaided reason. That is a somewhat curious dogma, but it is one of their dogmas. They had to introduce it because at one time the Freethinkers adopted the habit of saying that there were such and such arguments which mere reason might urge against the existence of God, but of course they knew as a matter of faith that God did exist. The arguments and the reasons were set out at great length, and the Catholic Church felt that they must stop it. Therefore they laid it down that the existence of God can be proved by the unaided reason, and they had to set up what they considered were arguments to prove it. There are, of course, a number of them, but I shall take only a few.

### THE FIRST CAUSE ARGUMENT

Perhaps the simplest and easiest to understand is the argument of the First Cause. (It is maintained that everything we see in this world has a cause, and as you go back in the chain of causes further and further you must come to a First Cause, and to that First Cause you give the name of God). That argument, I suppose, does not carry very much weight nowadays, because, in the first place, cause is not quite what it used to be. The philosophers and the men of science have got going on cause, and it has not anything like the vitality it used to have; but, apart from that, you can see that the argument that there must be a First Cause is one that cannot have any validity. I may say that when I was a young man and was debating these questions very seriously in my mind, I for a long time accepted the argument of the First Cause, until one day, at the age of eighteen, I read John Stuart Mill's Autobiography, and I there found this sentence: 'My father taught me that the question, "Who made me?" cannot be answered, since it immediately suggests the further question, "Who made God?"' That very simple sentence showed me, as I still think, the fallacy in the argument of the First Cause. If everything must have a cause, then God must have a cause. If there can be anything without a cause, it may just as well be the world as God, so that there cannot be any validity in that argument. It is exactly of the same nature as the Hindu's view, that the world rested upon an elephant and the elephant rested upon a tortoise; and when they said, 'How about the tortoise?' the Indian said, 'Suppose we change the subject.' The argument is really no better than that. There is no reason why the world could not have come into being without a cause; nor, on the other hand, is there any reason why it should not have always existed. There is no reason to suppose that the world had a beginning at all. The idea that things must have a beginning is really due to the poverty of our imagination. Therefore, perhaps, I need not waste any more time upon the argument about the First Cause.

### THE NATURAL LAW ARGUMENT

Then there is a very common argument from natural law. That was a favourite argument all through the eighteenth century, especially under the influence of Sir Isaac Newton and his cosmogony. People observed the planets going round the sun according to the law of gravitation, and they thought that God had given a behest to these planets to move in that particular fashion, and that was why they did so. That was, of course, a convenient and simple explanation that saved them the trouble of looking any further for explanations of the law of gravitation. Nowadays we explain the law of gravitation in a somewhat complicated fashion that Einstein has introduced. I do not propose to give you a lecture on the law of gravitation as interpreted by Einstein, because that again would take some time; at any rate, you no longer have the sort of natural law that you had in the Newtonian system, where, for some reason that nobody could understand, nature behaved in a uniform fashion. We now find that a great many things we thought were natural laws are really human conventions. You know that even in the remotest depths of stellar space there are still three feet to a yard. That is, no doubt, a very remarkable fact, but you would hardly call it a law of nature. And a great many things that have been regarded as laws of nature are of that kind. On the other hand, where you can get down to any knowledge of what atoms actually do, you will find they are much less subject to law than people thought, and that the laws at which you arrive are statistical averages of just the sort that would emerge from chance. There is, as we all know, a law that if you throw dice you will get double sixes only about once in thirty-six times, and we do not regard that as evidence that the fall of the dice is regulated by design; on the contrary, if the double sixes came every time we should think that there was design. The laws of nature are of that sort as regards a great many of them. They are statistical averages such as would emerge from the laws of chance; and that makes this whole business of natural law much less impressive than it formerly was. Quite apart from that, which represents the momentary state of science that may change tomorrow, the whole idea that natural laws imply a law-giver is due to a confusion between natural and human laws. Human laws are behests commanding you to behave a certain way, in which way you may choose to behave, or you may choose not to behave; but natural laws are a description of how things do in fact behave, and being a mere description of what they in fact do, you cannot argue that there must be somebody who told them to do that, because even supposing that there were you are then faced with the question, 'Why did God issue just those natural laws and no others?' If you say that He did it simply from His own good pleasure, and without any reason, you then find that there is something which is not subject to law, and so your train of natural law is interrupted. If you say, as more orthodox theologians do, that in all the laws which God issues He had a reason for giving those laws rather than others – the reason, of course, being to create the best universe, although you would never think it to look at it – if there was a reason for the laws which God gave, then God Himself was subject to law, and therefore you do not get any advantage by introducing God as an intermediary. You have really a law outside and anterior to the divine edicts, and God does not serve your purpose, because He is not the ultimate law-giver. In short, this whole argument about natural law no longer has anything like the strength that it used to have. I am travelling on in time in my review of the arguments. The arguments that are used for the existence of God change their character as time goes on. They were at first hard, intellectual arguments embodying certain quite definite fallacies. As we come to modern times they become less respectable intellectually and more and more affected by a kind of moralising vagueness.

### THE ARGUMENT FROM DESIGN

The next step in this process brings us to the argument from design. You all know the argument from design: everything in the world is made just so that we can manage to live in the world, and if the world was ever so little different we could not manage to live in it. That is the argument from design. It sometimes takes a rather curious form; for instance, it is argued that rabbits have white tails in order to be easy to shoot. I do not know how rabbits would view that application. It is an easy argument to parody. You all know Voltaire's remark, that obviously the nose was designed to be such as to fit spectacles. That sort of parody has turned out to be not nearly so wide of the mark as it might have seemed in the eighteenth century, because since the time of Darwin we understand much better why living creatures are adapted to their environment. It is not that their environment was made to be suitable to them, but that they grew to be suitable to it, and that is the basis of adaptation. There is no evidence of design about it.

When you come to look into this argument from design, it is a most astonishing thing that people can believe that this world, with all the things that are in it, with all its defects, should be the best that omnipotence and omniscience has been able to produce in millions of years. I really cannot believe it. Do you think that, if you were granted omnipotence and omniscience and millions of years in which to perfect your world, you could produce nothing better than the Ku-Klux-Klan or the Fascists? Moreover, if you accept the ordinary laws of science, you have to suppose that human life and life in general on this planet will die out in due course: it is a stage in the decay of the solar system; at a certain stage of decay you get the sort of conditions of temperature and so forth which are suitable to protoplasm, and there is life for a short time in the life of the whole solar system. You see in the moon the sort of thing to which the earth is tending – something dead, cold, and lifeless.

I am told that that sort of view is depressing, and people will sometimes tell you that if they believed that they would not be able to go on living. Do not believe it; it is all nonsense. Nobody really worries much about what is going to happen millions of years hence. Even if they think they are worrying much about that, they are really deceiving themselves. They are worried about something much more mundane, or it may merely be a bad digestion; but nobody is really seriously rendered unhappy by the thought of something that is going to happen to this world millions of years hence. Therefore, although it is of course a gloomy view to suppose that life will die out – at least I suppose we may say so, although sometimes when I contemplate the things that people do with their lives I think it is almost a consolation – it is not such as to render life miserable. It merely makes you turn your attention to other things.

THE MORAL ARGUMENTS FOR DEITY

Now we reach one stage further in what I shall call the intellectual descent that the Theists have made in their argumentations, and we come to what are called the moral arguments for the existence of God. You all know, of course, that there used to be in the old days three intellectual arguments for the existence of God, all of which were disposed of by Immanuel Kant in the *Critique of Pure Reason*; but no sooner had he disposed of those arguments than he invented a new one, a moral argument, and that quite convinced him. He was like many people: in intellectual matters he was sceptical, but in moral matters he believed implicitly in the maxims that he had imbibed at his mother's knee. That illustrates what the psycho-analysts so much emphasise – the immensely stronger hold upon us that our very early associations have than those of later times.

Kant, as I say, invented a new moral argument for the existence of God, and that in varying forms was extremely popular during the nineteenth century. It has all sorts of forms. One form is to say that there would be no right or wrong unless God existed. I am not for the moment concerned with whether there is a difference between right and wrong, or whether there is not: that is another question. The point I am concerned with is that, if you are quite sure there is a difference between right and wrong, you are then in this situation: is that difference due to God's fiat or is it not? If it is due to God's fiat, then for God Himself there is no difference between right and wrong, and it is no longer a significant statement to say that God is good. If you are going to say, as theologians do, that God is good, you must then say that right and wrong have some meaning which is independent of God's fiat, because God's fiats are good and not bad independently of the mere fact that He made them. If you are going to say that, you will then have to say that it is not only through God that right and wrong came into being, but that they are in their essence logically anterior to God. You could, of course, if you liked, say that there was a superior deity who gave orders to the God who made this world, or could take up the line that some of the gnostics took up – a line which I often thought was a very plausible one – that as a matter of fact this world that we know was made by the devil at a moment when God was not looking. There is a good deal to be said for that, and I am not concerned to refute it.

### THE ARGUMENT FOR THE REMEDYING OF INJUSTICE

Then there is another very curious form of moral argument, which is this: they say that the existence of God is required in order to bring justice into the world. In the part of this universe that we know there is great injustice, and often the good suffer, and often the wicked prosper, and one hardly knows which of those is the more annoying; but if you are going to have justice in the universe as a whole you have to suppose a future life to redress the balance of life here on earth. So they say that there must be a God, and there must be heaven and hell in order that in the long run there may be justice. That is a very curious argument. If you looked at the matter from a scientific point of view, you would say: 'After all, I know only this world. I do not know about the rest of the universe, but so far as one can argue at all on probabilities one would say that probably this world is a fair sample, and if there is injustice here the odds are that there is injustice elsewhere also.' Supposing you got a crate of oranges that you opened, and you found all the top layer of oranges bad, you would not argue: 'The underneath ones must be good, so as to redress the balance.' You would say: 'Probably the whole lot is a bad consignment'; and that is really what a scientific person would argue about the universe. He would say: 'Here we find in this world a great deal of injustice and so far as that goes that is a reason for supposing that justice does not rule in the world; and therefore so far as it goes it affords a moral argument against deity and not in favour of one.' Of course I know that the sort of intellectual arguments that I have been talking to you about are not what really moves people. What really moves people to believe in God is not any intellectual argument at all. Most people believe in God because they have been taught from early infancy to do it, and that is the main reason.

Then I think that the next most powerful reason is the wish for safety, a sort of feeling that there is a big brother who will look after you. That plays a very profound part in influencing people's desire for a belief in God.

### THE CHARACTER OF CHRIST

I now want to say a few words upon a topic which I often think is not quite sufficiently dealt with by Rationalists, and that is the question whether Christ was the best and the wisest of men. It is generally taken for granted that we shall all agree that that was so. I do not myself. I think that there are a good many points upon which I agree with Christ a great deal more than the professing Christians do. I do not know that I could go with Him all the way, but I could go with Him much farther than most professing Christians can. You will remember that He said: 'Resist not evil, but whosoever shall smite thee on thy right cheek, turn to him the other also.' That is not a new precept or a new principle. It was used by Lao-Tze and Buddha some five or six hundred years before Christ, but it is not a principle which as a matter of fact Christians accept. I have no doubt that the present Prime Minister,[1] for instance, is a most sincere Christian, but I should not advise any of you to go and smite him on one cheek. I think you might find that he thought this text was intended in a figurative sense.

[1] Stanley Baldwin.

Then there is another point which I consider is excellent. You will remember that Christ said: 'Judge not lest ye be judged.' That principle I do not think you would find was popular in the law courts of Christian countries. I have known in my time quite a number of judges who were very earnest Christians, and they none of them felt that they were acting contrary to Christian principles in what they did. Then Christ says: 'Give to him that asketh thee, and from him that would borrow of thee turn not thou away.' That is a very good principle.

Your Chairman has reminded you that we are not here to talk politics, but I cannot help observing that the last general election was fought on the question of how desirable it was to turn away from him that would borrow of thee, so that one must assume that the Liberals and Conservatives of this country are composed of people who do not agree with the teaching of Christ, because they certainly did very emphatically turn away on that occasion.

Then there is one other maxim of Christ which I think has a great deal in it, but I do not find that it is very popular among some of our Christian friends. He says: 'If thou wilt be perfect, go and sell that thou hast, and give to the poor.' That is a very excellent maxim, but, as I say, it is not much practised. All these, I think, are good maxims, although they are a little difficult to live up to. I do not profess to live up to them myself; but then after all, it is not quite the same thing as for a Christian.

#### DEFECTS IN CHRIST'S TEACHING

Having granted the excellence of these maxims, I come to certain points in which I do not believe that one can grant either the superlative wisdom or the superlative goodness of Christ as depicted in the Gospels; and here I may say that one is not concerned with the historical question. Historically it is quite doubtful whether Christ ever existed at all, and if He did we do not know anything about Him, so that I am not concerned with the historical question, which is a very difficult one. I am concerned with Christ as He appears in the Gospels, taking the Gospel narrative as it stands, and there one does find some things that do not seem to be very wise. For one thing, He certainly thought that His second coming would occur in clouds of glory before the death of all the people who were living at that time. There are a great many texts that prove that. He says, for instance: 'Ye shall not have gone over the cities of Israel, till the Son of Man be come.' Then He says: 'There are some standing here which shall not taste death till the Son of Man comes into His kingdom'; and there are a lot of places where it is quite clear that He believed that His second coming would happen during the lifetime of many then living. That was the belief of His earlier followers, and it was the basis of a good deal of His moral teaching. When He said, 'Take no thought for the morrow,' and things of that sort, it was very largely because He thought that the second coming was going to be very soon, and that all ordinary mundane affairs did not count. I have, as a matter of fact, known some Christians who did believe that the second coming was imminent. I knew a parson who frightened his congregation terribly by telling them that the second coming was very imminent indeed, but they were much consoled when they found that he was planting trees in his garden. The early Christians did really believe it, and they did abstain from such things as planting trees in their gardens, because they did accept from Christ the belief that the second coming was imminent. In that respect clearly He was not so wise as some other people have been, and he was certainly not superlatively wise.

THE MORAL PROBLEM

Then you come to moral questions. There is one very serious defect to my mind in Christ's moral character, and that is that He believed in hell. I do not myself feel that any person who is really profoundly humane can believe in everlasting punishment. Christ certainly as depicted in the Gospels did believe in everlasting punishment, and one does find repeatedly a vindictive fury against those people who would not listen to His preaching – an attitude which is not uncommon with preachers, but which does somewhat detract from superlative excellence. You do not, for instance, find that attitude in Socrates. You find him quite bland and urbane towards the people who would not listen to him; and it is, to my mind, far more worthy of a sage to take that line than to take the line of indignation. You probably all remember the sort of things that Socrates was saying when he was dying, and the sort of things that he generally did say to people who did not agree with him.

You will find that in the Gospels Christ said: 'Ye serpents, ye generation of vipers, how can ye escape the damnation of hell?' That was said to people who did not like His preaching. It is not really to my mind quite the best tone, and there are a great many of these things about hell. There is, of course, the familiar text about the sin against the Holy Ghost: 'Whosoever speaketh against the Holy Ghost it shall not be forgiven him neither in this world nor in the world to come.' That text has caused an unspeakable amount of misery in the world, for all sorts of people have imagined that they have committed the sin against the Holy Ghost, and thought that it would not be forgiven them either in this world or in the world to come. I really do not think that a person with a proper degree of kindliness in his nature would have put fears and terrors of that sort into the world.

Then Christ says: 'The Son of Man shall send forth His angels, and they shall gather out of His kingdom all things that offend, and them which do iniquity, and shall cast them into a furnace of fire; there shall be wailing and gnashing of teeth'; and He goes on about the wailing and gnashing of teeth. It comes in one verse after another, and it is quite manifest to the reader that there is a certain pleasure in contemplating wailing and gnashing of teeth, or else it would not occur so often. Then you all, of course, remember about the sheep and the goats; how at the second coming to divide the sheep and the goats He is going to say to the goats: 'Depart from me, ye cursed, into everlasting fire.' He continues: 'And these shall go away into everlasting fire.' Then He says again: 'If thy hand offend thee, cut it off; it is better for thee to enter into life maimed, than having two hands to go into hell, into the fire that never shall be quenched; where the worm dieth not and the fire is not quenched.' He repeats that again and again also. I must say that I think all this doctrine, that hell-fire is a punishment for sin, is a doctrine of cruelty. It is a doctrine that put cruelty into the world and gave the world generations of cruel torture; and the Christ of the Gospels, if you could take Him as His chroniclers represent Him, would certainly have to be considered partly responsible for that.

There are other things of less importance. There is the instance of the Gadarene swine where it certainly was not very kind to the pigs to put the devils into them and make them rush down the hill to the sea. You must remember that He was omnipotent, and He could have made the devils simply go away; but He chooses to send them into the pigs. Then there is the curious story of the fig-tree, which always rather puzzled me. You remember what happened about the fig-tree. 'He was hungry; and seeing a fig-tree afar off having leaves, He came if haply He might find anything thereon; and when He came to it He found nothing but leaves, for the time of figs was not yet. And Jesus answered and said unto it: "No man eat fruit of thee hereafter for ever," ... and Peter ... saith unto Him: "Master, behold the fig-tree which thou cursedst is withered away".' This is a very curious story, because it was not the right time of year for figs, and you really could not blame the tree. I cannot myself feel that either in the matter of wisdom or in the matter of virtue Christ stands quite as high as some other people known to history. I think I should put Buddha and Socrates above Him in those respects.

### THE EMOTIONAL FACTOR

As I said before, I do not think that the real reason why people accept religion has anything to do with argumentation. They accept religion on emotional grounds. One is often told that it is a very wrong thing to attack religion, because religion makes men virtuous. So I am told; I have not noticed it. You know, of course, the parody of that argument in Samuel Butler's book, *Erewhon Revisited*. You will remember that in *Erewhon* there is a certain Higgs who arrives in a remote country, and after spending some time there he escapes from that country in a balloon. Twenty years later he comes back to that country and finds a new religion, in which he is worshipped under the name of the 'Sun Child', and it is said that he ascended into Heaven. He finds that the Feast of the Ascension is about to be celebrated, and he hears Professors Hanky and Panky say to each other that they never set eyes on the man Higgs, and they hope they never will; but they are the high priests of the religion of the Sun Child. He is very indignant, and he comes up to them, and he says: 'I am going to expose all this humbug and tell the people of Erewhon that it was only I, the man Higgs, and I went up in a balloon.' He was told: 'You must not do that, because all the morals of this country are bound round this myth, and if they once know that you did not ascend into heaven they will all become wicked'; and so he is persuaded of that and he goes quietly away.

That is the idea – that we should all be wicked if we did not hold to the Christian religion. It seems to me that the people who have held to it have been for the most part extremely wicked. You find this curious fact, that the more intense has been the religion of any period and the more profound has been the dogmatic belief, the greater has been the cruelty and the worse has been the state of affairs. In the so-called ages of faith, when men really did believe the Christian religion in all its completeness, there was the Inquisition, with its tortures; there were millions of unfortunate women burnt as witches; and there was every kind of cruelty practised upon all sorts of people in the name of religion.

You find as you look around the world that every single bit of progress in humane feeling, every improvement in the criminal law, every step towards the diminution of war, every step towards better treatment of the coloured races, or every mitigation of slavery, every moral progress that there has been in the world, has been consistently opposed by the organised Churches of the world. I say quite deliberately that the Christian religion, as organised in its Churches, has been and still is the principal enemy of moral progress in the world.

### HOW THE CHURCHES HAVE RETARDED PROGRESS

You may think that I am going too far when I say that that is still so. I do not think that I am. Take one fact. You will bear with me if I mention it. It is not a pleasant fact, but the Churches compel one to mention facts that are not pleasant. Supposing that in this world that we live in today an inexperienced girl is married to a syphilitic man, in that case the Catholic Church says: 'This is an indissoluble sacrament. You must stay together for life.' And no steps of any sort must be taken by that woman to prevent herself from giving birth to syphilitic children. That is what the Catholic Church says. I say that that is fiendish cruelty, and nobody whose natural sympathies have not been warped by dogma, or whose moral nature was not absolutely dead to all sense of suffering, could maintain that it is right and proper that that state of things should continue.

That is only an example. There are a great many ways in which at the present moment the Church, by its insistence upon what it chooses to call morality, inflicts upon all sorts of people undeserved and unnecessary suffering. And of course, as we know, it is in its major part an opponent still of· progress and of improvement in all the ways that diminish suffering in the world, because it has chosen to label as morality a certain narrow set of rules of conduct which have nothing to do with human happiness; and when you say that this or that ought to be done because it would make for human happiness, they think that has nothing to do with the matter at all. 'What has human happiness to do with morals? The object of morals is not to make people happy.'

### FEAR THE FOUNDATION OF RELIGION

Religion is based, I think, primarily and mainly upon fear. It is partly the terror of the unknown, and partly, as I have said, the wish to feel that you have a kind of elder brother who will stand by you in all your troubles and disputes. Fear is the basis of the whole thing – fear of the mysterious, fear of defeat, fear of death. Fear is the parent of cruelty, and therefore it is no wonder if cruelty and religion have gone hand-in-hand. It is because fear is at the basis of those two things. In this world we can now begin a little to understand things, and a little to master them by help of science, which has forced its way step by step against the Christian religion, against the Churches, and against the opposition of all the old precepts. Science can help us to get over this craven fear in which mankind has lived for so many generations. Science can teach us, and I think our own hearts can teach us, no longer to look round for imaginary supports, no longer to invent allies in the sky, but rather to look to our own efforts here below to make this world a fit place to live in, instead of the sort of place that the churches in all these centuries have made it.

### WHAT WE MUST DO

We want to stand upon our own feet and look fair and square at the world – its good facts, its bad facts, its beauties, and its ugliness; see the world as it is, and be not afraid of it. Conquer the world by intelligence, and not merely by being slavishly subdued by the terror that comes from it. The whole conception of God is a conception derived from the ancient Oriental despotisms. It is a conception quite unworthy of free men. When you hear people in church debasing themselves and saying that they are miserable sinners, and all the rest of it, it seems contemptible and not worthy of self-respecting human beings. We ought to stand up and look the world frankly in the face. We ought to make the best we can of the world, and if it is not so good as we wish, after all it will still be better than what these others have made of it in all these ages. A good world needs knowledge, kindliness, and courage; it does not need a regretful hankering after the past, or a fettering of the free intelligence by the words uttered long ago by ignorant men. It needs a fearless outlook and a free intelligence. It needs hope for the future, not looking back all the time towards a past that is dead, which we trust will be far surpassed by the future that our intelligence can create.

*Chapter 2*

# Has Religion Made Useful Contributions to Civilisation?[1]

My own view on religion is that of Lucretius. I regard it as a disease born of fear and as a source of untold misery to the human race. I cannot, however, deny that it has made some contributions to civilisation. It helped in early days to fix the calendar, and it caused Egyptian priests to chronicle eclipses with such care that in time they became able to predict them. These two services I am prepared to acknowledge, but I do not know of any others.

The word 'religion' is used nowadays in a very loose sense. Some people, under the influence of extreme Protestantism, employ the word to denote any serious personal convictions as to morals or the nature of the universe. This use of the word is quite unhistorical. Religion is primarily a social phenomenon. Churches may owe their origin to teachers with strong individual convictions, but these teachers have seldom had much influence upon the Churches that they founded, whereas Churches have had enormous influence upon the communities in which they flourished. To take the case that is of most interest to members of Western civilisation: the teaching of Christ, as it appears in the Gospels, has had extraordinarily little to do with the ethics of Christians. The most important thing about Christianity, from a social and historical point of view, is not Christ but the Church, and if we are to judge of Christianity as a social force we must not go to the Gospels for our material. Christ taught that you should give your goods to the poor, that you should not fight, that you should not go to church, and that you should not punish adultery. Neither Catholics nor Protestants have shown any strong desire to follow His teaching in any

[1] First published in 1930.

of these respects. Some of the Franciscans, it is true, attempted to teach the doctrine of apostolic poverty, but the Pope condemned them, and their doctrine was declared heretical. Or, again, consider such a text as 'Judge not that ye be not judged,' and ask yourself what influence such a text has had upon the Inquisition and the Ku-Klux-Klan.

What is true of Christianity is equally true of Buddhism. The Buddha was amiable and enlightened; on his death-bed he laughed at his disciples for supposing that he was immortal. But the Buddhist priesthood – as it exists, for example, in Tibet – has been obscurantist, tyrannous, and cruel in the highest degree.

There is nothing accidental about this difference between a Church and its Founder. As soon as absolute truth is supposed to be contained in the sayings of a certain man, there is a body of experts to interpret his sayings, and these experts infallibly acquire power, since they hold the key to truth. Like any other privileged caste, they use their power for their own advantage. They are, however, in one respect worse than any other privileged caste, since it is their business to expound an unchanging truth, revealed once for all in utter perfection, so that they become necessarily opponents of all intellectual and moral progress. The Church opposed Galileo and Darwin; in our own day it opposes Freud. In the days of its greatest power it went further in its opposition to the intellectual life. Pope Gregory the Great wrote to a certain bishop a letter beginning: 'A report has reached us which we cannot mention without a blush, that thou expoundest grammar to certain friends.' The bishop was compelled by pontifical authority to desist from this wicked labour, and Latinity did not recover until the Renaissance. It is not only intellectually, but also morally, that religion is pernicious. I mean by this that it teaches ethical codes which are not conducive to human happiness. When, a few years ago, a plebiscite was taken in Germany as to whether the deposed royal houses should still be allowed to enjoy their private property, the Churches in Germany officially stated that it would be contrary to the teaching of Christianity to deprive them of it. The Churches, as everyone knows, opposed the abolition of slavery as long as they dared, and with a few well-advertised exceptions they oppose at the present day every movement towards economic justice. The Pope has officially condemned Socialism.

### CHRISTIANITY AND SEX

The worst feature of the Christian religion, however, is its attitude towards sex – an attitude so morbid and so unnatural that it can be understood only when taken in relation to the sickness of the civilised world at the time when the Roman Empire was decaying. We sometimes hear talk to the effect that Christianity improved the status of women. This is one of the grossest perversions of history that it is possible to make. Women cannot enjoy a tolerable position in society where it is considered of the utmost importance that they should not infringe a very rigid moral code. Monks have always regarded Woman primarily as the temptress; they have thought of her mainly as the inspirer of impure lusts. The teaching of the Church has been, and still is, that virginity is best, but that for those who find this impossible marriage is permissible. 'It is better to marry than to burn,' as St Paul brutally puts it. By making marriage indissoluble, and by stamping out all knowledge of the *ars amandi*, the Church did what it could to secure that the only form of sex which it permitted should involve very little pleasure and a great deal of pain. The opposition to birth control has, in fact, the same motive: if a woman has a child a year until she dies worn out, it is not to be supposed that she will derive much pleasure from her married life; therefore birth control must be discouraged.

The conception of Sin which is bound up with Christian ethics is one that does an extraordinary amount of harm, since it affords people an outlet for their sadism which they believe to be legitimate, and even noble. Take, for example, the question of the prevention of syphilis. It is known that, by precautions taken in advance, the danger of contracting this disease can be made negligible. Christians, however, object to the dissemination of knowledge of this fact, since they hold it good that sinners should be punished. They hold this so good that they are even willing that punishment should extend to the wives and children of sinners. There are in the world at the present moment many thousands of children suffering from congenital syphilis who would never have been born but for the desire of Christians to see sinners punished. I cannot understand how doctrines leading to this fiendish cruelty can be considered to have any good effect upon morals.

It is not only in regard to sexual behaviour, but also in regard to knowledge on sex subjects, that the attitude of Christians is dangerous to human welfare. Every person who has taken the trouble to study the question in an unbiased spirit knows that the artificial ignorance on sex subjects which orthodox Christians attempt to enforce upon the young is extremely dangerous to mental and physical health, and causes in those who pick up their knowledge by the way of 'improper' talk, as most children do, an attitude that sex is in itself indecent and ridiculous. I do not think there can be any defence for the view that knowledge is ever undesirable. I should not put barriers in the way of the acquisition of knowledge by anybody at any age. But in the particular case of sex knowledge there are much weightier arguments in its favour than in the case of most other knowledge. A person is much less likely to act wisely when he is ignorant than when he is instructed, and it is ridiculous to give young people a sense of sin because they have a natural curiosity about an important matter.

Every boy is interested in trains. Suppose we told him that an interest in trains is wicked; suppose we kept his eyes bandaged whenever he is in a train or on a railway station; suppose we never allowed the word 'train' to be mentioned in his presence and preserved an impenetrable mystery as to the means by which he is transported from one place to another. The result would not be that he would cease to be interested in trains; on the contrary, he would become more interested than ever, but would have a morbid sense of sin, because this interest had been represented to him as improper. Every boy of active intelligence could by this means be rendered in a greater or less degree neurasthenic. This is precisely what is done in the matter of sex; but, as sex is more interesting than trains, the results are worse. Almost every adult in a Christian community is more or less diseased nervously as a result of the taboo on sex knowledge when he or she was young. And the sense of sin which is thus artificially implanted is one of the causes of cruelty, timidity, and stupidity in later life. There is no rational ground of any sort or kind for keeping a child ignorant of anything that he may wish to know, whether on sex or on any other matter. And we shall never get a sane population until this fact is recognised in early education, which is impossible so long as the Churches are able to control educational politics.

Leaving these comparatively detailed objections on one side, it is clear that the fundamental doctrines of Christianity demand a great deal of ethical perversion before they can be accepted. The world, we are told, was created by a God who is both good and omnipotent. Before He created the world He foresaw all the pain and misery that it would contain; He is therefore responsible for all of it. It is useless to argue that the pain in the world is due to sin. In the first place, this is not true; it is not sin that causes rivers to overflow their banks or volcanoes to erupt. But even if it were true, it would make no difference. If I were going to beget a child knowing that the child was going to be a homicidal maniac, I should be responsible for his crimes. If God knew in advance the sins of which man would be guilty, He was clearly responsible for all the consequences of those sins when He decided to create man. The usual Christian argument is that the suffering in the world is a purification for sin, and is therefore a good thing. This argument is, of course, only a rationalisation of sadism; but in any case it is a very poor argument. I would invite any Christian to accompany me to the children's ward of a hospital, to watch the suffering that is there being endured, and then to persist in the assertion that those children are so morally abandoned as to deserve what they are suffering. In order to bring himself to say this, a man must destroy in himself all feelings of mercy and compassion. He must, in short, make himself as cruel as the God in whom he believes. No man who believes that all is for the best in this suffering world can keep his ethical values unimpaired, since he is always having to find excuses for pain and misery.

### THE OBJECTIONS TO RELIGION

The objections to religion are of two sorts – intellectual and moral. The intellectual objection is that there is no reason to suppose any religion true; the moral objection is that religious precepts date from a time when men were more cruel than they are, and therefore tend to perpetuate inhumanities which the moral conscience of the age would otherwise outgrow.

To take the intellectual objection first; there is a certain tendency in our practical age to consider that it does not much matter whether religious teaching is true or not, since the important question is whether it is useful. One question cannot, however, well be decided without the other. If we believe the Christian religion, our notions of what is good will be different from what they will be if we do not believe it. Therefore to Christians the effects of Christianity may seem good, while to unbelievers they may seem bad. Moreover, the attitude that one ought to believe such and such a proposition, independently of the question whether there is evidence in its favour, is an attitude which produces hostility to evidence and causes us to close our minds to every fact that does not suit our prejudices.

A certain kind of scientific candour is a very important quality, and it is one which can hardly exist in a man who imagines that there are things which it is his duty to believe. We cannot, therefore, really decide whether religion does good without investigating the question whether religion is true. To Christians, Mohammedans, and Jews the most fundamental question involved in the truth of religion is the existence of God. In the days when religion was still triumphant the word 'God' had a perfectly definite meaning; but as a result of the onslaughts of Rationalists the word has become paler and paler, until it is difficult to see what people mean when they assert that they believe in God. Let us take for purposes of argument Matthew Arnold's definition: 'A power not ourselves that makes for righteousness.' Perhaps we might make this even more vague, and ask ourselves whether we have any evidence of purpose in the universe apart from the purposes of living beings on the surface of this planet.

The usual argument of religious people on this subject is roughly as follows: 'I and my friends are persons of amazing intelligence and virtue. It is hardly conceivable that so much intelligence and virtue could have come about by chance. There must, therefore, be someone at least as intelligent and virtuous as we are, who set the cosmic machinery in motion with a view to producing us.' I am sorry to say that I do not find this argument so impressive as it is found by those who use it. The universe is large; yet, if we are to believe Eddington, there are probably nowhere else in the universe beings as intelligent as men. If you consider the total amount of matter in the world and compare it with the amount forming the bodies of intelligent beings, you will see that the latter bears an almost infinitesimal proportion to the former. Consequently, even if it is enormously improbable that the laws of chance will produce an organism capable of intelligence out of a casual selection of atoms, it is nevertheless probable that there will be in the universe that very small number of such organisms that we do in fact find. Then again, considered as the climax to such a vast process, we do not really seem to be sufficiently marvellous. Of course, I am aware that many divines are far more marvellous than I am, and that I cannot wholly appreciate merits so far transcending my own. Nevertheless, even after making allowances under this head, I cannot but think that Omnipotence operating through all eternity might have produced something better. And then we have to reflect that even this result is only a flash in the pan. The earth will not always remain habitable; the human race will die out, and if the cosmic process is to justify itself hereafter it will have to do so elsewhere than on the surface of our planet. And even if this should occur, it must stop sooner or later. The second law of thermodynamics makes it scarcely possible to doubt that the universe is running down, and that ultimately nothing of the slightest interest will be possible anywhere. Of course, it is open to us to say that when that time comes God will wind up the machinery again; but if we do say this, we can base our assertion only upon faith, not upon one shred of scientific evidence. So far as scientific evidence goes, the universe has crawled by slow stages to a somewhat pitiful result on this earth, and is going to crawl by still more pitiful stages to a condition of universal death. If this is to be taken as evidence of purpose, I can only say that the purpose is one that does not appeal to me. I see no reason therefore to believe in any sort of God, however vague and however attenuated. I leave on one side the old metaphysical arguments, since religious apologists themselves have thrown them over.

### THE SOUL AND IMMORTALITY

The Christian emphasis on the individual soul has had a profound influence upon the ethics of Christian communities. It is a doctrine fundamentally akin to that of the Stoics, arising as theirs did in communities that could no longer cherish political hopes. The natural impulse of the vigorous person of decent character is to attempt to do good, but if he is deprived of all political power and of all opportunity to influence events he will be deflected from his natural course and will decide that the important thing is to be good. This is what happened to the early Christians; it led to a conception of personal holiness as something quite independent of beneficent action, since holiness had to be something that could be achieved by people who were impotent in action. Social virtue came therefore to be excluded from Christian ethics. To this day conventional Christians think an adulterer more wicked than a politician who takes bribes, although the latter probably does a thousand times as much harm. The mediaeval conception of virtue, as one sees in their pictures, was of something wishy-washy, feeble, and sentimental. The most virtuous man was the man who retired from the world; the only men of action who were regarded as saints were those who wasted the lives and substance of their subjects in fighting the Turks, like St Louis. The Church would never regard a man as a saint because he reformed the finances, or the criminal law, or the judiciary. Such mere contributions to human welfare would be regarded as of no importance. I do not believe there is a single saint in the whole calendar whose saintship is due to work of public utility. With this separation between the social and the moral person there went an increasing separation between soul and body, which has survived in Christian metaphysics and in the systems derived from Descartes. One may say, broadly speaking, that the body represents the social and public part of a man, whereas the soul represents the private part. In emphasising the soul Christian ethics has made itself completely individualistic. I think it is clear that the net result of all the centuries of Christianity has been to make men more egotistic, more shut up in themselves, than nature made them; for the impulses that naturally take a man outside the walls of his ego are those of sex, parenthood, and patriotism or herd instinct. Sex the Church did everything it could to decry and degrade; family affection was decried by Christ Himself and by the bulk of His followers; and patriotism could find no place among the subject populations of the Roman Empire. The polemic against the family in the Gospels is a matter that has not received the attention it deserves. The Church treats the Mother of Christ with reverence, but He Himself showed little of this attitude. 'Woman, what have I to do with thee?' (John ii. 4) is His way of speaking to her. He says also that He has come to set a man at variance against his father, the daughter against her mother, and the daughter-in-law against her mother-in-law, and that he that loveth father and mother more than Him is not worthy of Him (Matt. x. 35–7). All this means the break-up of the biological family tie for the sake of creed – an attitude which had a great deal to do with the intolerance that came into the world with the spread of Christianity.

This individualism culminated in the doctrine of the immortality of the individual soul, which was to enjoy hereafter endless bliss or endless woe according to circumstances. The circumstances upon which this momentous difference depended were somewhat curious. For example, if you died immediately after a priest had sprinkled water upon you while pronouncing certain words, you inherited eternal bliss; whereas, if after a long and virtuous life you happened to be struck by lightning at a moment when you were using bad language because you had broken a bootlace, you would inherit eternal torment. I do not say that the modern Protestant Christian believes this, nor even perhaps the modern Catholic Christian who has not been adequately instructed in theology; but I do say that this is the orthodox doctrine and was firmly believed until recent times. The Spaniards in Mexico and Peru used to baptise Indian infants, and then immediately dash their brains out: by this means they secured that these infants went to Heaven. No orthodox Christian can find any logical reason for condemning their action, although all nowadays do so. In countless ways the doctrine of personal immortality in its Christian form has had disastrous effects upon morals, and the metaphysical separation of soul and body has had disastrous effects upon philosophy.

## SOURCES OF INTOLERANCE

The intolerance that spread over the world with the advent of Christianity is one of its most curious features, due, I think, to the Jewish belief in righteousness and in the exclusive reality of the Jewish God. Why the Jews should have had these peculiarities I do not know. They seem to have developed during the captivity as a reaction against the attempt to absorb the Jews into alien populations. However that may be, the Jews, and more especially the prophets, invented emphasis upon personal righteousness and the idea that it is wicked to tolerate any religion except one. These two ideas have had an extraordinarily disastrous effect upon Occidental history. The Church has made much of the persecution of Christians by the Roman State before the time of Constantine. This persecution, however, was slight and intermittent and wholly political. At all times, from the age of Constantine to the end of the seventeenth century, Christians were far more fiercely persecuted by other Christians than they ever were by the Roman emperors. Before the rise of Christianity this persecuting attitude was unknown to the ancient world except among the Jews. If you read, for example, Herodotus, you find a bland and tolerant account of the habits of the foreign nations he has visited. Sometimes, it is true, a peculiarly barbarous custom may shock him, but in general he is hospitable to foreign gods and foreign customs. He is not anxious to prove that people who call Zeus by some other name will suffer eternal perdition, and ought to be put to death in order that their punishment may begin as soon as possible. This attitude has been reserved for Christians. It is true that the modern Christian is less robust, but that is not thanks to Christianity; it is thanks to the generations of Freethinkers, who, from the Renaissance to the present day, have made Christians ashamed of many of their traditional beliefs. It is amusing to hear the modern Christian telling you how mild and rationalistic Christianity really is, and ignoring the fact that all its mildness and rationalism is due to the teaching of men who in their own day were persecuted by all orthodox Christians. Nobody nowadays believes that the world was created in 4004 BC; but not so very long ago scepticism on this point was thought an abominable crime. My great-great-grandfather, after observing the depth of the lava on the slopes of Etna, came to the conclusion that the world must be older than the orthodox supposed, and published this opinion in a book. For this offence he was cut by the County and ostracised from society. Had he been a man in humbler circumstances, his punishment would doubtless have been more severe. It is no credit to the orthodox that they do not now believe all the absurdities that were believed 150 years ago. The gradual emasculation of the Christian doctrine has been effected in spite of the most vigorous resistance, and solely as the result of the onslaughts of Freethinkers.

## THE DOCTRINE OF FREE-WILL

The attitude of the Christians on the subject of natural law has been curiously vacillating and uncertain. There was, on the one hand, the doctrine of free-will, in which the great majority of Christians believed; and this doctrine required that the acts of human beings at least should not be subject to natural law. There was, on the other hand, especially in the eighteenth and nineteenth centuries, a belief in God as the Lawgiver and in natural law as one of the main evidences of the existence of a Creator. In recent times the objection to the reign of law in the interests of free-will has begun to be felt more strongly than the belief in natural law as affording evidence for a Lawgiver. Materialists used the laws of physics to show, or attempt to show, that the movements of human bodies are mechanically determined, and that consequently everything that we say and every change of position that we effect fall outside the sphere of any possible free-will. If this be so, whatever may be left for our unfettered volitions is of little value. If, when a man writes a poem or commits a murder, the bodily movements involved in his act result solely from physical causes, it would seem absurd to put up a statue to him in the one case and to hang him in the other. There might in certain metaphysical systems remain a region of pure thought in which the will would be free; but, since that can be communicated to others only by means of bodily movement, the realm of freedom would be one that could never be the subject of communication, and could never have any social importance.

Then, again, evolution has had a considerable influence upon those Christians who have accepted it. They have seen that it will not do to make claims on behalf of man which are totally different from those which are made on behalf of other forms of life. Therefore, in order to safeguard free-will in man, they have objected to every attempt at explaining the behaviour of living matter in terms of physical and chemical laws. The position of Descartes, to the effect that all lower animals are automata, no longer finds favour with liberal theologians. The doctrine of continuity makes them inclined to go a step further still and maintain that even what is called dead matter is not rigidly governed in its behaviour by unalterable laws. They seem to have overlooked the fact that, if you abolish the reign of law, you also abolish the possibility of miracles, since miracles are acts of God which contravene the laws governing ordinary phenomena. I can, however, imagine the modern liberal theologian maintaining with an air of profundity that all creation is miraculous, so that he no longer needs to fasten upon certain occurrences as special evidence of Divine intervention.

Under the influence of this reaction against natural law, some Christian apologists have seized upon the latest doctrines of the atom, which tend to show that the physical laws in which we have hitherto believed have only an approximate and average truth as applied to large numbers of atoms, while the individual electron behaves pretty much as it likes. My own belief is that this is a temporary phase, and that the physicists will in time discover laws governing minute phenomena, although these laws may differ very considerably from those of traditional physics. However that may be, it is worth while to observe that the modern doctrines as to minute phenomena have no bearing upon anything that is of practical importance. Visible motions, and indeed all motions that make any difference to anybody, involve such large numbers of atoms that they come well within the scope of the old laws. To write a poem or commit a murder (reverting to our previous illustration), it is necessary to move an appreciable mass of ink or lead. The electrons composing the ink may be dancing freely round their little ballroom, but the ballroom as a whole is moving according to the old laws of physics, and this alone is what concerns the poet and his publisher. The modern doctrines, therefore, have no appreciable bearing upon any of those problems of human interest with which the theologian is concerned.

The free-will question consequently remains just where it was. Whatever may be thought about it as a matter of ultimate metaphysics, it is quite clear that nobody believes in it in practice. Everyone has always believed that it is possible to train character; everyone has always known that alcohol or opium will have a certain effect on behaviour. The apostle of free-will maintains that a man can by will power avoid getting drunk, but he does not maintain that when drunk a man can say 'British Constitution' as clearly as if he were sober. And everybody who has ever had to do with children knows that a suitable diet does more to make them virtuous than the most eloquent preaching in the world. The one effect that the free-will doctrine has in practice is to prevent people from following out such common-sense knowledge to its rational conclusion. When a man acts in ways that annoy us we wish to think him wicked, and we refuse to face the fact that his annoying behaviour is a result of antecedent causes which, if you follow them long enough, will take you beyond the moment of his birth, and therefore to events for which he cannot be held responsible by any stretch of imagination.

No man treats a motor-car as foolishly as he treats another human being. When the car will not go, he does not attribute its annoying behaviour to sin; he does not say: 'You are a wicked motor-car, and I shall not give you any more petrol until you go.' He attempts to find out what is wrong, and to set it right. An analogous way of treating human beings is, however, considered to be contrary to the truths of our holy religion. And this applies even in the treatment of little children. Many children have bad habits which are perpetuated by punishment, but will probably pass away of themselves if left unnoticed. Nevertheless, nurses with very few exceptions consider it right to inflict punishment, although by so doing they run the risk of causing insanity. When insanity has been caused it is cited in courts of law as a proof of the harmfulness of the habit, not of the punishment. (I am alluding to a recent prosecution for obscenity in the State of New York.)

Reforms in education have come very largely through the study of the insane and feeble-minded, because they have not been held morally responsible for their failures, and have therefore been treated more scientifically than normal children. Until very recently it was held that, if a boy could not learn his lessons, the proper cure was caning or flogging. This view is nearly extinct in the treatment of children, but it survives in the criminal law. It is evident that a man with a propensity to crime must be stopped, but so must a man who has hydrophobia and wants to bite people, although nobody considers him morally responsible. A man who is suffering from plague has to be imprisoned until he is cured, although nobody thinks him wicked. The same thing should be done with a man who suffers from a propensity to commit forgery; but there should be no more idea of guilt in the one case than in the other. And this is only common sense, though it is a form of common sense to which Christian ethics and metaphysics are opposed.

To judge of the moral influence of any institution upon a community, we have to consider the kind of impulse which is embodied in the institution, and the degree to which the institution increases the efficacy of the impulse in that community. Sometimes the impulse concerned is quite obvious, sometimes it is more hidden. An Alpine club, for example, obviously embodies the impulse to adventure, and a learned society embodies the impulse towards knowledge. The family as an institution embodies jealousy and parental feeling; a football club or a political party embodies the impulse towards competitive play; but the two great social institutions – namely, the Church and the State – are more complex in their psychological motivation. The primary purpose of the State is clearly security against both internal criminals and external enemies. It is rooted in the tendency of children to huddle together when they are frightened, and to look for a grown-up person who will give them a sense of security. The Church has more complex origins. Undoubtedly the most important source of religion is fear; this can be seen at the present day, since anything that causes alarm is apt to turn people's thoughts to God. Battle, pestilence, and shipwreck all tend to make people religious. Religion has, however, other appeals besides that of terror; it appeals especially to our human self-esteem. If Christianity is true, mankind are not such pitiful worms as they seem to be; they are of interest to the Creator of the universe, who takes the trouble to be pleased with them when they behave well and displeased when they behave badly. This is a great compliment. We should not think of studying an ants' nest to find out which of the ants performed their formicular duty, and we should certainly not think of picking out those individual ants who were remiss and putting them into a bonfire. If God does this for us, it is a compliment to our importance; and it is even a pleasanter compliment if He awards to the good among us everlasting happiness in heaven. Then there is the comparatively modern idea that cosmic evolution is all designed to bring about the sort of results which we call good – that is to say, the sort of results that give us pleasure. Here again it is flattering to suppose that the universe is controlled by a Being who shares our tastes and prejudices.

## THE IDEA OF RIGHTEOUSNESS

The third psychological impulse which is embodied in religion is that which has led to the conception of righteousness. I am aware that many Freethinkers treat this conception with great respect, and hold that it should be preserved in spite of the decay of dogmatic religion. I cannot agree with them on this point. The psychological analysis of the idea of righteousness seems to me to show that it is rooted in undesirable passions, and ought not to be strengthened by the *imprimatur* of reason. Righteousness and unrighteousness must be taken together; it is impossible to stress the one without stressing the other also. Now, what is 'unrighteousness' in practice? It is in practice behaviour of a kind disliked by the herd. By calling it unrighteousness, and by arranging an elaborate system of ethics round this conception, the herd justifies itself in wreaking punishment upon the objects of its own dislike, while at the same time, since the herd is righteous by definition, it enhances its own self-esteem at the very moment when it lets loose its impulse to cruelty. This is the psychology of lynching, and of the other ways in which criminals are punished. The essence of the conception of righteousness, therefore, is to afford an outlet for sadism by cloaking cruelty as justice.

But, it will be said, the account you have been giving of righteousness is wholly inapplicable to the Hebrew prophets, who, after all, on your own showing, invented the idea. There is truth in this: righteousness in the mouths of the Hebrew prophets meant what was approved by them and Yahveh. One finds the same attitude expressed in the Acts of the Apostles, where the Apostles began a pronouncement with the words: 'For it seemed good to the Holy Ghost, and to us' (Acts xv. 28). This kind of individual certainty as to God's tastes and opinions cannot, however, be made the basis of any institution. That has always been the difficulty with which Protestantism has had to contend: a new prophet could maintain that his revelation was more authentic than those of his predecessors, and there was nothing in the general outlook of Protestantism to show that this claim was invalid. Consequently Protestantism split into innumerable sects, which weakened each other; and there is reason to suppose that a hundred years hence Catholicism will be the only effective representative of the Christian faith. In the Catholic Church inspiration such as the prophets enjoyed has its place; but it is recognised that phenomena which look rather like genuine divine inspiration may be inspired by the Devil, and it is the business of the Church to discriminate, just as it is the business of an art connoisseur to know a genuine Leonardo from a forgery. In this way revelation becomes institutionalised at the same time. Righteousness is what the Church approves, and unrighteousness is what it disapproves. Thus the effective part of the conception of righteousness is a justification of herd antipathy.

It would seem, therefore, that the three human impulses embodied in religion are fear, conceit and hatred. The purpose of religion, one may say, is to give an air of respectability to these passions, provided they run in certain channels. It is because these passions make on the whole for human misery that religion is a force for evil, since it permits men to indulge these passions without restraint, where but for its sanction they might, at least to a certain degree, control them.

I can imagine at this point an objection, not likely to be urged perhaps by most orthodox believers, but nevertheless worthy to be examined. Hatred and fear, it may be said, are essential human characteristics; mankind has always felt them and always will. The best that you can do with them, I may be told, is to direct them into certain channels in which they are less harmful than they would be in certain other channels. A Christian theologian might say that their treatment by the Church is analogous to its treatment of the sex impulse, which it deplores. It attempts to render concupiscence innocuous by confining it within the bounds of matrimony. So, it may be said, if mankind must inevitably feel hatred, it is better to direct this hatred against those who are really harmful, and this is precisely what the Church does by its conception of righteousness.

To this contention there are two replies – one comparatively superficial; the other going to the root of the matter. The superficial reply is that the Church's conception of righteousness is not the best possible; the fundamental reply is that hatred and fear can, with our present psychological knowledge and our present industrial technique, be eliminated altogether from human life.

To take the first point first. The Church's conception of righteousness is socially undesirable in various way – first and foremost in its depreciation of intelligence and science. This defect is inherited from the Gospels. Christ tells us to become as little children, but little children cannot understand the differential calculus, or the principles of currency, or the modern methods of combating disease. To acquire such knowledge is no part of our duty, according to the Church. The Church no longer contends that knowledge is in itself sinful, though it did so in its palmy days; but the acquisition of knowledge, even though not sinful, is dangerous, since it may lead to pride of intellect, and hence to a questioning of the Christian dogma. Take, for example, two men, one of whom has stamped out yellow fever throughout some large region in the tropics, but has in the course of his labours had occasional relations with women to whom he was not married; while the other has been lazy and shiftless, begetting a child a year until his wife died of exhaustion, and taking so little care of his children that half of them died from preventable causes, but never indulging in illicit sexual intercourse. Every good Christian must maintain that the second of these men is more virtuous than the first. Such an attitude is, of course, superstitious and totally contrary to reason. Yet something of this absurdity is inevitable so long as avoidance of sin is thought more important than positive merit, and so long as the importance of knowledge as a help to a useful life is not recognised.

The second and more fundamental objection to the utilisation of fear and hatred in the way practised by the Church is that these emotions can now be almost wholly eliminated from human nature by educational, economic and political reforms. The educational reforms must be the basis, since men who feel hate and fear will also admire these emotions and wish to perpetuate them, although this admiration and wish will be probably unconscious, as it is in the ordinary Christian. An education designed to eliminate fear is by no means difficult to create. It is only necessary to treat a child with kindness, to put him in an environment where initiative is possible without disastrous results, and to save him from contact with adults who have irrational terrors, whether of the dark, of mice, or of social revolution. A child must also not be subject to severe punishment, or to threats, or to grave and excessive reproof. To save a child from hatred is a somewhat more elaborate business. Situations arousing jealousy must be very carefully avoided by means of scrupulous and exact justice as between different children. A child must feel himself the object of warm affection on the part of some at least of the adults with whom he has to do, and he must not be thwarted in his natural activities and curiosities except when danger to life or health is concerned. In particular, there must be no taboo on sex knowledge, or on conversation about matters which conventional people consider improper. If these simple precepts are observed from the start, the child will be fearless and friendly.

On entering adult life, however, a young person so educated will find himself or herself plunged into a world full of injustice, full of cruelty, full of preventable misery. The injustice, the cruelty, and the misery that exist in the modern world are an inheritance from the past, and their ultimate source is economic, since life-and-death competition for the means of subsistence was in former days inevitable. It is not inevitable in our age. With our present industrial technique we can, if we choose, provide a tolerable subsistence for everybody. We could also secure that the world's population should be stationary if we were not prevented by the political influence of Churches which prefer war, pestilence, and famine to contraception. The knowledge exists by which universal happiness can be secured; the chief obstacle to its utilisation for that purpose is the teaching of religion. Religion prevents our children from having a rational education; religion prevents us from removing the fundamental causes of war; religion prevents us from teaching the ethic of scientific co-operation in place of the old fierce doctrines of sin and punishment. It is possible that mankind is on the threshold of a golden age; but, if so, it will be necessary first to slay the dragon that guards the door, and this dragon is religion.

## Chapter 3

# What I Believe

What I Believe *was published as a little book in 1925. In it, Russell wrote in the preface, 'I have tried to say what I think of man's place in the universe, and of his possibilities in the way of achieving the good life. . . . In human affairs, we can see that there are forces making for happiness, and forces making for misery. We do not know which will prevail, but to act wisely we must be aware of both.' In the New York court proceedings in 1948* What I Believe *was one of the books presented as evidence that Russell was unfit to teach at City College. Extracts from it were also widely quoted in the press, usually in such a way as to give quite a false impression of Russell's views.*

## I NATURE AND MAN

Man is a part of Nature, not something contrasted with Nature. His thoughts and his bodily movements follow the same laws that describe the motions of stars and atoms. The physical world is large compared with Man – larger than it was thought to be in Dante's time, but not so large as it seemed a hundred years ago. Both upward and downward, both in the large and in the small, science seems to be reaching limits. It is thought that the universe is of finite extent in space, and that light could travel round it in a few hundred millions of years. It is thought matter consists of electrons and protons, which are of finite size and of which there are only a finite number in the world. Probably their changes are not continuous, as used to be thought, but proceed by jerks, which are never smaller than a certain minimum jerk. The laws of these changes can apparently be summed up in a small number of very general principles, which determine the past and the future of the world when any small section of its history is known.

Physical science is thus approaching the stage when it will be complete, and therefore uninteresting. Given the laws governing the motions of electrons and protons, the rest is merely geography – a collection of particular facts telling their distribution throughout some portion of the world's history. The total number of facts of geography required to determine the world's history is probably finite; theoretically they could all be written down in a big book to be kept at Somerset House with a calculating machine attached which, by turning a handle, would enable the inquirer to find out the facts at other times than those recorded. It is difficult to imagine anything less interesting or more different from the passionate delights of incomplete discovery. It is like climbing a high mountain and finding nothing at the top except a restaurant where they sell ginger beer, surrounded by fog but equipped with wireless. Perhaps in the times of Ahmes the multiplication table was exciting.

Of this physical world, uninteresting in itself, Man is a part. His body, like other matter, is composed of electrons and protons, which, so far as we know, obey the same laws as those not forming part of animals or plants. There are some who maintain that physiology can never be reduced to physics, but their arguments are not very convincing and it seems prudent to suppose that they are mistaken. What we call our 'thoughts' seem to depend upon the organisation of tracks in the brain in the same sort of way in which journeys depend upon roads and railways. The energy used in thinking seems to have a chemical origin; for instance, a deficiency of iodine will turn a clever man into an idiot. Mental phenomena seem to be bound up with material structure. If this be so, we cannot suppose that a solitary electron or proton can 'think'; we might as well expect a solitary individual to play a football match. We also cannot suppose that an individual's thinking survives bodily death, since that destroys the organisation of the brain, and dissipates the energy which utilised the brain tracks.

God and immortality, the central dogmas of the Christian religion, find no support in science. It cannot be said that either doctrine is essential to religion, since neither is found in Buddhism. (With regard to immortality, this statement in an unqualified form might be misleading, but it is correct in the last analysis.) But we in the West have come to think of them as the irreducible minimum of theology. No doubt people will continue to entertain these beliefs, because they are pleasant, just as it is pleasant to think ourselves virtuous and our enemies wicked. But for my part I cannot see any ground for either. I do not pretend to be able to prove that there is no God. I equally cannot prove that Satan is a fiction. The Christian God may exist; so may the Gods of Olympus, or of ancient Egypt, or of Babylon. But no one of these hypotheses is more probable than any other: they lie outside the region of even probable knowledge, and therefore there is no reason to consider any of them.

I shall not enlarge upon this question, as I have dealt with it else-where.[1]

The question of personal immortality stands on a somewhat different footing. Here evidence either way is possible. Persons are part of the everyday world with which science is concerned, and the conditions which determine their existence are discoverable. A drop of water is not immortal; it can be resolved into oxygen and hydrogen. If, therefore, a drop of water were to maintain that it had a quality of aqueousness which would survive its dissolution we should be inclined to be sceptical. In like manner we know that the brain is not immortal, and that the organised energy of a living body becomes, as it were, demobilised at death, and therefore not available for collective action. All the evidence goes to show that what we regard as our mental life is bound up with brain structure and organised bodily energy. Therefore it is rational to suppose that mental life ceases when bodily life ceases. The argument is only one of probability, but it is as strong as those upon which most scientific conclusions are based.

There are various grounds upon which this conclusion might be attacked. Psychical research professes to have actual scientific evidence of survival, and undoubtedly its procedure is, in principle, scientifically correct. Evidence of this sort might be so overwhelming that no one with a scientific temper could reject it. The weight to be attached to the evidence, however, must depend upon the antecedent probability of the hypothesis of survival. There are always different ways of accounting for any set of phenomena and of these we should prefer the one which is antecedentally least improbable. Those who already think it likely that we survive death will be ready to view this theory as the best explanation of psychical phenomena. Those who, on other grounds, regard this theory as implausible will seek for other explanations. For my part, I consider the evidence so far adduced by psychical research in favour of survival much weaker than the physiological evidence on the other side. But I fully admit that it might at any moment become stronger, and in that case it would be unscientific to disbelieve in survival.

Survival of bodily death is, however, a different matter from immortality: it may only mean a postponement of psychical death. It is immortality that men desire to believe in. Believers in immortality will object to physiological arguments, such as I have been using, on the ground that soul and body are totally disparate, and that the soul is something quite other than its empirical manifestations

[1] See my *Philosophy of Leibniz*, Chapter XV.

through our bodily organs. I believe this to be a metaphysical super-stition. Mind and matter alike are for certain purposes convenient terms, but are not ultimate realities. Electrons and protons, like the soul, are logical fictions; each is really a history, a series of events, not a single persistent entity. In the case of the soul, this is obvious from the facts of growth. Whoever considers conception, gestation, and infancy cannot seriously believe that the soul in any indivisible something, perfect and complete throughout this process. It is evi-dent that it grows like the body, and that it derives both from the spermatozoon and from the ovum, so that it cannot be indivisible. This is not materialism: it is merely the recognition that everything interesting is a matter of organisation, not of primal substance.

Metaphysicians have advanced innumerable arguments to prove that the soul must be immortal. There is one simple test by which all these arguments can be demolished. They all prove equally that the soul must pervade all space. But as we are not so anxious to be fat as to live long, none of the metaphysicians in question have ever no-ticed this application of their reasonings. This is an instance of the amazing power of desire in blinding even very able men to fallacies which would otherwise be obvious at once. If we were not afraid of death, I do not believe that the idea of immortality would ever have arisen.

Fear is the basis of religious dogma, as of so much else in human life. Fear of human beings, individually or collectively, dominates much of our social life, but it is fear of nature that gives rise to religion. The antithesis of mind and matter is, as we have seen, more or less illusory; but there is another antithesis which is more import-ant – that, namely, between things that can be affected by our desires and things that cannot be so affected. The line between the two is neither sharp nor immutable – as science advances, more and more things are brought under human control. Nevertheless there remain things definitely on the other side. Among these are all the *large* facts of our world, the sort of facts that are dealt with by astronomy. It is only facts on or near the surface of the earth that we can, to some extent, mould to suit our desires. And even on the surface of the earth our powers are very limited. Above all, we cannot prevent death, although we can often delay it.

Religion is an attempt to overcome this antithesis. If the world is controlled by God, and God can be moved by prayer, we acquire a share in omnipotence. In former days, miracles happened in answer to prayer; they still do in the Catholic Church, but Protestants have lost this power. However, it is possible to dispense with miracles, since Providence has decreed that the operation of natural laws shall produce the best possible results. Thus belief in God still serves to humanise the world of nature, and to make men feel that physical forces are really their allies. In like manner immortality removes the terror from death. People who believe that when they die they will inherit eternal bliss may be expected to view death without horror, though, fortunately for medical men, this does not invariably happen. It does, however, soothe men's fears somewhat even when it cannot allay them wholly.

Religion, since it has its source in terror, has dignified certain kinds of fear, and made people think them not disgraceful. In this it has done mankind a great disservice: *all* fear is bad. I believe that when I die I shall rot, and nothing of my ego will survive. I am not young, and I love life. But I should scorn to shiver with terror at the thought of annihilation. Happiness is none the less true happiness because it must come to an end, nor do thought and love lose their value because they are not everlasting. Many a man has borne himself proudly on the scaffold; surely the same pride should teach us to think truly about man's place in the world. Even if the open windows of science at first make us shiver after the cosy indoor warmth of traditional humanising myths, in the end the fresh air brings vigour, and the great spaces have a splendour of their own.

The philosophy of nature is one thing, the philosophy of value is quite another. Nothing but harm can come of confusing them. What we think good, what we should like, has no bearing whatever upon what is, which is the question for the philosophy of nature. On the other hand, we cannot be forbidden to value this or that on the ground that the non-human world does not value it, nor can we be compelled to admire anything because it is a 'law of nature'. Undoubtedly we are part of nature, which has produced our desires, our hopes and fears, in accordance with laws which the physicist is beginning to discover. In this sense we are part of nature, we are subordinated to nature, the outcome of natural laws, and their victims in the long run.

The philosophy of nature must not be unduly terrestrial; for it, the earth is merely one of the smaller planets of one of the smaller stars of the Milky Way. It would be ridiculous to warp the philosophy of nature in order to bring out results that are pleasing to the tiny parasites of this insignificant planet. Vitalism as a philosophy, and evolutionism, show, in this respect, a lack of sense of proportion and logical relevance. They regard the facts of life, which are personally interesting to us, as having a cosmic significance, not a significance confined to the earth's surface. Optimism and pessimism, as cosmic philosophies, show the same naïve humanism; the great world, so far as we know it from the philosophy of nature, is neither good nor bad, and is not concerned to make us happy or unhappy. All such philosophies spring from self-importance, and are best corrected by a little astronomy.

But in the philosophy of value the situation is reversed. Nature is only a part of what we can imagine; everything, real or imagined, can be appraised by us, and there is no outside standard to show that our valuation is wrong. We are ourselves the ultimate and irrefutable arbiters of value, and in the world of value Nature is only a part. Thus in this world we are greater than Nature. In the world of values, Nature in itself is neutral, neither good nor bad, deserving of neither admiration nor censure. It is we who create value and our desires which confer value. In this realm we are kings, and we debase our kingship if we bow down to Nature. It is for us to determine the good life, not for Nature – not even for Nature personified as God.

II THE GOOD LIFE

There have been at different times and among different people many varying conceptions of the good life. To some extent the differences were amenable to argument; this was when men differed as to the means to achieve a given end. Some think that prison is a good way of preventing crime; others hold that education would be better. A difference of this sort can be decided by sufficient evidence. But some differences cannot be tested in this way. Tolstoy condemned all war; others have held the life of a soldier doing battle for the right to be very noble. Here there was probably involved a real difference as to ends. Those who praise the soldier usually consider the punishment of sinners a good thing in itself; Tolstoy did not think so. On such a matter no argument is possible. I cannot, therefore, prove that my view of the good life is right; I can only state my view, and hope that as many as possible will agree. My view is this:

*The good life is one inspired by love and guided by knowledge.*

Knowledge and love are both indefinitely extensible; therefore, however good a life may be, a better life can be imagined. Neither love without knowledge, nor knowledge without love can produce a good life. In the Middle Ages, when pestilence appeared in a country, holy men advised the population to assemble in churches and pray for deliverance; the result was that the infection spread with extraordinary rapidity among the crowded masses of supplicants. This was an example of love, without knowledge. The late war afforded an example of knowledge without love. In each case, the result was death on a large scale.

Although both love and knowledge are necessary, love is in a sense more fundamental, since it will lead intelligent people to seek knowledge, in order to find out how to benefit those whom they love. But if people are not intelligent, they will be content to believe what they have been told, and may do harm in spite of the most genuine benevolence. Medicine affords, perhaps, the best example of what I mean. An able physician is more useful to a patient than the most devoted friend, and progress in medical knowledge does more for the health of the community than ill-informed philanthropy. Nevertheless, an element of benevolence is essential even here if any but the rich are to profit by scientific discoveries.

Love is a word which covers a variety of feelings; I have used it purposely, as I wish to include them all. Love as an emotion – which is what I am speaking about, for love 'on principle' does not seem to me genuine – moves between two poles: on one side, pure delight in contemplation; on the other, pure benevolence. Where inanimate objects are concerned, delight alone enters in; we cannot feel benevolence towards a landscape or a sonata. This type of enjoyment is presumably the source of art. It is stronger, as a rule, in very young children than in adults, who are apt to view objects in a utilitarian spirit. It plays a large part in our feelings towards human beings, some of whom have charm and some the reverse, when considered simply as objects of aesthetic contemplation.

The opposite pole of love is pure benevolence. Men have sacrificed their lives to helping lepers; in such a case the love they felt cannot have had any element of aesthetic delight. Parental affection, as a rule, is accompanied by pleasure in the child's appearance, but remains strong when this element is wholly absent. It would seem odd to call a mother's interest in a sick child 'benevolence', because we are in the habit of using this word to describe a pale emotion nine parts humbug. But it is difficult to find any other word to describe the desire for another person's welfare. It is a fact that a desire of this sort may reach any degree of strength in the case of parental feeling. In other cases it is far less intense; indeed it would seem likely that all altruistic emotion is a sort of overflow of parental feeling, or sometimes a sublimation of it. For want of a better word, I shall call this emotion 'benevolence'. But I want to make it clear that I am speaking of an emotion, not a principle, and that I do not include in it any feeling of superiority such as is sometimes associated with the word. The word 'sympathy' expresses part of what I mean, but leaves out the element of activity that I wish to include.

Love at its fullest is an indissoluble combination of the two elements, delight and well-wishing. The pleasure of a parent in a beautiful and successful child combines both elements; so does sexlove at its best. But in sex-love benevolence will only exist where there is secure possession, since otherwise jealousy will destroy it, while perhaps actually increasing the delight in contemplation. Delight without well-wishing may be cruel; well-wishing without delight easily tends to become cold and a little superior. A person who wishes to be loved wishes to be the object of a love containing both elements, except in cases of extreme weakness, such as infancy and severe illness. In these cases benevolence may be all that is desired. Conversely, in cases of extreme strength, admiration is more desired than benevolence: this is the state of mind of potentates and famous beauties. We only desire other people's good wishes in proportion as we feel ourselves in need of help or in danger of harm from them. At least, that would seem to be the biological logic of the situation, but it is not quite true to life. We desire affection in order to escape from the feeling of loneliness, in order to be, as we say, 'understood'. This is a matter of sympathy, not merely of benevolence; the person whose affection is satisfactory to us must not merely wish us well, but must know in what our happiness consists. But this belongs to the other element of the good life, namely knowledge.

In a perfect world, every sentient being would be to every other the object of the fullest love, compounded of delight, benevolence, and understanding inextricably blended. It does not follow that, in this actual world, we ought to attempt to have such feelings towards all the sentient beings whom we encounter. There are many in whom we cannot feel delight, because they are disgusting; if we were to do violence to our nature by trying to see beauties in them, we should merely blunt our susceptibilites to what we naturally find beautiful. Not to mention human beings there are fleas and bugs and lice. We should have to be as hard pressed as the Ancient Mariner before we could feel delight in contemplating these creatures. Some saints, it is true, have called them 'pearls of God', but what these men delighted in was the opportunity of displaying their own sanctity.

Benevolence is easier to extend widely, but even benevolence has its limits. If a man wished to marry a lady, we should not think the better of him for withdrawing if he found that someone else also wished to marry her: we should regard this as a fair field for competition. Yet his feelings towards a rival cannot be *wholly* benevolent. I think that in all descriptions of the good life here on earth we must assume a certain basis of animal vitality and animal instinct; without this, life becomes tame and uninteresting. Civilisation should be something added to this, not substituted for it; the ascetic saint and the detached sage fail in this respect to be complete human beings. A small number of them may enrich a community; but a world composed of them would die of boredom.

These considerations lead to a certain emphasis on the element of delight as an ingredient in the best love. Delight, in this actual world, is unavoidably selective, and prevents us from having the same feelings towards all mankind. When conflicts arise between delight and benevolence, they must, as a rule, be decided by a compromise, not by a complete surrender of either. Instinct has its rights, and if we do violence to it beyond a point it takes vengeance in subtle ways. Therefore in aiming at a good life the limits of human possibility must be borne in mind. Here again, however, we are brought back to the necessity of knowledge.

When I speak of knowledge as an ingredient of the good life, I am not thinking of ethical knowledge, but of scientific knowledge and knowledge of particular facts. I do not think there is, strictly speaking, such a thing as ethical knowledge. If we desire to achieve some end, knowledge may show us the means, and this knowledge may loosely pass as ethical. But I do not believe that we can decide what sort of conduct is right or wrong except by reference to its probable consequences. Given an end to be achieved, it is a question for science to discover how to achieve it. All moral rules must be tested by examining whether they tend to realise ends that we desire. I say ends that we desire, not ends that we *ought* to desire. What we 'ought' to desire is merely what someone else wishes us to desire. Usually it is what the authorities wish us to desire – parents, schoolmasters, policemen, and judges. If you say to me 'you ought to do so-and-so', the motive power of your remark lies in my desire for your approval – together, possibly, with rewards or punishments attached to your approval or disapproval. Since all behaviour springs from desire, it is clear that ethical notions can have no importance except as they influence desire. They do this through the desire for approval and the fear of disapproval. These are powerful social forces, and we shall naturally endeavour to win them to our side if we wish to realise any social purpose. When I say that the morality of conduct is to be judged by its probable consequences, I mean that I desire to see approval given to behaviour likely to realise social purposes which we desire, and disapproval to opposite behaviour. At present this is not done; there are certain traditional rules according to which approval and disapproval are meted out quite regardless of consequences. But this is a topic with which we shall deal in the next section.

The superfluity of theoretical ethics is obvious in simple cases. Suppose, for instance, your child is ill. Love makes you wish to cure it, and science tells you how to do so. There is not an intermediate stage of ethical theory, where it is demonstrated that your child had better be cured. Your act springs directly from desire for an end, together with knowledge of means. This is equally true of all acts, whether good or bad. The ends differ, and the knowledge is more adequate in some cases than in others. But there is no conceivable way of making people do things they do not wish to do. What is possible is to alter their desires by a system of rewards and penalties, among which social approval and disapproval are not the least potent. The question for the legislative moralist is, therefore: How shall this system of rewards and punishments be arranged so as to secure the maximum of what is desired by the legislative authority? If I say that the legislative authority has bad desires, I mean merely that its desires conflict with those of some section of the community to which I belong. Outside human desires there is no moral standard.

Thus, what distinguishes ethics from science is not any special kind of knowledge but merely desire. The knowledge required in ethics is exactly like the knowledge elsewhere; what is peculiar is that certain ends are desired, and that right conduct is what conduces to them. Of course, if the definition of right conduct is to make a wide appeal, the ends must be such as large sections of mankind desire. If I defined right conduct as that which increases my own income, readers would disagree. The whole effectiveness of any ethical argument lies in its scientific part, i.e. in the proof that one kind of conduct, rather than some other, is a means to an end which is widely desired. I distinguish, however, between ethical argument and ethical education. The latter consists in strengthening certain desires and weakening others. This is quite a different process, which will be separately discussed at a later stage.

We can now explain more exactly the purport of the definition of the good life with which this chapter began. When I said that the good life consists of love guided by knowledge, the desire which prompted me was the desire to live such a life as far as possible, and to see others living it; and the logical content of the statement is that, in a community where men live in this way, more desires will be satisfied than in one where there is less love or less knowledge. I do not mean that such a life is 'virtuous' or that its opposite is 'sinful', for these are conceptions which seem to me to have no scientific justification.

### III MORAL RULES

The practical need of morals arises from the conflict of desires, whether of different people or of the same person at different times or even at one time. A man desires to drink, and also to be fit for his work next morning. We think him immoral if he adopts the course which gives him the smaller total satisfaction of desire. We think ill of people who are extravagant or reckless, even if they injure no one but themselves. Bentham supposed that the whole of morality could be derived from 'enlightened self-interest', and that a person who always acted with a view to his own maximum satisfaction in the long run would always act rightly. I cannot accept this view. Tyrants have existed who derived exquisite pleasure from watching the infliction of torture; I cannot praise such men when prudence led them to spare their victims' lives with a view to further sufferings another day. Nevertheless, other things being equal, prudence is a part of the good life. Even Robinson Crusoe had occasion to practise industry, self-control and foresight which must be reckoned as moral qualities, since they increased his total satisfaction without counterbalancing injury to others. This part of morals plays a great part in the training of young children, who have little inclination to think of the future. If it were more practised in later life, the world would quickly become a paradise, since it would be quite sufficient to prevent wars, which are acts of passion, not reason. Nevertheless, in spite of the importance of prudence, it is not the most interesting part of morals. Nor is it the part that raises intellectual problems, since it does not require an appeal to anything beyond self-interest.

The part of morality that is not included in prudence, is, in essence, analogous to law, or the rules of a club. It is a method of enabling men to live together in a community in spite of the possibility that their desires may conflict. But here two very different methods are possible. There is the method of criminal law, which aims at a merely external harmony by attaching disagreeable consequences to acts which thwart other men's desires in certain ways. This is also the method of social censure: to be thought ill of by one's own society is a form of punishment, to avoid which most people avoid being known to transgress the code of their set. But there is another method, more fundamental, and far more satisfactory when it succeeds. This is to alter men's characters and desires in such a way as to minimise occasions of conflict by making the success of one man's desires as far as possible consistent with that of another's. That is why love is better than hate, because it brings harmony instead of conflict into the desires of the person concerned. Two people between whom there is love succeed or fail together, but when two people hate each other the success of either is the failure of the other.

If we were right in saying that the good life is inspired by love and guided by knowledge, it is clear that the moral code of any community is not ultimate and self-sufficient, but must be examined with a view to seeing whether it is such as wisdom and benevolence would have decreed. Moral codes have not always been faultless. The Aztecs considered it their painful duty to eat human flesh for fear the light of the sun should grow dim. They erred in their science; and perhaps they would have perceived the scientific error if they had had any love for the sacrificial victims. Some tribes immure girls in the dark from the age of 10 to the age of 17, for fear the sun's rays should render them pregnant. But surely our modern codes of morals contain nothing analogous to these savage practices? Surely we only forbid things which are really harmful, or at any rate so abominable that no decent person could defend them? I am not so sure.

Current morality is a curious blend of ultilitarianism and superstition, but the superstitious part has the stronger hold, as is natural, since superstition is the origin of moral rules. Originally, certain acts were thought displeasing to the gods, and were forbidden by law because the divine wrath was apt to descend upon the community, not merely upon the guilty individuals. Hence arose the conception of sin, as that which is displeasing to God. No reason can be assigned as to why certain acts should be thus displeasing; it would be very difficult to say, for instance, why it was displeasing that the kid should be seethed in its mother's milk. But it was known by Revelation that this was the case. Sometimes the Divine commands have been curiously interpreted. For example, we are told not to work on Saturdays, and Protestants take this to mean that we are not to play on Sundays. But the same sublime authority is attributed to the new prohibition as to the old.

It is evident that a man with a scientific outlook on life cannot let himself be intimidated by texts of Scripture or by the teaching of the Church. He will not be content to say 'such-and-such an act is sinful, and that ends the matter'. He will inquire whether it does any harm or whether, on the contrary, the belief that it is sinful does harm. And he will find that, especially in what concerns sex, our current morality contains a very great deal of which the origin is purely superstitious. He will find also that this superstition, like that of the Aztecs, involves needless cruelty, and would be swept away if people were actuated by kindly feelings towards their neighbours. But the defenders of traditional morality are seldom people with warm hearts, as may be seen from the love of militarism displayed by Church dignitaries. One is tempted to think that they value morals as affording a legitimate outlet for their desire to inflict pain; the sinner is fair game, and therefore away with tolerance!

Let us follow an ordinary human life from conception to the grave, and note the points where superstitious morals inflict preventable suffering. I begin with conception, because here the influence of superstition is particularly noteworthy. If the parents are not married, the child has a stigma, as clearly undeserved as anything could be. If either of the parents has venereal disease, the child is likely to inherit it. If they already have too many children for the family income, there will be poverty, underfeeding, overcrowding, very likely incest. Yet the great majority of moralists agree that the parents had better not know how to prevent this misery by preventing conception.[1] To please these moralists, a life of torture is inflicted upon millions of human beings who ought never to have existed, merely because it is supposed that sexual intercourse is wicked unless accompanied by desire for offspring, but not wicked when this desire is present, even though the offspring is humanly certain to be wretched. To be killed suddenly and then eaten, which was the fate of the Aztecs' victims, is a far less degree of suffering than is inflicted upon a child born in miserable surroundings and tainted with venereal disease. Yet it is the greater suffering which is deliberately inflicted by bishops and politicians in the name of morality. If they had even the smallest spark of love or pity for children they could not adhere to a moral code involving this fiendish cruelty.

At birth, and in early infancy, the average child suffers more from economic causes than from superstition. When well-to-do women have children, they have the best doctors, the best nurses, the best diet, the best rest and the best exercise. Working-class women do not enjoy these advantages, and frequently their children die for lack of

[1] This is fortunately no longer true. The vast majority of Protestant and Jewish leaders do not now object to birth control. Russell's statement is a perfectly accurate description of conditions in 1925. It is also significant that, with one or two exceptions, all the great pioneers of contraception – Francis Place, Richard Carlile, Charles Knowlton, Charles Bradlaugh and Margaret Sanger – were prominent Freethinkers. (Editor's note.)

them. A little is done by the public authorities in the way of care of mothers, but very grudgingly. At a moment when the supply of milk to nursing mothers is being cut down to save expense, public authorities will spend vast sums on paving rich residential districts where there is little traffic. They must know that in taking this decision they are condemning a certain number of working-class children to death for the crime of poverty. Yet the ruling party are supported by the immense majority of ministers of religion, who, with the Pope at their head, have pledged the vast forces of superstition throughout the world to the support of social injustice.

In all stages of education the influence of superstition is disastrous. A certain percentage of children have the habit of thinking; one of the aims of education is to cure them of this habit. Inconvenient questions are met with 'hush, hush', or with punishment. Collective emotion is used to instil certain kinds of belief, more particularly nationalistic kinds. Capitalists, militarists, and ecclesiastics co-operate in education, because all depend for their power upon the prevalence of emotionalism and the rarity of critical judgement. With the aid of human nature, education succeeds in increasing and intensifying these propensities of the average man.

Another way in which superstition damages education is through its influence on the choice of teachers. For economic reasons, a woman teacher must not be married; for moral reasons, she must not have extra-marital sexual relations. And yet everybody who has taken the trouble to study morbid psychology knows that prolonged virginity is, as a rule, extraordinarily harmful to women, so harmful that, in a sane society, it would be severely discouraged in teachers. The restrictions imposed lead more and more to a refusal, on the part of energetic and enterprising women, to enter the teaching profession. This is all due to the lingering influence of superstitious asceticism.  ·

At middle and upper class schools the matter is even worse. There are chapel services, and the care of morals is in the hands of clergymen. Clergymen, almost necessarily, fail in two ways as teachers of morals. They condemn acts which do not harm and they condone acts which do great harm. They all condemn sexual relations between unmarried people who are fond of each other but not yet sure that they wish to live together all their lives. Most of them condemn birth control. None of them condemns the brutality of a husband who causes his wife to die of too frequent pregnancies. I knew a fashionable clergyman whose wife had nine children in nine years. The doctors told him that if she had another she would die. Next year she had another and died. No one condemned; he retained his benefice and married again. So long as clergymen continue to condone cruelty and condemn innocent pleasure, they can only do harm as guardians of the morals of the young.

Another bad effect of superstition on education is the absence of instruction about the facts of sex. The main physiological facts ought to be taught quite simply and naturally before puberty at a time when they are not exciting. At puberty, the elements of an unsuperstitious sexual morality ought to be taught. Boys and girls should be taught that nothing can justify sexual intercourse unless there is mutual inclination. This is contrary to the teaching of the Church, which holds that, provided the parties are married and the man desires another child, sexual intercourse is justified however great may be the reluctance of the wife. Boys and girls should be taught respect for each other's liberty; they should be made to feel that nothing gives one human being rights over another, and that jealousy and possessiveness kill love. They should be taught that to bring another human being into the world is a very serious matter, only to be undertaken when the child will have a reasonable prospect of health, good surroundings, and parental care. But they should also be taught methods of birth control, so as to insure that children shall only come when they are wanted. Finally, they should be taught the dangers of venereal disease, and the methods of prevention and cure. The increase of human happiness to be expected from sex education on these lines is immeasurable.

It should be recognised that, in the absence of children, sexual relations are a purely private matter, which does not concern either the State or the neighbours. Certain forms of sex which do not lead to children are at present punished by the criminal law: this is purely superstitious, since the matter is one which affects no one except the parties directly concerned. Where there are children, it is a mistake to suppose that it is necessarily to their interest to make divorce very difficult. Habitual drunkenness, cruelty, insanity are grounds upon which divorce is necessary for the children's sake quite as much as for the sake of the wife or husband. The peculiar importance attached, at present, to adultery is quite irrational. It is obvious that many forms of misconduct are more fatal to married happiness than an occasional infidelity. Masculine insistence on a child a year, which is not conventionally misconduct or cruelty, is the most fatal of all.

Moral rules ought not to be such as to make instinctive happiness impossible. Yet that is an effect of strict monogamy in a community where the numbers of the two sexes are very unequal. Of course, under such circumstances, the moral rules are infringed. But when the rules are such that they can only be obeyed by greatly diminishing the happiness of the community, and when it is better they should be infringed than observed, surely it is time that the rules were changed. If this is not done, many people who are acting in a way not contrary to the public interest are faced with the undeserved alternative of hypocrisy or obloquy. The Church does not mind hypocrisy, which is a flattering tribute to its power; but elsewhere it has come to be recognised as an evil which we ought not lightly to inflict.

Even more harmful than theological superstition is the superstition of nationalism, of duty to one's own State and to no other. But I do not propose on this occasion to discuss the matter beyond pointing out that limitation to one's compatriots is contrary to the principle of love which we recognised as constituting the good life. It is also, of course, contrary to enlightened self-interest, since an exclusive nationalism does not pay even the victorious nations.

One other respect in which our society suffers from the theological conception of 'sin' is the treatment of criminals. The view that criminals are 'wicked' and 'deserve' punishment is not one which a rational morality can support. Undoubtedly certain people do things which society wishes to prevent, and does right in preventing as far as possible. We may take murder as the plainest case. Obviously, if a community is to hold together and we are to enjoy its pleasures and advantages, we cannot allow people to kill each other whenever they feel an impulse to do so. But this problem should be treated in a purely scientific spirit. We should ask simply: What is the best method of preventing murder? Of two methods which are equally effective in preventing murder, the one involving least harm to the murderer is to be preferred. The harm to the murderer is wholly regrettable, like the pain of a surgical operation. It may be equally necessary, but it is not a subject for rejoicing. The vindictive feeling called 'moral indignation' is merely a form of cruelty. Suffering to the criminal can never be justified by the notion of vindictive punishment. If education combined with kindness is equally effective, it is to be preferred; still more is it to be preferred if it is more effective. Of course, the prevention of crime and the punishment of crime are two different questions; the object of causing pain to the criminal is presumably deterrent. If prisons were so humanised that a prisoner got a good education for nothing, people might commit crimes in order to qualify for entrance. No doubt prison must be less pleasant than freedom; but the best way to secure this result is to make freedom more pleasant than it sometimes is at present. I do not wish, however, to embark upon the subject of Penal Reform. I merely wish to suggest that we should treat the criminal as we treat a man suffering from plague. Each is a public danger, each must have his liberty curtailed until he has ceased to be a danger. But the man suffering from plague is an object of sympathy and commiseration, whereas the criminal is an object of execration. This is quite irrational. And it is because of this difference of attitude that our prisons are so much less successful in curing criminal tendencies than our hospitals are in curing disease.

IV SALVATION: INDIVIDUAL AND SOCIAL

One of the defects of traditional religion is its individualism, and this defect belongs also to the morality associated with it. Traditionally, the religious life was, as it were, a duologue between the soul and God. To obey the will of God was virtue; and this was possible for the individual quite regardless of the state of the community. Protestant sects developed the idea of 'finding salvation', but it was always present in Christian teaching. This individualism of the separate soul had its value at certain stages of history, but in the modern world we need rather a social than an individual conception of welfare. I want to consider, in this section, how this affects our conception of the good life.

Christianity arose in the Roman Empire among populations, wholly destitute of political power, whose national States had been destroyed and merged in a vast impersonal aggregate. During the first three centuries of the Christian era the individuals who adopted Christianity could not alter the social or political institutions under which they lived, although they were profoundly convinced of their badness. In these circumstances, it was natural that they should adopt the belief that an individual may be perfect in an imperfect world, and that the good life has nothing to do with this world. What I mean may become plain by comparison with Plato's Republic. When Plato wanted to describe the good life, he described a whole community, not an individual; he did so in order to define justice, which is an essentially social conception. He was accustomed to citizenship of a republic, and political responsibility was something which he took for granted. With the loss of Greek freedom comes the rise of Stoicism, which is like Christianity, and unlike Plato, in having an individualistic conception of the good life.

We, who belong to great democracies, should find a more appropriate morality in free Athens than in despotic Imperial Rome. In

India, where the political circumstances are very similar to those of
Judea in the time of Christ, we find Gandhi preaching a very similar morality to Christ's and being punished for it by the chris-
tianised successors of Pontius Pilate. But the more extreme Indian
nationalists are not content with individual salvation: they want
national salvation. In this they have taken on the outlook of the free
democracies of the West. I want to suggest some respects in which
this outlook, owing to Christian influences, is not yet sufficiently
bold and self-conscious, but is still hampered by the belief in individual salvation.

The good life, as we conceive it, demands a multitude of social
conditions, and cannot be realised without them. The good life, we
said, is a life inspired by love and guided by knowledge. The knowledge required can only exist where governments or millionaires
devote themselves to its discovery and diffusion. For example, the
spread of cancer is alarming – what are we to do about it? At the
moment, no one can answer the question for lack of knowledge; and
the knowledge is not likely to emerge except through endowed research. Again, knowledge of science, history, literature and art
ought to be attainable by all who desire it; this requires elaborate
arrangements on the part of public authorities, and is not to be
achieved by means of religious conversion. Then there is foreign
trade, without which half the inhabitants of Great Britain would
starve; and if we were starving very few of us would live the good
life. It is needless to multiply examples. The important point is that,
in all that differentiates between a good life and a bad one, the world
is a unity, and the man who pretends to live independently is a
conscious or unconscious parasite.

The idea of individual salvation, with which the early Christians
consoled themselves for their political subjection, becomes impossible as soon as we escape from a very narrow conception of the
good life. In the orthodox Christian conception, the good life is the
virtuous life, and virtue consists in obedience to the will of God, and
the will of God is revealed to each individual through the voice of
conscience. This whole conception is that of men subject to an alien
despotism. The good life involves much beside virtue – intelligence,
for instance. And conscience is a most fallacious guide, since it
consists of vague reminiscences of precepts heard in early youth, so
that it is never wiser than its possessor's nurse or mother. To live a
good life in the fullest sense a man must have a good education,
friends, love, children (if he desires them), a sufficient income to
keep him from want and grave anxiety, good health, and work
which is not uninteresting. All these things, in varying degrees,

depend upon the community, and are helped or hindered by political events. The good life must be lived in a good society, and is not fully possible otherwise.

This is the fundamental defect of the aristocratic ideal. Certain good things, such as art and science and friendship, can flourish very well in an aristocratic society. They existed in Greece on a basis of slavery; they exist among ourselves on a basis of exploitation. But love, in the form of sympathy, or benevolence, cannot exist freely in an aristocratic society. The aristocrat has to persuade himself that the slave or proletarian or coloured man is of inferior clay, and that his sufferings do not matter. At the present moment, polished English gentlemen flog Africans so severely that they die after hours of unspeakable anguish. Even if these gentlemen are well-educated, artistic, and admirable conversationalists, I cannot admit that they are living the good life. Human nature imposes some limitation of sympathy, but not such a degree as that. In a democratically-minded society, only a maniac would behave in this way. The limitation of sympathy involved in the aristocratic ideal is its condemnation. Salvation is an aristocratic ideal, because it is individualistic. For this reason, also, the idea of personal salvation, however interpreted and expanded, cannot serve for the definition of the good life.

Another characteristic of salvation is that it results from a catastrophic change, like the conversion of St Paul. Shelley's poems afford an illustration of this conception applied to societies; the moment comes when everybody is converted, the 'anarchs' fly, and 'the world's great age begins anew'. It may be said that a poet is an unimportant person, whose ideas are of no consequence. But I am persuaded that a large proportion of revolutionary leaders have had ideas extremely like Shelley's. They have thought that misery and cruelty and degradation were due to tyrants or priests or capitalists or Germans, and that if these sources of evil were overthrown there would be a general change of heart and we should all live happy ever after. Holding these beliefs, they have been willing to wage a 'war to end war'. Comparatively fortunate were those who had suffered defeat or death; those who had the misfortune to emerge victorious were reduced to cynicism and despair by the failure of all their glowing hopes. The ultimate source of these hopes was the Christian doctrine of catastrophic conversion as the road to salvation.

I do not wish to suggest that revolutions are never necessary, but I do wish to suggest that they are not short cuts to the millennium. There is no short cut to the good life, whether individual or social. To build up the good life, we must build up intelligence, self-control and sympathy. This is a quantitative matter, a matter of gradual improvement, of early training, of educational experiment. Only impatience prompts the belief in the possibility of sudden improvement. The gradual improvement that is possible, and the methods by which it may be achieved, are a matter for future science. But something can be said now. Some part of what can be said I shall try to indicate in a final section.

<h3 style="text-align:center">V SCIENCE AND HAPPINESS</h3>

The purpose of the moralist is to improve men's behaviour. This is a laudable ambition, since their behaviour is for the most part deplorable. But I cannot praise the moralist either for the particular improvements he desires or for the methods he adopts for achieving them. His ostensible method is moral exhortation; his real method (if he is orthodox) is a system of economic rewards and punishments. The former effects nothing permanent or important; the influence of revivalists, from Savonarola downwards, has always been very transitory. The latter – the rewards and punishments – have a very considerable effect. They cause a man, for example, to prefer casual prostitutes to a quasi-permanent mistress, because it is necessary to adopt the method which is most easily concealed. They thus keep up the numbers of a very dangerous profession, and secure the prevalence of venereal disease. These are not the objects desired by the moralist, and he is too unscientific to notice that they are the objects which he actually achieves.

Is there anything better to be substituted for this unscientific mixture of preaching and bribery? I think there is.

Men's actions are harmful either from ignorance or from bad desires. 'Bad' desires, when we are speaking from a social point of view, may be defined as those which tend to thwart the desires of others, or more exactly, those which thwart more desires than they assist. It is not necessary to dwell upon the harmfulness that springs from ignorance; here, more knowledge is all that is wanted, so that the road to improvement lies in more research and more education. But the harmfulness that springs from bad desires is a more difficult matter.

In the ordinary man and woman there is a certain amount of active malevolence, both special ill-will directed to particular enemies and general impersonal pleasure in the misfortunes of others. It is customary to cover this over with fine phrases; about half of conventional morality is a cloak for it. But it must be faced if the moralists' aim of improving our actions is to be achieved. It is shown in a thousand ways, great and small: in the glee with which people repeat and believe scandal, in the unkind treatment of criminals in spite of clear proof that better treatment would have more effect in reforming them, in the unbelievable barbarity with which all white races treat Negroes, and in the gusto with which old ladies and clergymen pointed out the duty of military service to young men during the War. Even children may be the objects of wanton cruelty: David Copperfield and Oliver Twist are by no means imaginary. This active malevolence is the worst feature of human nature and the one which it is most necessary to change if the world is to grow happier. Probably this one cause has more to do with war than all the economic and political causes put together.

Given this problem of preventing malevolence, how shall we deal with it? First let us try to understand its causes. These are, I think, partly social, partly physiological. The world, now as much as at any former time, is based upon life-and-death competition; the question at issue in the War was whether German or Allied children should die of want and starvation. (Apart from malevolence on both sides there was not the slightest reason why both should not survive.) Most people have in the background of their minds a haunting fear of ruin; this is especially true of people who have children. The rich fear that Bolsheviks will confiscate their investments; the poor fear that they will lose their job or their health. Everyone is engaged in the frantic pursuit of 'security' and imagines that this is to be achieved by keeping potential enemies in subjection. It is in moments of panic that cruelty becomes most widespread and most atrocious. Reactionaries everywhere appeal to fear: in England, to fear of Bolshevism; in France, to fear of Germany; in Germany, to fear of France. And the sole effect of their appeals is to increase the danger against which they wish to be protected.

It must, therefore, be one of the chief concerns of the scientific moralist to combat fear. This can be done in two ways: by increasing security, and by cultivating courage. I am speaking of fear as an irrational passion, not of the rational prevision of possible misfortune. When a theatre catches fire, the rational man foresees disaster just as clearly as the man stricken with panic, but he adopts methods likely to diminish the disaster, whereas the man stricken with panic increases it. Europe since 1914 has been like a panic-stricken audience in a theatre on fire; what is needed is calm, authoritative directions as to how to escape without trampling each other to pieces in the process. The Victorian Age, for all its humbug, was a period of rapid progress, because men were dominated by hope rather than fear. If we are again to have progress, we must again be dominated by hope.

Everything that increases the general security is likely to diminish cruelty. This applies to prevention of war, whether through the instrumentality of the League of Nations or otherwise; to prevention of destitution; to better health by improvement in medicine, hygiene, and sanitation; and to all other methods of lessening the terrors that lurk in the abysses of men's minds and emerge as nightmares when they sleep. But nothing is accomplished by an attempt to make a portion of mankind secure at the expense of another portion – Frenchmen at the expense of Germans, capitalists at the expense of wage-earners, white men at the expense of yellow men, and so on. Such methods only increase terror in the dominant group, lest just resentment should lead the oppressed to rebel. Only justice can give security; and by 'justice' I mean the recognition of the equal claims of all human beings.

In addition to social changes designed to bring security there is, however, another and more direct means of diminishing fear, namely by a regimen designed to increase courage. Owing to the importance of courage in battle, men early discovered means of increasing it by education and diet – eating human flesh, for example, was supposed to be useful. But military courage was to be the prerogative of the ruling caste: Spartans were to have more than helots, British officers than Indian privates, men than women, and so on. For centuries it was supposed to be the privilege of the aristocracy. Every increase of courage in the ruling caste was used to increase the burdens on the oppressed, and therefore to increase the grounds for fear in the oppressors, and therefore to leave the causes of cruelty undiminished. Courage must be democratised before it can make men humane.

To a great extent, courage has already been democratised by recent events. The suffragettes showed that they possessed as much courage as the bravest men; this demonstration was essential in winning them the vote. The common soldier in the War needed as much courage as a captain or lieutenant, and much more than a general; this had much to do with his lack of servility after demobilisation. The Bolsheviks, who proclaim themselves the champions of the proletariat, are not lacking in courage, whatever else may be said of them; this is proved by their pre-revolutionary record. In Japan, where formerly the Samurai had a monopoly of martial ardour, conscription brought the need of courage throughout the male population. Thus among all the Great Powers much has been done during the past half-century to make courage no longer an aristocratic monopoly: if this were not the case, the danger to democracy would be far greater than it is.

But courage in fighting is by no means the only form, nor perhaps even the most important. There is courage in facing poverty, courage in facing derision, courage in facing the hostility of one's own herd. In these, the bravest soldiers are often lamentably deficient. And above all there is the courage to think calmly and rationally in the face of danger, and to control the impulse of panic fear or panic rage. These are certainly things which education can help to give. And the teaching of every form of courage is rendered easier by good health, good physique, adequate nourishment, and free play for fundamental vital impulses. Perhaps the physiological sources of courage could be discovered by comparing the blood of a cat with that of a rabbit. In all likelihood there is no limit to what science could do in the way of increasing courage, by example, experience of danger, an athletic life, and a suitable diet. All these things our upper class boys to a great extent enjoy, but as yet they are in the main the prerogative of wealth. The courage so far encouraged in the poorer sections of the community is courage under orders, not the kind that involves initiative and leadership. When the qualities that now confer leadership have become universal, there will no longer be leaders and followers, and democracy will have been realised at last.

But fear is not the only source of malevolence; envy and disappointment also have their share. The envy of cripples and hunchbacks is proverbial as a source of malignity, but other misfortunes than theirs produce similar results. A man or woman who has been thwarted sexually is apt to be full of envy; this generally takes the form of moral condemnation of the more fortunate. Much of the driving force of revolutionary movements is due to envy of the rich. Jealousy is, of course, a special form of envy – envy of love. The old often envy the young; when they do, they are apt to treat them cruelly.

There is, so far as I know, no way of dealing with envy except to make the lives of the envious happier and fuller, and to encourage in youth the idea of collective enterprises rather than competition. The worst forms of envy are in those who have not had a full life in the way of marriage, or children, or career. Such misfortunes could in most cases be avoided by better social institutions. Still, it must be admitted that a residuum of envy is likely to remain. There are many instances in history of generals so jealous of each other that they preferred defeat to enhancement of the other's reputation. Two politicians of the same party, or two artists of the same school, are almost sure to be jealous of one another. In such cases, there seems nothing to be done except to arrange, as far as possible, that each competitor shall be unable to injure the other, and shall only be able to win by superior merit. An artist's jealousy of a rival does little harm usually, because the only effective way of indulging it is to paint better pictures than his rival's, since it is not open to him to destroy his rival's pictures. Where envy is unavoidable it must be used as a stimulus to one's own efforts, not to the thwarting of the efforts of rivals.

The possibilities of science in the way of increasing human happiness are not confined to diminishing those aspects of human nature which make for mutual defeat, and which we therefore call 'bad'. There is probably no limit to what science can do in the way of increasing positive excellence. Health has already been greatly improved; in spite of the lamentations of those who idealise the past, we live longer and have fewer illnesses than any class or nation in the eighteenth century. With a little more application of the knowledge we already possess, we might be much healthier than we are. And future discoveries are likely to accelerate this process enormously.

So far, it has been physical science that has had most effect upon our lives, but in the future physiology and psychology are likely to be far more potent. When we have discovered how character depends upon physiological conditions, we shall be able, if we choose, to produce far more of the type of human being that we admire. Intelligence, artistic capacity, benevolence – all these things no doubt could be increased by science. There seems scarcely any limit to what *could* be done in the way of producing a good world, if only men would use science wisely. I have expressed elsewhere my fears that men may not make a wise use of the power they derive from science.[1] At present I am concerned with the good that men could do if they chose, not with the question whether they will choose rather to do harm.

There is a certain attitude about the application of science to human life with which I have some sympathy, though I do not, in the last analysis, agree with it. It is the attitude of those who dread what is 'unnatural'. Rousseau is, of course, the great protagonist of this view in Europe. In Asia, Lao-Tze has set it forth even more persuasively, and 2400 years sooner. I think there is a mixture of truth and falsehood in the admiration of 'nature', which it is important to disentangle. To begin with, what is 'natural'? Roughly speaking, anything to which the speaker was accustomed in childhood. Lao-Tze objects to roads and carriages and boats, all of which

[1] See *Icarus.*

were probably unknown in the village where he was born. Rousseau has got used to these things, and does not regard them as against nature. But he would no doubt have thundered against railways if he had lived to see them. Clothes and cooking are too ancient to be denounced by most of the apostles of nature, though they all object to new fashions in either. Birth control is thought wicked by people who tolerate celibacy, because the former is a new violation of nature and the latter an ancient one. In all these ways those who preach 'nature' are inconsistent, and one is tempted to regard them as mere conservatives.

Nevertheless, there is something to be said in their favour. Take for instance vitamins, the discovery of which has produced a revulsion in favour of 'natural' foods. It seems, however, that vitamins can be supplied by cod liver oil and electric light, which are certainly not part of the 'natural' diet of a human being. This case illustrates that, in the absence of knowledge, unexpected harm may be done by a new departure from nature; but when the harm has come to be understood it can usually be remedied by some new artificiality. As regards our physical environment and our physical means of gratifying our desires, I do not think the doctrine of 'nature' justifies anything beyond a certain experimental caution in the adoption of new expedients. Clothes, for instance, are contrary to nature, and need to be supplemented by another unnatural practice, namely washing, if they are not to bring disease. But the two practices together make a man healthier than the savage who eschews both.

There is more to be said for 'nature' in the realm of human desires. To force upon man, woman or child a life which thwarts their strongest impulses is both cruel and dangerous; in this sense, a life according to 'nature' is to be commended with certain provisos. Nothing could be more artificial than an underground electric railway, but no violence is done to a child's nature when it is taken to travel in one; on the contrary, almost all children find the experience delightful. Artificialities which gratify the desires of ordinary human beings are good, other things being equal. But there is nothing to be said for ways of life which are artificial in the sense of being imposed by authority or economic necessity. Such ways of life are, no doubt, to some extent necessary at present; ocean travel would become very difficult if there were no stokers on steamers. But necessities of this kind are regrettable, and we ought to look for ways of avoiding them. A certain amount of work is not a thing to complain of; indeed, in nine cases out of ten, it makes a man happier than complete idleness. But the amount and kind of work that most people have to do at present is a grave evil: especially bad is the life-long bondage to routine. Life should not be too closely regulated or too methodical; our impulses, when not positively destructive or injurious to others, ought if possible to have free play; there should be room for adventure. Human nature we should respect, because our impulses and desires are the stuff out of which our happiness is to be made. It is no use to give men something abstractedly considered 'good'; we must give them something desired or needed if we are to add to their happiness. Science may learn in time to mould our desires so that they shall not conflict with those of other people to the same extent as they do now; then we shall be able to satisfy a larger proportion of our desires than at present. In that sense, but in that sense only, our desires will then have become 'better'. A single desire is no better and no worse, considered in isolation, than any other; but a group of desires is better than another group if all of the first group can be satisfied simultaneously, while in the second group some are inconsistent with others. That is why love is better than hatred.

To respect physical nature is foolish; physical nature should be studied with a view to making it serve human ends as far as possible, but it remains ethically neither good nor bad. And where physical nature and human nature interact, as in the population question, there is no need to fold our hands in passive adoration and accept war, pestilence and famine as the only possible means of dealing with excessive fertility. The divines say: it is wicked, in this matter, to apply science to the physical side of the problem; we must (they say) apply morals to the human side and practise abstinence. Apart from the fact that everyone, including the divines, knows that their advice will not be taken, why should it be wicked to solve the population question by adopting physical means for preventing conception? No answer is forthcoming except one based upon antiquated dogmas. And clearly the violence to nature advocated by the divines is at least as great as that involved in birth control. The divines prefer a violence to human nature, which, when successfully practised, involves unhappiness, envy, a tendency to persecution, often madness. I prefer a 'violence' to physical nature which is of the same sort as that involved in the steam engine or even in the use of an umbrella. This instance shows how ambiguous and uncertain is the application of the principle that we should follow 'nature'.

Nature, even human nature, will cease more and more to be an absolute datum; more and more it will become what scientific manipulation has made it. Science can, if it chooses, enable our grand-children to live the good life, by giving them knowledge, self-control, and characters productive of harmony rather than strife. At present it is teaching our children to kill each other, because many men of science are willing to sacrifice the future of mankind to their own momentary prosperity. But this phase will pass when men have acquired the same domination over their own passions that they already have over the physical forces of the external world. Then at last we shall have won our freedom.

## Chapter 4

# Do We Survive Death?

*This piece was first published in 1936 in a book entitled* The Mysteries of Life and Death. *The article by Bishop Barnes to which Russell refers appeared in the same work.*

Before we can profitably discuss whether we shall continue to exist after death, it is well to be clear as to the sense in which a man is the same person as he was yesterday. Philosophers used to think that there were definite substances, the soul and the body that each lasted on from day to day; that a soul, once created, continued to exist throughout all future time, whereas a body ceased temporarily from death till the resurrection of the body.

The part of this doctrine which concerns the present life is pretty certainly false. The matter of the body is continually changing by processes of nutriment and wastage. Even if it were not, atoms in physics are no longer supposed to have continuous existence; there in no sense in saying: this is the same atom as the one that existed a few minutes ago. The continuity of a human body is a matter of appearance and behaviour, not of substance.

The same thing applies to the mind. We think and feel and act, but there is not, in addition to thoughts and feelings and actions, a bare entity, the mind or the soul, which does or suffers these occurrences. The mental continuity of a person is a continuity of habit and memory: there was yesterday one person whose feelings I can remember, and that person I regard as myself of yesterday; but in fact, myself of yesterday was only certain mental occurrences which are now remembered, and are regarded as part of the person who now recollects them. All that constitutes a person is a series of experiences connected by memory and by certain similarities of the sort we call habit.

If, therefore, we are to believe that a person survives death, we must believe that the memories and habits which constitute the person will continue to be exhibited in a new set of occurrences.

No one can prove that this will not happen. But it is easy to see that it is very unlikely. Our memories and habits are bound up with the structure of the brain, in much the same way in which a river is connected with the river-bed. The water in the river is always changing, but it keeps to the same course because previous rains have worn a channel. In like manner, previous events have worn a channel in the brain, and our thoughts flow along this channel. This is the cause of memory and mental habits. But the brain, as a structure, is dissolved at death, and memory therefore may be expected to be also dissolved. There is no more reason to think otherwise than to expect a river to persist in its old course after an earthquake has raised a mountain where a valley used to be.

All memory, and therefore (one may say) all minds, depend upon a property which is very noticeable in certain kinds of material structures, but exists little if at all in other kinds. This is the property of forming habits as a result of frequent similar occurrences. For example: a bright light makes the pupils of the eyes contract; and if you repeatedly flash a light in a man's eyes and beat a gong at the same time, the gong alone will, in the end, cause his pupils to contract. This is a fact about the brain and nervous system, that is to say, about a certain material structure. It will be found that exactly similar facts explain our response to language and our use of it, our memories and the emotions they arouse, our moral or immoral habits of behaviour, and indeed everything that constitutes our mental personality, except the part determined by heredity. The part determined by heredity is handed on to our posterity, but cannot, in the individual, survive the disintegration of the body. Thus both the hereditary and the acquired parts of a personality are, so far as our experience goes, bound up with the characteristics of certain bodily structures. We all know that memory may be obliterated by an injury to the brain, that a virtuous person may be rendered vicious by encephalitis lethargica, and that a clever child can be turned into an idiot by lack of iodine. In view of such familiar facts, it seems scarcely probable that the mind survives the total destruction of brain structure which occurs at death.

It is not rational arguments, but emotions, that cause belief in a future life.

The most important of these emotions is fear of death, which is instinctive and biologically useful. If we genuinely and wholeheartedly believe in the future life, we should cease completely to fear death. The effects would be curious, and probably such as most of us would deplore. But our human and sub-human ancestors have fought and exterminated their enemies throughout many geological ages, and have profited by courage; it is therefore an advantage to the victors in the struggle for life to be able, on occasion, to overcome the natural fear of death. Among animals and savages, instinctive pugnacity suffices for this purpose; but at a certain stage of development, as the Mohammedans first proved, belief in Paradise has considerable military value as reinforcing natural pugnacity. We should therefore admit that militarists are wise in encouraging the belief in immortality, always supposing that this belief does not become so profound as to produce indifference to the affairs of the world.

Another emotion which encourages the belief in survival is admiration of the excellence of man. As the Bishop of Birmingham says: 'His mind is a far finer instrument than anything that had appeared earlier – he knows right and wrong. He can build Westminster Abbey. He can make an aeroplane. He can calculate the distance of the sun ... Shall, then, man at death perish utterly? Does that incomparable instrument, his mind, vanish when life ceases?'

The Bishop proceeds to argue that 'the universe has been shaped and is governed by an intelligent purpose', and that it would have been unintelligent, having made man, to let him perish.

To this argument there are many answers. In the first place, it has been found, in the scientific investigation of Nature, that the intrusion of moral or aesthetic values has always been an obstacle to discovery. It used to be thought that the heavenly bodies must move in circles because the circle is the most perfect curve, that species must be immutable because God would only create what was perfect and what therefore stood in no need of improvement, that it was useless to combat epidemics except by repentance because they were sent as a punishment for sin, and so on. It has been found, however, that, so far as we can discover, Nature is indifferent to our values, and can only be understood by ignoring our notions of good and bad. The universe may have a purpose, but nothing that we know suggests that, if so, this purpose has any similarity to ours.

Nor is there in this anything surprising. Dr Barnes tells us that Man 'knows right and wrong'. But in fact, as anthropology shows, men's views of right and wrong have varied to such an extent that no single item has been permanent. We cannot say, therefore, that Man knows right and wrong, but only that some men do. Which men? Nietzsche argued in favour of an ethic profoundly different from Christ's, and some powerful governments have accepted his teaching. If knowledge of right and wrong is to be an argument for immortality, we must first settle whether to believe Christ or Nietzsche, and then argue that Christians are immortal, but Hitler and Mussolini are not, or vice versa. The decision will obviously be made on the battlefield, not in the study. Those who have the best poison gas will have the ethic of the future, and will therefore be the immortal ones.

Our feelings and beliefs on the subject of good and evil are, like everything else about us, natural facts, developed in the struggle for existence, and not having any divine or supernatural origin. In one of Aesop's fables, a lion is shown pictures of huntsmen catching lions, and remarks that, if he had painted them, they would have shown lions catching huntsmen. Man, says Dr Barnes, is a fine fellow because he can make aeroplanes. A little while ago there was a popular song about the cleverness of flies in walking upside down on the ceiling, with the chorus: 'Could Lloyd George do it? Could Mr Baldwin do it? Could Ramsay Mac do it? Why, NO.' On this basis a very telling argument could be constructed by a theologically-minded fly, which no doubt the other flies would find most convincing.

Moreover, it is only when we think abstractly that we have such a high opinion of Man. Of men in the concrete, most of us think the vast majority very bad. Civilised states spend more than half their revenue on killing each other's citizens. Consider the long history of the activities inspired by moral fervour: human sacrifices, persecutions of heretics, witch-hunts, pogroms, leading up to wholesale extermination by poison gases, which one at least of Dr Barnes's episcopal colleagues must be supposed to favour, since he holds pacifism to be un-Christian. Are these abominations, and the ethical doctrines by which they are prompted, really evidence of an intelligent Creator? And can we really wish that the men who practised them should live for ever? The world in which we live can be understood as a result of muddle and accident; but if it is the outcome of deliberate purpose, the purpose must have been that of a fiend. For my part, I find accident a less painful and more plausible hypothesis.

## Chapter 5

# Seems, Madam?
# Nay, it is

*This essay, written in 1899, has not been published before. It is reproduced here chiefly because of its historical interest since it represents Russell's first revolt against the Hegelian philosophy of which he was an adherent in his early days at Cambridge. Although his opposition to religion was not in those days as pronounced as it has been since the First World War, some of his criticisms were based on the same grounds.*

Philosophy, in the days when it was still fat and prosperous, claimed to perform, for its votaries, a variety of the most important services. It offered them comfort in adversity, explanation in intellectual difficulty, and guidance in moral perplexity. No wonder if the Younger Brother, when an instance of its uses was presented to him, exclaimed with the enthusiasm of youth:

> How charming is divine Philosophy!
> Not harsh and crabbed, as dull fools suppose,
> But musical as is Apollo's lute.

But those happy days are past. Philosophy, by the slow victories of its own offspring, has been forced to forgo, one by one, its high pretensions. Intellectual difficulties, for the most part, have been acquired by science – philosophy's anxious claims on the few exceptional questions, which it still endeavours to answer, are regarded by most people as a remnant of the Dark Ages, and are being transferred with all speed to the rigid science of Mr F. W. H. Myers. Moral perplexities – which, until recently, were unhesitatingly assigned by philosophers to their own domain – have been abandoned by McTaggart and Mr Bradley to the whimsies of statistics and common sense. But the power of giving comfort and consolation – the last power of the powerless – is still supposed by McTaggart to belong to philosophy. It is this last possession of which, tonight, I wish to rob the decrepit parent of our modern gods.

It might seem, at first sight, that the question could be settled very briefly. 'I know that Philosophy can give comfort,' McTaggart might say, 'because it certainly comforts me.' I shall try to prove, however, that those conclusions which give him comfort are conclusions which do not follow from his general position – which, indeed, admittedly do not follow, and are retained, it would seem, only *because* they give him comfort.

As I do not wish to discuss the truth of philosophy, but only its emotional value, I shall assume a metaphysic which rests on the distinction between Appearance and Reality, and regards the latter as timeless and perfect. The principle of any such metaphysic may be put in a nutshell. 'God's in His heaven, all's wrong with the world' – that is its last word. But it seems to be supposed that, since He is in His heaven, and always has been there, we may expect Him some day to descend to earth – if not to judge the quick and the dead, at least to reward the faith of the philosophers. His long resignation, however, to a purely heavenly existence, would seem to suggest, as regards the affairs of the earth, a stoicism on which it would be rash to found our hopes.

But to speak seriously. The emotional value of a doctrine, as a comfort in adversity, appears to depend upon its prediction of the future. The future, emotionally speaking, is more important than the past, or even than the present. 'All's well that ends well' is the dictum of unanimous common sense. 'Many a dull morning turns out a fine day' is optimism; whereas pessimism says:

> Full many a glorious morning have I seen
> Flatter the mountain tops with sovereign eye,
> Kissing with golden face the meadows green,
> Gilding pale streams with heavenly alchemy,
> Anon, permit the basest clouds to ride
> With ugly rack on his celestial face,
> And from the forlorn world his visage hide
> Stealing unseen to west with this disgrace.

And so, emotionally, our view of the universe as good or bad depends on the future, on what it will be; we are concerned always with appearances in time, and unless we are assured that the future is to be better than the present, it is hard to see where we are to find consolation.

So much, indeed, is the future bound up with optimism that McTaggart himself, while all his optimism depends upon the denial of time, is compelled to represent the Absolute as a future state of things, as 'a harmony which must some day become explicit'. It would be unkind to urge this contradiction, as it is mainly McTaggart himself who has made me aware of it. But what I do wish to urge is, that any comfort which may be derived from the doctrine that Reality is timeless and eternally good, is derived only and exclusively by means of this contradiction. A timeless Reality can have no more intimate connection with the future than with the past: if its perfection has not appeared hitherto, there is no reason to suppose it ever will – there is, indeed, every likelihood that God will stay in his heaven. We might, with equal propriety, speak of a harmony which must once *have been* explicit; it may be that 'my grief lies onward and my joy behind' – and it is obvious how little comfort this would afford us.

All our experience is bound up with time, nor is it possible to imagine a timeless experience. But even if it were possible, we could not, without contradiction, suppose that we ever *shall* have such an experience. All experience, therefore, for aught that philosophy can show, is likely to resemble the experience we know – if this seems bad to us, no doctrine of a Reality distinguished from Appearances can give us hope of anything better. We fall, indeed, into a hopeless dualism; on the one side we have the world we know, with its events, pleasant and unpleasant, its deaths and failures and disasters; on the other hand an imaginary world, which we christen the world of Reality, atoning, by the largeness of the Reality, for the absence of every other sign that there really is such a world. Now our only ground for this world of Reality is, that this is what Reality would have to be if we could understand it. But if the result of our purely ideal construction turns out so very different from the world we know – from the real world, in fact – if, moreover, it follows from this very construction that we never shall experience the so-called world of Reality, except in a sense in which already we experience nothing else – then I cannot see what, as concerns comfort for present ills, we have gained by all our metaphysicising. Take, for example, such a question as immortality. People have desired immortality either as a redress for the injustices of this world or, which is the more respectable motive, as affording a possibility of meeting again after death those whom they have loved. The latter desire is one which we all feel, and for whose sastisfaction, if philosophy could satisfy it, we should be immeasurably grateful. But philosophy, at best, can only assure us that the soul is a timeless reality. At what points of time, if any, it may happen to appear, is thus wholly irrelevant to it, and there is no legitimate inference from such a doctrine to existence after death. Keats may still regret:

> That I shall never look upon thee more,
> Never have relish in the faery power
> Of unreflecting love!

and it cannot much console him to be told that 'fair creature of an hour' is not a metaphysically accurate phrase. It is still true that 'Time will come and take my love away', and that 'This thought is as a death which cannot choose But weep to have that which it fears to lose.' And so with every part of the doctrines of timelessly perfect Reality. Whatever now seems evil – and it is the lamentable prerogative of evil that to seem so is to be so – whatever evil now appears may remain, for ought we know, throughout all time, to torment our latest descendants. And in such a doctrine there is, to my mind, no vestige of comfort or consolation.

It is true that Christianity, and all previous optimisms, have represented the world as eternally ruled by a beneficent Providence, and thus metaphysically good. But this has been, at bottom, only a device by which to prove the future excellence of the world – to prove, for example, that good men would be happy after death. It has always been this deduction – illegitimately made of course – which has given comfort. 'He's a good fellow, and 't *will* all be well.'

It may be said, indeed, that there is comfort in the mere abstract doctrine that Reality is good. I do not myself accept the proof of this doctrine, but even if true, I cannot see why it should be comforting. For the essence of my contention is that Reality, as constructed by metaphysics, bears no sort of relation to the world of experience. It is an empty abstraction, from which no single inference can be validly made as to the world of appearance, in which world, nevertheless, all our interests lie. Even the pure intellectual interest, from which metaphysics springs, is an interest in explaining the world of appearance. But instead of really explaining this actual palpable sensible world, metaphysics constructs another fundamentally different world, so different, so unconnected with actual experience, that the world of daily life remains wholly unaffected by it, and goes on its way just as if there were no world of Reality at all. If even one were allowed to regard the world of Reality as an 'other world', as a heavenly city existing somewhere in the skies, there might no doubt be comfort in the thought that others have a perfect experience which we lack. But to be told that our experience, as we know it, is that perfect experience, must leave us cold, since it cannot prove our experience to be better than it is. On the other hand, to say that our actual experience is not that perfect experience constructed by philosophy, is to cut off the only sort of existence which philosophical reality can have – since God in His heaven cannot be maintained as a separate person. Either, then, our existing experience is perfect – which is an empty phrase, leaving it no better than before – or there is no perfect experience, and our world of Reality, being experienced by no one, exists only in the metaphysics books. In either case, it seems to me, we cannot find in philosophy the consolations of religion.

There are, of course, several senses in which it would be absurd to deny that philosophy may give us comfort. We may find philosophising a pleasant way of passing our mornings – in this sense, the comfort derived may even, in extreme cases, be comparable to that of drinking as a way of passing our evenings. We may, again, take philosophy aesthetically, as probably most of us take Spinoza. We may use metaphysics, like poetry and music, as a means of producing a mood, of giving us a certain view of the universe, a certain attitude towards life – the resulting state of mind being valued on account of, and in proportion to, the degree of poetic emotion aroused, not in proportion to the truth of the beliefs entertained. Our satisfaction, indeed, seems to be, in these moods, the exact opposite of the metaphysician's professions. It is the satisfaction of forgetting the real world and its evils, and persuading ourselves, for the moment, of the reality of a world we have ourselves created. This seems to be one of the grounds on which Bradley justifies metaphysics. 'When poetry, art and religion,' he says, 'have ceased wholly to interest, or when they show no longer any tendency to struggle with ultimate problems and come to an understanding with them; when the sense of mystery and enchantment no longer draw the mind to wander aimlessly and love it knows not what; when, in short, twilight has no charm – then metaphysics will be worthless.' What metaphysics does for us in this way is essentially what, say, *The Tempest* does for us – but its value on this view is quite independent of its truth. It is not because Prospero's magic makes us acquainted with the world of spirits that we value *The Tempest*; it is not, aesthetically, because we are informed of a world of spirit that we value metaphysics. And this brings out the essential difference between the aesthetic satisfaction, which I allow, and the religious comfort, which I deny to philosophy. For aesthetic satisfaction, intellectual conviction is unnecessary, and we may therefore choose, when we seek it, the metaphysic which gives us the most of it. For religious comfort, on the other hand, belief is essential, and I am contending that we do not get religious comfort from the metaphysics which we believe.

It is possible, however, to introduce a refinement into the argument by adopting a more or less mystical theory of the aesthetic emotion. It may be contended that, although we can never wholly experience Reality as it really is, yet some experiences approach it more nearly than others, and such experiences, it may be said, are given by art and philosophy. And under the influence of the experiences which art and philosophy sometimes give us, it seems easy to adopt this view. For those who have the metaphysical passion, there is probably no emotion so rich and beautiful, so wholly desirable, as that mystic sense, which philosophy sometimes gives, of a world transformed by the beatific vision. As Bradley again says, 'Some in one way, some in another, we seem to touch and have communion with what is beyond the visible world. In various manners we find something higher, which both supports and humbles, both chastens and supports us. And, with certain persons, the intellectual effort to understand the Universe is a principal way of thus experiencing the Deity ... And this appears,' he continues, 'to be another reason for some persons pursuing the study of ultimate truth.'

But is it not equally a reason for hoping that these persons will not find ultimate truth? If indeed ultimate truth bears any resemblance to the doctrines set forth in *Appearance and Reality*. I do not deny the value of the emotion, but I do deny that, strictly speaking, it is in any peculiar sense a beatific vision, or an experience of the Deity. In one sense, of course, all experience is experience of the Deity, but in another, since all experience equally is in time, and the Deity is timeless, no experience is experience of the Deity – 'as such' pedantry would bid me add. The gulf between Appearance and Reality is so profound that we have no grounds, so far as I can see, for regarding some experiences as nearer than others to the perfect experience of Reality. The value of the experiences in question must, therefore, be based wholly on their emotional quality, and not, as Bradley would seem to suggest, on any superior degree of truth which may attach to them. But if so, they are at best the consolations of philosophising, not of philosophy. They constitute a reason for the pursuit of ultimate truth, since they are flowers to be gathered by the way; but they do not constitute a reward for its attainment, since by all that appears, the flowers grow only at the beginning of the road, and disappear long before we have reached our journey's end.

The view which I have advocated is no doubt not an inspiring one, nor yet one which, if generally accepted, would be likely to promote the study of philosophy. I might justify my paper, if I wished to do so, on the maxim that, 'where all is rotten, it is a man's work to cry stinking fish'. But I prefer to suggest that metaphysics, when it seeks to supply the place of religion, has really mistaken its function. That it can supply this place, I admit; but it supplies it, I maintain, at the expense of being bad metaphysics. Why not admit that metaphysics, like science, is justified by intellectual curiosity, and ought to be guided by intellectual curiosity alone? The desire to find comfort in metaphysics has, we must all admit, produced a great deal of fallacious reasoning and intellectual dishonesty. From this, at any rate, the abandonment of religion would deliver us. And since intellectual curiosity exists in some people, it is probable that they would be freed from certain hitherto persistent fallacies. 'The man,' to quote Bradley once more, 'whose nature is such that by one path alone his chief desire will reach consummation, will try to find it on that path, whatever it may be, and whatever the world thinks of it; and if he does not, he is contemptible.'

## Chapter 6

# On Catholic and Protestant Sceptics[1]

Any person who has had much contact with free-thinking people of different countries and diverse antecedents must have been struck by the remarkable difference between those of Catholic and of Protestant origin, however much they may imagine that they have thrown off the theology that they were taught in youth. The difference between Protestant and Catholic is just as marked among Freethinkers as it is among believers; indeed, the essential differences are perhaps easier to discover, since they are not hidden behind the ostensible divergences of dogma. There is, of course, a difficulty, which is that most of the Protestant atheists are English or German, while most of the Catholic ones are French. And those Englishmen who, like Gibbon, have been brought into intimate contact with French thought acquire the characteristics of Catholic Freethinkers in spite of their Protestant origin. Nevertheless, the broad difference remains, and it may be entertaining to endeavour to find out in what it consists.

One may take as a completely typical Protestant Freethinker James Mill, as he appears in his son's autobiography. 'My father,' says John Stuart Mill, 'educated in the creed of Scotch Presbyterianism, had by his own studies and reflections been early led to reject not only the belief in Revelation, but the foundations of what is commonly called Natural Religion. My father's rejection of all that is called religious belief, was not, as many might suppose, primarily a matter of logic and evidence: the grounds of it were moral, still more than intellectual. He found it impossible to believe that a world so full of evil was the work of an Author combining infinite power with perfect goodness and righteousness ... His aversion to religion, in the sense usually attached to the term, was of the same kind with that of Lucretius: he regarded it with the feelings due not

[1] Written in 1928.

to mere mental delusion, but to a great moral evil. It would have been wholly inconsistent with my father's ideas of duty, to allow me to acquire impressions contrary to his convictions and feelings respecting religion: and he impressed on me from the first that the manner in which the world came into existence was a subject on which nothing was known.' Nevertheless, there was no doubt that James Mill remained a Protestant. 'He taught me to have the strongest interest in the Reformation, as the great and decisive contest against priestly tyranny for liberty of thought.'

In all this James Mill was only carrying out the spirit of John Knox. He was a nonconformist, though of an extreme sect, and retained the moral earnestness and the interest in theology which distinguished his forerunners. Protestants, from the first, have been distinguished from their opponents by what they do not believe; to throw over one more dogma is, therefore, merely to carry the movement one stage farther. Moral fervour is the essence of the matter.

This is only one of the distinctive differences between Protestant and Catholic morality. To the Protestant the exceptionally good man is one who opposes the authorities and the received doctrines, like Luther at the Diet of Worms. The Protestant conception of goodness is of something individual and isolated. I was myself educated as a Protestant, and one of the texts most impressed upon my youthful mind was 'Thou shalt not follow a multitude to do evil.' I am conscious that to this day this text influences me in my most serious actions. The Catholic has quite a different conception of virtue: to him there is in all virtue an element of submission, not only to the voice of God as revealed in conscience, but also to the authority of the Church as the repository of Revelation. This gives to the Catholic a conception of virtue far more social than that of the Protestant, and makes the wrench much greater when he severs his connection with the Church. The Protestant who leaves the particular Protestant sect in which he had been brought up is only doing what the founders of that sect did not so very long ago, and his mentality is adapted to the foundation of a new sect. The Catholic, on the other hand, feels himself lost without the support of the Church. He can, of course, join some other institution such as the freemasons, but he remains conscious, none the less, of desperate revolt. And he generally remains convinced, at any rate subconsciously, that the moral life is confined to members of the Church, so that for the Freethinker the highest kinds of virtue have become impossible. This conviction takes him in different ways according to his temperament; if he is of a cheerful and easy-going disposition he enjoys what William James calls a moral holiday. The most perfect example of this type is Montaigne, who allowed himself also an intellectual holiday in the shape of hostility to systems and deductions. Moderns do not always realise to what extent the Renaissance was an anti-intellectual movement. In the Middle Ages it was the custom to prove things; the Renaissance invented the habit of observing them. The only syllogisms to which Montaigne is friendly are those which prove a particular negative, as for example, when he brings his erudition to bear in order to demonstrate that not all those who died as Arius died were heretics. After enumerating various bad men who have died in this or the like manner, he proceeds: 'But what! Ireneus is found to be in like fortune: God's intent being to teach us that the good have something else to hope for, and the wicked something else to fear, than the good or bad fortune of this world.' Something of this dislike of system has remained characteristic of the Catholic as opposed to the Protestant Freethinker; the reason being again that the system of Catholic theology is so imposing as not to permit an individual (unless he possesses heroic force) to set up another in competition with it.

The Catholic Freethinker accordingly tends to eschew solemnity both moral and intellectual, whereas the Protestant Freethinker is very prone to both. James Mill taught his son 'that the question "Who made me?" could not be answered, because we have no experience or authentic information from which to answer it; and that any answer only throws the difficulty a step farther back, since the question immediately presents itself "Who made God?".' Compare with this what Voltaire has to say about God in the *Dictionnaire Philosophique*. The article 'Dieu' in that work begins as follows: 'During the reign of Arcadius, Logomacos, lecturer in theology of Constantinople, went to Scythia and halted at the foot of the Caucasus, in the fertile plains of Zephirim, on the frontier of Colchis. That worthy old man Dondindac was in his great hall, between his huge sheepfold and his vast barn; he was kneeling with his wife, his five sons and five daughters, his parents and his servants, and after a light meal they were all singing God's praises.'

The article proceeds in the same vein and winds up with the conclusion: 'Since that time I resolved never to argue.' One cannot imagine a time when James Mill would have resolved to argue no longer, nor a subject, even had it been less sublime, which he would have illustrated by a fable. Nor could he have practised the art of skilful irrelevance, as Voltaire does when he says of Leibniz: 'He declared in the North of Germany that God could make only one world.' Or compare the moral fervour with which James Mill asserted the existence of evil with the following passage in which

Voltaire says the same thing: 'To deny that there exists evil could be said jokingly by a Lucullus who is in fine health and who is eating a good dinner with his friends and his mistress in the parlour of Apollo; but let him look out of the window and he would see some miserable human beings; let him suffer from fever and he would be miserable himself.'

Montaigne and Voltaire are the supreme examples of cheerful sceptics. Many Catholic Freethinkers, however, have been far from cheerful, and have always felt the need of a rigid faith and a directing Church. Such men sometimes become Communists; of this Lenin was the supreme example. Lenin took over his faith from a Protestant Freethinker (for Jews and Protestants are mentally indistinguishable), but his Byzantine antecedents compelled him to create a Church as the visible embodiment of the faith. A less successful example of the same attempt is August Comte. Men with his temperament, unless they have abnormal force, relapse sooner or later into the bosom of the Church. In the realm of philosophy a very interesting example is Mr Santayana, who has always loved orthodoxy in itself, but hankered after some intellectually less abhorrent form than that provided by the Catholic Church. He liked always in Catholicism the institution of the Church and its political influence; he liked, speaking broadly, what the Church has taken over from Greece and from Rome, but he did not like what the Church has taken over from the Jews, including, of course, whatever it owes to its Founder. He could have wished that Lucretius had succeeded in founding a Church based upon the tenets of Democritus, for materialism has always appealed to his intellect, and, at any rate in his earlier works, he came nearer to worshipping matter than to awarding this distinction to anything else. But in the long run he seems to have come to feel that any Church which actually exists is to be preferred to a Church confined to the realm of essence. Mr Santayana, however, is an exceptional phenomenon, and hardly fits into any of our modern categories. He is really pre-Renaissance, and belongs if anything with the Ghibellines whom Dante found suffering in Hell for their adherence to the doctrines of Epicurus. This outlook is, no doubt, reinforced by the nostalgia for the past which an unwilling and prolonged contact with America was bound to produce in a Spanish temperament.

Everybody knows how George Eliot taught F. W. H. Myers that there is no God, and yet we must be good. George Eliot in this typified the Protestant Freethinker. One may say, broadly speaking, that Protestants like to be good and have invented theology in order to keep themselves so, whereas Catholics like to be bad and have invented theology in order to keep their neighbours good. Hence the social character of Catholicism and the individual character of Protestatism. Jeremy Bentham, a typical Protestant Freethinker, considered that the greatest of all pleasures is the pleasure of self-approbation. He was therefore not tempted to eat or drink to excess, to be guilty of loose living, or to steal his neighbour's purse, for none of these would have given him that exquisite thrill that he shared with Jack Horner, but not on such easy terms, since he had to forgo the Christmas pie in order to get it. In France, on the other hand, it was ascetic morality that first broke down; theological doubt came later and as a consequence. This distinction is probably national rather than one of creeds.

The connection between religion and morals is one which deserves impartial geographical study. I remember in Japan coming across a Buddhist sect in which the priesthood was hereditary. I inquired how this could be since the general Buddhist priests are celibate; nobody could inform me, but I at last ascertained the facts in a book. It appeared that the sect had started from the doctrine of justification by faith, and had deduced that so long as the faith remained pure, sin did not matter; consequently, the priesthood all decided to sin, but the only sin that tempted them was marriage. From that day to our own the priests of this sect have married, but have otherwise lived blameless lives. Perhaps if Americans could be made to believe that marriage is a sin they would no longer feel the need for divorce. Perhaps it is of the essence of a wise social system to label a number of harmless actions 'Sin', but tolerate those who perform them. In this way the pleasure of wickedness can be obtained without harm to anyone. This point has been forced upon me in dealing with children. Every child wishes at times to be naughty, and if he has been taught rationally, he can only gratify the impulse to naughtiness by some really harmful action, whereas if he has been taught that it is wicked to play cards on Sunday, or, alternatively, to eat meat on Friday, he can gratify the impulse to sin without injuring anyone. I do not say that I act upon this principle in practice; nevertheless, the case of the Buddhist sect which I spoke of just now suggests that it might be wise to do so.

It would not do to insist too rigidly upon the distinction that we have been trying to make between Protestant and Catholic Freethinkers; for example, the *Encyclopédistes* and *Philosophe*s of the late eighteenth century were Protestant types, and Samuel Butler I should regard, though with some hesitation, as a Catholic type. The chief distinction that one notices is that in the Protestant type departure from tradition is primarily intellectual, whereas in the Catholic type it is primarily practical. The typical Protestant Free-thinker has not the slightest desire to do anything of which his neighbours disapprove apart from the advocacy of heretical opinions. *Home Life with Herbert Spencer*, by Two (one of the most delightful books in existence), mentions the common opinion of that philosopher to the effect that 'There is nothing to be said for him but that he has a good moral character.' It would not have occurred to Herbert Spencer, to Bentham, to the Mills, or to any of the other British Freethinkers who maintained in their works that pleasure is the end of life – it would not have occurred, I say, to any of these men to seek pleasure themselves, whereas a Catholic who arrived at the same conclusions would have to set to work to live in accordance with them. It must be said that in this respect the world is changing. The Protestant Freethinker of the present day is apt to take liberties in action as well as in thought, but that is only a symptom of the general decay of Protestantism. In the good old days a Protestant Freethinker would have been capable of deciding in the abstract in favour of free love, and nevertheless living all his days a life of strict celibacy. I think the change is regrettable. Great ages and great individuals have arisen from the breakdown of a rigid system: the rigid system has given the necessary discipline and co-herence, while its breakdown has released the necessary energy. It is a mistake to suppose that the admirable consequences achieved in the first moment of breakdown can continue indefinitely. No doubt the ideal is a certain rigidity of action, plus a certain plasticity of thought, but this is difficult to achieve in practice except during brief transitional periods. And it seems likely that if the old ortho-doxies decay, new rigid creeds will grow up through the necessities of conflict. There will come to be Bolshevik atheists in Russia who will throw doubt upon the divinity of Lenin, and infer that it is not wicked to love one's children. There will be Kuomintang atheists in China who will have reservations about Sun Yat-Sen, and a scarcely avowed respect for Confucius. I fear the decay of liberalism will make it increasingly difficult for men to refrain from adherence to some fighting creed. Probably the various kinds of atheists will have to combine in a secret society and revert to the methods invented by Bayle in his dictionary. There is, at any rate, this consolation, that persecution of opinion has an admirable effect upon literary style.

*Chapter 7*

# Life in the Middle Ages[1]

Our picture of the Middle Ages, perhaps even more than that of other periods, has been falsified to suit our own prejudices. Sometimes the picture has been too black, sometimes too rosy. The eighteenth century, which had no doubt of itself, regarded mediaeval times as merely barbarous: to Gibbon, the men of those days would have been our 'rude forefathers'. The reaction against the French Revolution produced the romantic admiration of absurdity, based upon the experience that reason led to the guillotine. This engendered a glorification of the supposed 'age of chivalry', popularised among English-speaking people by Sir Walter Scott. The average boy or girl is probably still dominated by the romantic view of the Middle Ages: he or she imagines a period when knights wore armour, carried lances, said 'quotha' and 'by my halidom', and were invariably either courteous or wrathful; when all ladies were beautiful and distressed, but were sure to be rescued at the end of the story. There is a third view, quite different, though, like the second, it admires the Middle Ages; this is the ecclesiastical view, engendered by dislike of the Reformation. The emphasis here is on piety, orthodoxy, the scholastic philosophy, and the unification of Christendom by the Church. Like the romantic view, it is a reaction against reason, but a less naïve reaction, cloaking itself in the forms of reason, appealing to a great system of thought which once dominated the world and may dominate it again.

In all these views there are elements of truth: the Middle Ages were rude, they were knightly, they were pious. But if we wish to see a period truly, we must not see it contrasted with our own, whether to its advantage or disadvantage: we must try to see it as it was to those who lived in it. Above all, we must remember that, in every epoch, most people are ordinary people, concerned with their daily

[1] Written in 1925.

bread rather than with the great themes of which historians treat. Such ordinary mortals are portrayed by Miss Eileen Power in a delightful book, *Medieval People*, which ranges from the time of Charlemagne to that of Henry VII. The only eminent person in her gallery is Marco Polo; the other five are more or less obscure individuals, whose lives are reconstructed by means of documents which happen to survive. Chivalry, which was an aristocratic affair, does not appear in these democratic annals; piety is displayed by peasants and British merchants, but is much less in evidence in ecclesiastical circles; and everybody is much less barbaric than the eighteenth century would have expected. There is, however, in favour of the 'barbaric' view, one very striking contrast brought out in the book: the contrast between Venetian art just before the Renaissance and Chinese art in the fourteenth century. Two pictures are reproduced: one a Venetian illustration of Marco Polo's embarkation, the other a Chinese fourteenth-century landscape of Chao Meng-fu. Miss Powers says: 'The one [that by Chao Meng-fu] is so obviously the work of a highly developed and the other by an almost naïve and childish civilisation.' No one who compares the two can fail to agree.

Another recent book, *The Waning of the Middle Ages*, by Professor Huizinga of Leiden, gives an extraordinarily interesting picture of the fourteenth and fifteenth centuries in France and Flanders. In this book chivalry receives its fair share of attention, not from the romantic point of view, but as an elaborate game which the upper classes invented to beguile the intolerable tedium of their lives. An essential part of chivalry was the curious courtly conception of love, as something which it was pleasant to leave unsatisfied. 'When in the twelfth century unsatisfied desire was placed by the troubadours of Provence in the centre of the poetic conception of love, an important turn in the history of civilisation was effected. Courtly poetry ... makes desire itself the essential motif, and so creates a conception of love with a negative ground-note.' And again:

'The existence of an upper class whose intellectual and moral notions are enshrined in an *ars amandi* remains a rather exceptional fact in history. In no other epoch did the ideal of civilisation amalgamate to such a degree with that of love. Just as scholasticism represents the grand effort of the mediaeval spirit to unite all philosophic thought in a single centre, so the theory of courtly love, in a less elevated sphere, tends to embrace all that appertains to the noble life.'

A great deal of the Middle Ages may be interpreted as a conflict between Roman and Germanic traditions: on the one side the Church, on the other the State; on the one side theology and philosophy, on the other chilvalry and poetry; on the one side the law, on the other pleasure, passion, and all the anarchic, impulses of very headstrong men. The Roman tradition was not that of the great days of Rome, it was that of Constantine and Justinian; but even so it contained something which the turbulent nations needed, and without which civilisation could not have re-emerged from the Dark Ages. Because men were fierce, they could only be curbed by an awful severity: terror was employed until it lost its effect through familiarity. After describing the Dance of Death, a favourite subject of late mediaeval art, in which skeletons dance with living men, Dr Huizinga proceeds to tell of the churchyard of the Innocents in Paris, where Villon's contemporaries promenaded for pleasure:

'Skulls and bones were heaped up in charnel-houses along the cloisters enclosing the ground on three sides, and lay there open to the eye by thousands, preaching to all the lesson of equality. ... Under the cloisters the death dance exhibited its images and its stanzas. No place was better suited to the simian figure of grinning death, dragging along pope and emperor, monk and fool. The Duke of Berry, who wished to be buried there, had the history of the three dead and the three living men carved at the portal of the church. A century later, this exhibition of funeral symbols was completed by a large statue of Death, now in the Louvre, and the only remnant of it all. Such was the place which the Parisians of the fifteenth century frequented as a sort of lugubrious counterpart of the Palais Royal of 1789. Day after day, crowds of people walked under the cloisters, looking at the figures and reading the simple verses, which reminded them of the approaching end. In spite of the incessant burials and exhumations going on there, it was a public lounge and rendezvous. Shops were established before the charnel-houses and prostitutes strolled under the cloisters. A female recluse was immured on one of the sides of the church. Friars came to preach and processions were drawn up there. ... Even feasts were given there. To such an extent had the horrible become familiar.'

As might be expected from the love of the *macabre*, cruelty was one of the most highly prized pleasures of the populace. Mons purchased a brigand, solely in order to see him tortured, 'at which the people rejoiced more than if a new holy body had risen from the dead'. In 1488, some of the magistrates of Bruges, suspected of treason, were repeatedly tortured in the market-place for the delectation of the people. They begged to be killed, but the boon was refused, says Dr Huizinga, 'that the people may feast again upon their torments'.

Perhaps, after all, there is something to be said for the eighteenth-century view.

Dr Huizinga has some very interesting chapters on the art of the late Middle Ages. The exquisiteness of the painting was not equalled in architecture and sculpture, which became florid from the love of magnificence associated with feudal pomp. For example, when the Duke of Burgundy employed Sluter to make an elaborate Calvary at Champmol, the arms of Burgundy and Flanders appeared on the arms of the cross. What is still more surprising is that the figure of Jeremiah which formed part of the group had a pair of spectacles on its nose! The author draws a pathetic picture of a great artist controlled by a Philistine patron, and then proceeds to demolish it by suggesting that perhaps 'Sluter himself considered Jeremiah's spectacles a very happy find'. Miss Power mentions an equally surprising fact: that in the thirteenth century an Italian Bowdler, outdoing Tennyson in Victorian refinement, published a version of the Arthurian legends which omitted all reference to the loves of Lancelot and Guinevere. History is full of queer things, for example that a Japanese Jesuit was martyred at Moscow in the sixteenth century. I wish some erudite historian would write a book called 'facts that have astonished me.' In such a book Jeremiah's spectacles and the Italian Bowdler should certainly find a place.

*Chapter 8*

# The Fate of
# Thomas Paine[1]

Thomas Paine, though prominent in two Revolutions and almost hanged for attempting to raise a third, is grown, in our day, somewhat dim. To our great-grandfathers he seemed a kind of earthly Satan, a subversive infidel rebellious alike against his God and his King. He incurred the bitter hostility of three men not generally united: Pitt, Robespierre, and Washington. Of these the first two sought his death, while the third carefully abstained from measures designed to save his life. Pitt and Washington hated him because he was a democrat; Robespierre, because he opposed the execution of the King and the Reign of Terror. It was his fate to be always honoured by Opposition and hated by Governments: Washington, while he was still fighting the English, spoke of Paine in terms of highest praise; the French nation heaped honours upon him until the Jacobins rose to power; even in England, the most prominent Whig statesmen befriended him and employed him in drawing up manifestos. He had faults, like other men; but it was for his virtues that he was hated and successfully calumniated.

Paine's importance in history consists in the fact that he made the preaching of democracy democratic. There were, in the eighteenth century, democrats among French and English aristocrats, among *philosophes* and Nonconformist ministers. But all of them presented their political speculations in a form designed to appeal only to the educated. Paine, while his doctrine contained nothing novel, was an innovator in the manner of his writing, which was simple, direct, unlearned, and such as every intelligent working man could appreciate. This made him dangerous; and when he added religious unorthodoxy to his other crimes, the defenders of privilege seized the opportunity to load him with obloquy.

The first thirty-six years of his life gave no evidence of the talents

[1] Written in 1934.

which appeared in his later activities. He was born at Thetford in 1739, of poor Quaker parents, and was educated at the local grammar school up to the age of thirteen, when he became a stay-maker. A quiet life, however, was not his taste, and at the age of seventeen he tried to enlist on a privateer called *The Terrible*, whose captain's name was Death. His parents fetched him back and so probably saved his life, as 175 out of the crew of 200 were shortly afterwards killed in action. A little later, however, on the outbreak of the Seven Years War, he succeeded in sailing on another privateer, but nothing is known of his brief adventures at sea. In 1758 he was employed as a stay-maker in London, and in the following year he married, but his wife died after a few months. In 1763 he became an exciseman, but was dismissed two years later for professing to have made inspections while he was in fact studying at home. In great poverty, he became a schoolmaster at ten shillings a week, and tried to take Anglican orders. From such desperate expedients he was saved by being reinstated as an exciseman at Lewes, where he married a Quakeress from whom, for reasons unknown, he formally separated in 1774. In this year he again lost his employment, apparently because he organised a petition of the excisemen for higher pay. By selling all that he had, he was just able to pay his debts and leave some provision for his wife, but he himself was again reduced to destitution.

In London, where he was trying to present the exciseman's petition to Parliament, he made the acquaintance of Benjamin Franklin, who thought well of him. The result was that in October 1774, he sailed for America, armed with a letter of recommendation from Franklin describing him as an 'ingenious, worthy young man'. As soon as he arrived in Philadelphia, he began to show skill as a writer, and almost immediately became editor of a journal.

His first publication, in March 1775, was a forcible article against slavery and the slave trade, to which, whatever some of his American friends might say, he remained always an uncompromising enemy. It seems to have been largely owing to his influence that Jefferson inserted in the draft of the Declaration of Independence the passage on this subject which was afterwards cut out. In 1775, slavery still existed in Pennsylvania; it was abolished in that State by an Act of 1780, of which, it was generally believed, Paine wrote the preamble.

Paine was one of the first, if not the very first, to advocate complete freedom for the United States. In October 1775, when even those who subsequently signed the Declaration of Independence were still hoping for some accommodation with the British Government, he wrote:

'I hesitate not for a moment to believe that the Almighty will finally separate America from Britain. Call it Independency or what you will, if it is the cause of God and humanity it will go on. And when the Almighty shall have blest us, and made us a people *dependent only upon him*, then may our first gratitude be shown by an act of continental legislation, which shall put a stop to the importation of Negroes for sale, soften the hard fate of those already here, and in time procure their freedom.'

It was for the sake of freedom – freedom from monarchy, aristocracy, slavery, and every species of tyranny – that Paine took up the cause of America.

During the most difficult years of the War of Independence he spent his days campaigning and his evenings composing rousing manifestos published under the title 'Common Sense'. These had enormous success, and helped materially in winning the war. After the British had burnt the towns of Falmouth in Maine and Norfolk in Virginia, Washington wrote to a friend (January 31, 1776):

'A few more of such flaming arguments as were exhibited at Falmouth and Norfolk, added to the sound doctrine and unanswerable reasoning contained in the pamphlet *Common Sense*, will not leave numbers at a loss to decide upon the propriety of separation.'

The work was topical, and has now only an historical interest, but there are phrases in it that are still telling. After pointing out that the quarrel is not only with the King, but also with Parliament, he says: 'There is no body of men more jealous of their privileges than the Commons: Because they sell them.' At that date it was impossible to deny the justice of this taunt.

There is vigorous argument in favour of a Republic, and a triumphant refutation of the theory that monarchy prevents civil war. 'Monarchy and succession,' he says, after a summary of English history, 'have laid ... the world in blood and ashes. 'Tis a form of government which the word of God bears testimony against, and blood will attend it.' In December 1776, at a moment when the fortunes of war were adverse, Paine published a pamphlet called *The Crisis*, beginning:

'These are the times that try men's souls. The summer soldier and the sunshine patriot will, in this crisis, shrink from the service of their country; but he that stands it *now* deserves the love and thanks of man and woman.'

This essay was read to the troops, and Washington expressed to Paine a 'living sense of the importance of your works'. No other writer was so widely read in America, and he could have made large sums by his pen, but he always refused to accept any money at all for what he wrote. At the end of the War of Independence, he was universally respected in the United States, but still poor; however, one State legislature voted him a sum of money and another gave him an estate, so that he had every prospect of comfort for the rest of this life. He might have been expected to settle down into the respectability characteristic of revolutionaries who have succeeded. He turned his attention from politics to engineering, and demonstrated the possibility of iron bridges with longer spans than had previously been thought feasible. Iron bridges led him to England, where he was received in a friendly manner by Burke, the Duke of Portland, and other Whig notables. He had a large model of his iron bridge set up at Paddington; he was praised by eminent engineers, and seemed likely to spend his remaining years as an inventor.

However, France as well as England was interested in iron bridges. In 1788 he paid a visit to Paris to discuss them with Lafayette, and to submit his plans to the Académie des Sciences, which, after due delay, reported favourably. When the Bastille fell, Lafayette decided to present the key of the prison to Washington, and entrusted to Paine the task of conveying it across the Atlantic. Paine, however, was kept in Europe by the affairs of his bridge. He wrote a long letter to Washington informing him that he would find someone to take his place in transporting 'this early trophy of the spoils of despotism, and the first ripe fruits of American principles transplanted into Europe'. He goes on to say that 'I have not the least doubt of the final and compleat success of the French Revolution,' and that 'I have manufactured a Bridge (a single arch) of one hundred and ten feet span, and five feet high from the cord of the arch.'

For a time, the bridge and the Revolution remained thus evenly balanced in his interests, but gradually the Revolution conquered. In the hope of arousing a responsive movement in England, he wrote his *Rights of Man*, on which his fame as a democrat chiefly rests.

This work, which was considered madly subversive during the anti-Jacobin reaction, will astonish a modern reader by its mildness and common sense. It is, primarily, an answer to Burke, and deals at considerable length with contemporary events in France. The first part was published in 1791, the second in February 1792; there was therefore as yet no need to apologise for the Revolution. There is very little declamation about Natural Rights, but a great deal of sound sense about the British Government. Burke had contended that the Revolution of 1688 bound the British for ever to submit to the sovereigns appointed by the Act of Settlement. Paine contends that it is impossible to bind posterity, and that constitutions must be capable of revision from time to time.

Governments, he says, 'may all be comprehended under three heads. First, Superstition. Secondly, Power. Thirdly, the common interest of society and the common rights of man. The first was a government of priestcraft, the second of conquerors, the third of reason.' The two former amalgamated: 'the key of St Peter and the key of the Treasury became quartered on one another, and the wondering cheated multitude worshipped the invention'. Such general observations, however, are rare. The bulk of the work consists, first, of French history from 1789 to the end of 1791, and, secondly, of a comparison of the British Constitution with that decreed in France in 1791, of course to the advantage of the latter. It must be remembered that in 1791 France was still a monarchy. Paine was a republican and did not conceal the fact, but did not much emphasise it in the *Rights of Man*.

Paine's appeal, except in a few short passages, was to common sense. He argued against Pitt's finance, as Cobbett did later, on grounds which ought to have appealed to any Chancellor of the Exchequer; he described the combination of a small sinking fund with vast borrowings as setting a man with a wooden leg to catch a hare – the longer they run, the farther apart they are. He speaks of the 'Potter's field of paper money' – a phrase quite in Cobbett's style. It was, in fact, his writings on finance that turned Cobbett's former enmity into admiration. His objection to the hereditary principle, which horrified Burke and Pitt, is now common ground among all politicians, including even Mussolini and Hitler. Nor is his style in any way outrageous: it is clear, vigorous, and downright, but not nearly as abusive as that of his opponents.

Nevertheless, Pitt decided to inaugurate his reign of terror by prosecuting Paine and suppressing the *Rights of Man*. According to his niece, Lady Hester Stanhope, he 'used to say that Tom Paine was quite in the right, but then, he would add, what am I to do? As things are, if I were to encourage Tom Paine's opinions we should have a bloody revolution.' Paine replied to the prosecution by defiance and inflammatory speeches. But the September massacres were occurring, and the English Tories were reacting by increasing fierceness. The poet Blake – who had more worldly wisdom than Paine – persuaded him that if he stayed in England he would be hanged. He fled to France, missing the officers who had come to arrest him by a few hours in London and by twenty minutes in Dover, where he was allowed by the authorities to pass because he happened to have with him a recent friendly letter from Washington.

Although England and France were not yet at war, Dover and Calais belonged to different worlds. Paine, who had been elected a honorary French citizen, had been returned to the Convention by three different constituencies, of which Calais, which now welcomed him, was one. 'As the packet sails in a salute is fired from the battery; cheers sound along the shore. As the representative for Calais steps on French soil soldiers make his avenue, the officers embrace him, the national cockade is presented' – and so on through the usual French series of beautiful ladies, mayors, etc.

Arrived in Paris, he behaved with more public spirit than prudence. He hoped – in spite of the massacres – for an orderly and moderate Revolution such as he had helped to make in America. He made friends with the Girondins, refused to think ill of Lafayette (now in disgrace), and continued, as an American, to express gratitude to Louis XVI for his share in liberating the United States. By opposing the King's execution down to the last moment, he incurred the hostility of the Jacobins. He was first expelled from the Convention, and then imprisoned as a foreigner; he remained in prison throughout Robespierre's period of power and for some months longer. The responsibility rested only partly with the French; the American Minister, Gouverneur Morris, was equally to blame. He was a Federalist, and sided with England against France; he had, moreover, an ancient personal grudge against Paine for exposing a friend's corrupt deal during the War of Independence. He took the line that Paine was not an American, and that he could therefore do nothing for him. Washington, who was secretly negotiating Jay's treaty with England, was not sorry to have Paine in a situation in which he could not enlighten the French Government as to reactionary opinion in America. Paine escaped the guillotine by accident, but nearly died of illness. At last Morris was replaced by Monroe (of the 'Doctrine'), who immediately procured his release, took him into his own house, and restored him to health by eighteen months' care and kindness.

Paine did not know how great a part Morris had played in his misfortunes, but he never forgave Washington, after whose death, hearing that a statue was to be made of the great man, he addressed the following lines to the sculptor:

> Take from the mine the coldest, hardest stone,
> It needs no fashion: it is Washington.
> But if you chisel, let the stroke be rude,
> And on his heart engrave – Ingratitude.

This remained unpublished, but a long bitter letter to Washington was published in 1796, ending:

'And as to you, Sir, treacherous in private friendship (for so you have been to me, and that in the day of danger) and a hypocrite in pubilc life, the world will be puzzled to decide whether you are an apostate or an imposter; whether you have abandoned good principles, or whether you ever had any.'

To those who know only the statuesque Washington of the legend, these may seem wild words. But 1796 was the year of the first contest for the Presidency, between Jefferson and Adams, in which Washington's whole weight was thrown into support of the latter, in spite of his belief in monarchy and aristocracy; moreover, Washington was taking sides with England against France, and doing all in his power to prevent the spread of those republican and democratic principles to which he owed his own elevation. These public grounds, combined with a very grave personal grievance, show that Paine's words were not without justification.

It might have been more difficult for Washington to leave Paine languishing in prison if that rash man had not spent his last days of liberty in giving literary expression to the theological opinions which he and Jefferson shared with Washington and Adams, who, however, were careful to avoid all public avowals of unorthodoxy. Foreseeing his imprisonment, Paine set to work to write *The Age of Reason*, of which he finished Part I six hours before his arrest. This book shocked his contemporaries, even many of those who agreed with his politics. Nowadays, apart from a few passages in bad taste, there is very little that most clergymen would disagree with. In the first chapter he says:

'I believe in one God, and no more; and I hope for happiness beyond this life.

'I believe in the equality of man, and I believe that religious duties consist in doing justice, loving mercy, and endeavouring to make our fellow-creatures happy.'

These were not empty words. From the moment of his first participation in public affairs – his protest against slavery in 1775 – down to the day of his death, he was consistently opposed to every form of cruelty, whether practised by his own party or by his opponents. The Government of England at that time was a ruthless oligarchy, using Parliament as a means of lowering the standard of life in the poorest classes; Paine advocated political reform as the only cure for this abomination, and had to fly for his life. In France, for opposing unnecessary bloodshed, he was thrown into prison and narrowly escaped death. In America, for opposing slavery and upholding the principles of the Declaration of Independence, he was abandoned by the Government at the moment when he most needed its support. If, as he maintained and as many now believe, true religion consists in 'doing justice, loving mercy, and endeavouring to make our fellow-creatures happy', there was not one among his opponents who had as good a claim to be considered a religious man.

The greater part of *The Age of Reason* consists of criticism of the Old Testament from a moral point of view. Very few nowadays would regard the massacres of men, women and children recorded in the Pentateuch and the Book of Joshua as models of righteousness, but in Paine's day it was considered impious to criticise the Israelites when the Old Testament approved of them. Many pious divines wrote answers to him. The most liberal of those was the Bishop of Llandaff who went so far as to admit that parts of the Pentateuch were not written by Moses, and some of the Psalms were not composed by David. For such concessions he incurred the hostility of George III and lost all chance of translation to a richer see. Some of the Bishop's replies to Paine are curious. For example, *The Age of Reason* ventured to doubt whether God really commanded that all males and married women among the Midianites should be slaughtered, while the maidens should be preserved. The Bishop indignantly retorted that the maidens were not preserved for immoral purposes, as Paine had wickedly suggested, but as slaves, to which there could be no ethical objection. The orthodox of our day have forgotten what orthodoxy was like a hundred and forty years ago. They have forgotten still more completely that it was men like Paine, who, in face of persecution, caused the softening of dogma by which our age profits. Even the Quakers refused Paine's request for burial in their cemetery, although a Quaker farmer was one of the very few who followed his body to the grave.

After *The Age of Reason* Paine's work ceased to be important. For a long time he was very ill; when he recovered, he found no scope in the France of the Directoire and the First Consul. Napoleon did not ill-treat him, but naturally had no use for him, except as a possible agent of democratic rebellion in England. He became homesick for America, remembering his former success and popularity in that country, and wishing to help the Jeffersonians against the Federalists. But the fear of capture by the English, who would certainly have hanged him, kept him in France until the Treaty of Amiens. At length, in October 1802, he landed at Baltimore, and at once wrote to Jefferson (now President):

'I arrived here on Saturday from Havre, after a passage of sixty days. I have several cases of models, wheels, etc., and as soon as I can get them from the vessel and put them on board the packet for Georgetown I shall set off to pay my respects to you. Your much obliged fellow-citizen,

THOMAS PAINE'

He had no doubt that all his old friends, except such as were Federalists, would welcome him. But there was a difficulty: Jefferson had a hard fight for the Presidency, and in the campaign the most effective weapon against him – unscrupulously used by ministers of all denominations – had been the accusation of infidelity. His opponents magnified his intimacy with Paine, and spoke of the pair as 'the two Toms'. Twenty years later, Jefferson was still so much impressed by the bigotry of his compatriots that he replied to a Unitarian minister who wished to publish a letter of his: 'No, my dear Sir, not for the world! ... I should as soon undertake to bring the crazy skulls of Bedlam to sound understanding as to inculcate reason into that of an Athanasian... keep me therefore from the fire and faggot of Calvin and his victim Servetus.' It was not surprising that, when the fate of Servetus threatened them, Jefferson and his political followers should have fought shy of too close an association with Paine. He was treated politely, and had no cause to complain, but the old easy friendships were dead.

In other circles he fared worse. Dr Rush of Philadelphia, one of his first American friends, would have nothing to do with him: 'His principles,' he wrote, 'avowed in his *Age of Reason*, were so offensive to me that I did not wish to renew my intercourse with him.' In his own neighbourhood, he was mobbed, and refused a seat in the stage coach; three years before his death he was not allowed to vote, on the alleged ground of his being a foreigner. He was falsely accused of immorality and intemperance, and his last years were spent in solitude and poverty. He died in 1809. As he was dying, two clergymen invaded his room and tried to convert him, but he merely said, 'Let me alone; good morning!' Nevertheless, the orthodox invented a myth of deathbed recantation which was widely believed.

His posthumous fame was greater in England than in America. To publish his works was, of course, illegal, but it was done repeatedly, although many men went to prison for this offence. The last prosecution on this charge was that of Richard Carlile and his wife in 1819; he was sentenced to prison for three years and a fine of fifteen hundred pounds, she to one year and five hundred pounds. It was in this year that Cobbett brought Paine's bones to England and established his fame as one of the heroes in the fight for democracy in England. Cobbett did not, however, give his bones a permanent resting-place. 'The monument contemplated by Cobbett,' says Moncure Conway,[1] 'was never raised.' There was much parliamentary and municipal excitement. A Bolton town-crier was imprisoned nine weeks for proclaiming the arrival. In 1836 the bones passed with Cobbett's effects into the hands of a receiver (West). The Lord Chancellor refusing to regard them as an asset, they were kept by an old day-labourer until 1833, when they passed to B. Tilley, 13 Bedford Square, London, a furniture dealer. ... In 1854 Rev. R. Ainslie (Unitarian) told E. Truelove that he owned 'the skull and the right hand of Thomas Paine,' but evaded subsequent inquiries. No trace now remains, even of the skull and right hand.

Paine's influence in the world was twofold. During the American Revolution he inspired enthusiasm and confidence, and thereby did much to facilitate victory.

In France his popularity was transient and superficial, but in England he inaugurated the stubborn resistance of plebeian Radicals to the long tyranny of Pitt and Liverpool. His opinions on the Bible, though they shocked his contemporaries more than his unitarianism, were such as might now be held by an Archbishop, but his true followers were the men who worked in the movement that sprang from him – those whom Pitt imprisoned, those who suffered under the Six Acts, the Owenites, Chartists, Trade Unionists, and Socialists. To all these champions of the oppressed he set an example of courage, humanity, and single-mindedness. When public issues were involved, he forgot personal prudence. The world decided, as it usually does in such cases, to punish him for his lack of self-seeking; to this day his fame is less than it would have been if his character had been less generous. Some worldly wisdom is required even to secure praise for the lack of it.

---

[1] Whose biography of Paine and edition of his works are a monument of patient devotion and careful research.

## Chapter 9

# Nice People[1]

I intend to write an article in praise of nice people. But the reader may wish to know first who are the people that I consider nice. To get at their essential quality may perhaps be a little difficult, so I will begin by enumerating certain types who come under the heading. Maiden aunts are invariably nice, especially, of course, when they are rich; ministers of religion are nice, except those rare cases in which they elope to South Africa with a member of the choir after pretending to commit suicide. Young girls, I regret to say, are seldom nice nowadays. When I was young, most of them were quite nice; that is to say, they shared their mother's opinions, not only about topics but, what is more remarkable, about individuals, even young men. They said 'Yes, mamma,' and 'No, mamma,' at the appropriate moments; they loved their father because it was their duty so to do, and their mother because she preserved them from the slightest hint of wrong-doing. When they became engaged to be married they fell in love with decorous moderation; being married, they recognised it as a duty to love their husbands, but gave other women to understand that it was a duty that they performed with great difficulty. They behaved nicely to their parents-in-law, while making it clear that any less dutiful person would not have done so; they did not speak spitefully about other women, but pursed up their lips in such a way as to let it be seen what they might have said but for their angelic charitableness. This type is what is called a pure and noble woman. The type, alas, now hardly exists except among the old.

Mercifully the survivors still have great power: they control education, where they endeavour, not without success, to preserve a Victorian standard of hypocrisy; they control legislation on what are called 'moral issues', and have thereby created and endowed the great profession of bootlegging; they ensure that the young men who write for the newspapers shall express the opinions of the nice old ladies rather than their own, thereby enlarging the scope of the

[1] First published in 1931.

young men's style and the variety of their psychological imagination. They keep alive innumerable pleasures which otherwise
would be quickly ended by a surfeit: for example, the pleasure of
hearing bad language on the stage, or of seeing there a slightly larger
amount of bare skin than is customary. Above all, they keep alive the
pleasures of the hunt. In a homogeneous country population, such
as that of an English shire, people are condemned to hunt foxes; this
is expensive and sometimes even dangerous. Moreover, the fox
cannot explain very clearly how much he dislikes being hunted. In
all these respects the hunting of human beings is better sport, but if
it were not for the nice people, it would be difficult to hunt human
beings with a good conscience. Those whom the nice people condemn are fair game; at their call of 'Tally-ho!' the hunt assembles,
and the victim is pursued to prison or death. It is especially good
sport when the victim is a woman, since this gratifies the jealousy of
the women and the sadism of the men. I know at this moment a
foreign woman living in England, in happy though extra-legal
union with a man whom she loves and who loves her; unfortunately
her political opinions are not so conservative as could be wished,
though they are mere opinions, about which she does nothing.
The nice people, however, have used this excuse to set Scotland
Yard upon the scent, and she is to be sent back to her native country
to starve. In England, as in America, the foreigner is a morally de-
grading influence, and we all owe a debt of gratitude to the police
for the care which they take to see that only exceptionally virtuous
foreigners are allowed to reside among us.

It must not be supposed that all nice people are women, though,
of course, it is much commoner for a woman to be nice than for a
man. Apart from ministers of religion, there are many other nice
men. For example: those who have made large fortunes and have
now retired from business to spend their fortunes on charity; magistrates are also almost invariably nice men. It cannot, however, be
said that all supporters of law and order are nice men. When I was
young I remember hearing it advanced by a nice woman, as an
argument against capital punishment, that the hangman could
hardly be a nice man. I have never known any hangmen personally,
so I have not been able to test this argument empirically. I knew a
lady, however, who met the hangman in the train without knowing
who he was, and when she offered him a rug, the weather being cold,
he said, 'Ah, madam, you wouldn't do that if you knew who I am,'
which seems to show that he was a nice man after all. This, however,
must have been exceptional. The hangman in Dickens's *Barnaby
Rudge*, who is emphatically not a nice man, is probably more typical.

I do not think, however, that we ought to agree with the nice woman I quoted a moment ago in condemning capital punishment merely because the hangman is not likely to be nice. To be a nice person it is necessary to be protected from crude contact with reality, and those who do the protecting cannot be expected to share the niceness that they preserve. Imagine, for example, a wreck on a liner which is transporting a number of coloured labourers; the first-class female passengers, all of whom are presumably nice women, will be saved first, but in order that this may happen, there must be men who keep the coloured labourers from swamping the boats, and it is unlikely that these men will be able to succeed by nice methods. The women who have been saved, as soon as they are safe, will begin to feel sorry for the poor labourers who were drowned, but their tender hearts are rendered possible only by the rough men who defended them.

In general, nice people leave the policing of the world to hirelings because they feel the work to be not such as a person who is quite nice would wish to undertake. There is, however, one department which they do not delegate, namely the department of back-biting and scandal. People can be placed in a hierarchy of niceness by the power of their tongues. If A talks against B, and B talks against A, it will generally be agreed by the society in which they live that one of them is exercising a public duty, while the other is actuated by spite; the one who is exercising the public duty is the one who is the nicer of the two. Thus, for example, a headmistress in a school is nicer than an assistant mistress, but a lady who is on the school board is nicer than either. Well-directed tittle-tattle may easily cause its victim to lose his or her livelihood, and even when this extreme result is not achieved, it may turn a person into a pariah. It is, therefore, a great force for good, and we ought to be thankful that it is the nice people who wield it.

The chief characteristic of nice people is the laudable practice of improvement upon reality. God made the world, but nice people feel that they could have done the job better. There are many things in the Divine handiwork which, while it would be blasphemous to wish them otherwise, it would be by no means nice to mention. Divines have held that if our first parents had not eaten the apple the human race would have been replenished by some innocent mode of vegetation, as Gibbon calls it. The Divine plan in this respect is certainly mysterious. It is all very well to regard it, as the aforesaid divines do, in the light of a punishment of sin, but the trouble with this view is that while it may be a punishment for the nice people, the others, alas, find it quite pleasant. It would seem, therefore, as if the punishment had been made to fall in the wrong quarter. One of the main purposes of the nice people is to redress this no doubt unintended injustice. They endeavour to secure that the biologically ordained mode of vegetation shall be practised either furtively or frigidly, and that those who practise it furtively shall, when found out, be in the power of the nice people, owing to the damage that may be done to them by scandal. They endeavour to insure also that as little as possible shall be known on the subject in a decent way; they try to get the censor to forbid books and plays which represent the matter otherwise than as an occasion for sniggering nastiness; in this they are successful wherever and in so far as they control the laws and the police. It is not known why the Lord made the human body as he did, since one must suppose that omnipotence could have made it such as would not have shocked the nice people. Perhaps, however, there was a good reason. There has been in England, ever since the rise of the textile industry in Lancashire, a close alliance between missionaries and the cotton trade, for missionaries teach savages to cover up the human body and thereby increase the demand for cotton goods. If there had been nothing shameful about the human body, the textile trade would have lost this source of profit. This instance shows that we need never be afraid lest the spread of virtue should diminish our profits.

Whoever invented the phrase 'the naked truth' had perceived an important connection. Nakedness is shocking to all right-minded people, and so is truth. It matters little with what department you are concerned; you will soon find that truth is such as nice people will not admit into their consciousness. Whenever it has been my ill-fortune to be present in court during the hearing of a case about which I had some first-hand knowledge, I have been struck by the fact that no crude truth is allowed to penetrate within those august portals. The truth that gets into a law court is not the naked truth, but the truth in court dress, with all its less decent portions concealed. I do not say that this applies to the trial of straightforward crimes, such as murder or theft, but it applies to all those into which an element of prejudice enters, such as political trials, or trials for obscenity. I believe that in this respect England is worse than America, for England has brought to perfection the almost invisible and half-unconscious control of everything unpleasant by means of feelings of decency. If you wish to mention in a law court any unassimilable fact you will find that it is contrary to the laws of evidence to do so, and that not only the judge and the opposing counsel, but also counsel on your own side will prevent the said fact from coming out.

The same sort of unreality pervades politics, owing to the feelings of nice people. If you attempt to persuade any nice person that a politican of his own party is an ordinary mortal no better than the mass of mankind he will indignantly repudiate the suggestion. Consequently it is necessary to politicians to appear immaculate. At most times the politicians of all parties tacitly combine to prevent anything damaging to the profession from getting known, for difference of party usually does less to divide politicians than identity of profession does to unite them. In this way the nice people are able to preserve their fancy picture of the nation's great men, and school children can be made to believe that eminence is to be achieved only by the highest virtue. There are, it is true, exceptional times when politics become really bitter, and at all times there are politicians who are not considered sufficiently respectable to belong to the informal trade union. Parnell, for example, was first unsuccessfully accused of co-operation with murderers and then successfully convicted of an offence against morality, such as, of course, none of his accusers would have dreamed of committing. In our own day Communists in Europe and extreme Radicals and Labour agitators in America are outside the pale; no large body of nice people admires them, and if they offend against the conventional code they can expect no mercy. In this way the immovable moral convictions of nice people become linked with the defence of property, and thus once more prove their inestimable worth.

Nice people very properly suspect pleasure whenever they see it. They know that he that increaseth wisdom increaseth sorrow, and they infer that he that increaseth sorrow increaseth wisdom. They therefore feel that in spreading sorrow they are spreading wisdom; since wisdom is more precious than rubies, they are justified in feeling that they are conferring a benefit in so doing. They will, for example, make a public playground for children in order to per- suade themselves that they are philanthropic, and then impose so many regulations upon its use that no child can be as happy there as in the streets. They will do their best to prevent playgrounds, theatres, etc., from being open on a Sunday, because that is the day when they might be enjoyed. Young women in their employment are prevented as far as possible from talking with young men. The nicest people I have known carried this attitude into the bosom of the family and made their children play only instructive games. This degree of niceness, however, I regret to say, is becoming less common than it was. In old days children were taught that:

> One stroke of His almighty rod
> Can send young sinners quick to Hell,

and it was understood that this was likely to happen if children became boisterous or indulged in any activity such as was not calculated to fit them for the ministry. The education based upon this point of view is set forth in *The Fairchild Family*, an invaluable work on how to produce nice people. I know few parents, however, in the present day who live up to this high standard. It has become sadly common to wish children to enjoy themselves, and it is to be feared that those who have been educated on these lax principles will not display adequate horror of pleasure when they grow up.

The day of nice people, I fear, is nearly over; two things are killing it. The first is the belief that there is no harm in being happy, provided no one else is the worse for it; the second is the dislike of humbug, a dislike which is quite as much aesthetic as moral. Both these revolts were encouraged by the War, when the nice people in all countries were securely in control, and in the name of the highest morality induced the young people to slaughter one another. When it was all over the survivors began to wonder whether lies and misery inspired by hatred constituted the highest virtue. I am afraid it may be some time before they can again be induced to accept this fundamental doctrine of every really lofty ethic.

The essence of nice people is that they hate life as manifested in tendencies to co-operation, in the boisterousness of children, and above all in sex, with the thought of which they are obsessed. In a word, nice people are those who have nasty minds.

## Chapter 10

# The New Generation

*This piece is Russell's introduction to the book,* The New Generation,[1] *which contained contributions by a number of prominent psychologists and students of the social sciences. In connection with Russell's remark that in Russia alone 'the state is not in the grip of moral and religious prejudices' it should be emphasised that this was written in 1930. In the later years of the Stalin regime all attempts to establish a rational code of sexual morality were abandoned and legislation in this sphere became if anything more repressive and puritanical than in Western countries. Russell himself had predicted the likelihood of such a development as early as 1920.*

In the following pages, various branches of knowledge as affecting the welfare of children and the relations of children to parents are dealt with by contributors who have specialised in the several fields concerned. As an introduction to these studies I propose to consider the kind of way in which new knowledge has transformed, and still more is likely to transform, the traditional biological relations. I am thinking not only nor even chiefly of the deliberate and intended effects of knowledge, but also and more particularly of knowledge as a natural force producing unintended results of the most curious and unexpected kinds. I am sure that James Watt had no desire to establish a matriarchal family; yet by making it possible for men to sleep in places distant from those in which they work he has had this effect upon a great part of our urban populations. The place of the father in the modern suburban family is a very small one – particularly if he plays golf, which he usually does. It is a little difficult to see what he is purchasing when he pays for his children, and but for tradition it may be doubted whether he would consider children a good bargain. The patriarchal family in its heyday gave a man immense advantages: it gave him sons who would support him in his old age and defend him against his numerous enemies. Now, in

[1] London: George Allen & Unwin Ltd.

all those classes in which men live on investments or save out of their earnings, the son never becomes financially advantageous to the father however long they both may live.

New knowledge is the cause of the economic and psychological changes which make our age at once difficult and interesting. In the old days man was subject to nature: to inanimate nature as regards climate and the fertility of crops, to human nature as regards the blind urges which led him to beget and to fight. The resulting sense of impotence was utilised by religion in transforming fear into a duty and resignation into a virtue. The modern man, who as yet exists in only a few samples, has a different outlook. The material world is not to him a datum to be accepted with thankfulness or with prayerful supplication; it is raw material for his scientific manipulation. A desert is a place to which water must be brought, a malarial swamp is a place from which water must be taken away. Neither is allowed to maintain its natural hostility to man, so that in our struggles with physical nature we no longer have need of God to help us against Satan. What is perhaps as yet less appreciated is that an essentially similar change has begun to take place in regard to human nature. It has become clear that, while the individual may have difficulty in deliberately altering his character, the scientific psychologist, if allowed a free run with children, can manipulate human nature as freely as Californians manipulate the desert. It is no longer Satan who makes sin, but bad glands and unwise conditioning.

Perhaps at this point the reader will expect a definition of sin. This, however, offers no difficulty: sin is what is disliked by those who control education.

It must be confessed that this situation puts upon the holders of scientific power a new and grave responsibility. Hitherto mankind have survived because however foolish their purposes might be they had not the knowledge required to achieve them. Now that this knowledge is being acquired, a greater degree of wisdom than heretofore as regards the ends of life is becoming imperative. But where is such wisdom to be found in our distracted age?

The above general reflections are merely intended to suggest that all our institutions, even those most intimately connected with what used to be called instinct, are bound in the near future to become far more deliberate and conscious than they have been or are now, and that this must apply in particular to the getting and rearing of children. The new way may be better than the old; it also may easily be worse. But the new knowledge of our times has been thrust so rudely into the mechanism of traditional behaviour that the old patterns cannot survive, and new ones for good or evil have become imperative.

The family survives from the unspecialised past when a man made his own boots and baked his own bread. Male activities have passed beyond this stage, but it is held by the virtuous that there should be no corresponding change in the activities of females. Dealing with children is a specialised activity requiring specialised knowledge and a suitable environment. The rearing of children in the home is of a piece with the spinning wheel, and is equally uneconomic. With the growth of knowledge more and more departments of child-nurture have to be taken away from the home. It is no longer customary for the child to be born in the home. When he is ill he is not treated by the simple traditional lore which killed most of the children of his ancestors. Prayers are no longer taught at his mother's knee but in the Sunday School. Teeth are not extracted, as they still were when I was young, by tying a string to them and the door handle and then shutting the door. Medical knowledge possesses itself of one part of the child's life, knowledge of hygiene seizes another, child-psychology demands a third. In the end the distracted mother gives it up as a bad job, and under threat of the Oedipus complex begins to feel that all her natural affection smacks of sin.

One of the main causes of change is the diminution of births and deaths. Fortunately both have diminished together; for if either diminution had occurred without the other the result would have been disaster. The governments of the world, in combination with the churches, whose influence depends upon human misery and impotence, have done all that lay in their power to produce this disaster, since they have attempted to prevent any diminution in this birth rate correlative to the diminution in the death rate. In this respect, however, fortunately for mankind, individual selfishness has proved stronger than collective folly.

The smallness of the modern family has given parents a new sense of the value of the child. Parents who have only two children do not wish either to die, whereas out of the old-fashioned family of ten or fifteen, half could be sacrificed to carelessness with no great qualms. Modern scientific care of children is intimately bound up with the smallness of the modern family.

At the same time this change has made the family a less suitable psychological environment for the children and a less absorbing occupation for women. Having fifteen children most of whom died was no doubt an unpleasant life work, but at any rate it left little leisure for self-realisation. Having two or three children, on the other hand, is not felt to be an adequate life work, and yet so long as the old-fashioned home is preserved it interferes gravely with any other career. Thus the fewer children people have the more of a burden the children are felt to be.

In these days, when most people live in cities in cramped surroundings because of high rents, the home is as a rule physically the wrong environment for the child. The man who rears young trees in a nursery garden provides them with the right soil, the right light and air, the right space, and the right neighbours. He does not attempt to rear the trees one by one in separate cellars. Yet that is what has to be done with children so long as they remain in the modern urban home. Children, like young trees, require soil and light and air and neighbours of their own kind. Children ought to be in the country, where they can have freedom without excitement. The psychological atmosphere of a small urban apartment is as bad as the physical. Consider the one matter of noise. Busy grown-up people cannot be expected to endure a continual racket all round them, but to tell a child not to make a noise is a form of cruelty producing in him exasperation leading to grave moral faults. Much the same thing applies to the necessity for not breaking things. When a boy climbs on the kitchen shelves and breaks all the china, his parents are seldom quite pleased. Yet his activity is of a kind that is essential to his physical development. In an environment made for children such natural and healthy impulses need not be checked.

Psychological changes in the outlook of parents are inevitably produced by the scientific and economic changes affecting the family. With the growth of a sense of security there has gone inevitably an increase of individualism. What limited individualism in the past was fear and the need of mutual co-operation. A colony of settlers surrounded by Indians had of necessity a strong communal sense, for if not they would be wiped out. At present safety is provided by the State, not by voluntary co-operation, so that a man can afford to be individualistic in that part of his life which he individually controls. This applies in particular to the family relations. A man's part in the care of children is little more than financial, and his financial obligations will be enforced by the law if necessary, so that they make little demand upon his personal sense of duty. A woman, if she is vigorous and intelligent, is likely to feel that the truncated maternal duties remaining to her are inadequate as a career, the more so as most of them can be performed more scientifically by experts. This feeling would operate much more widely but for the lingering feeling on the part of men that they like their wives to be financially dependent upon them. This is, however, a kind of feeling surviving from an earlier age; it is already much weakened and likely to disappear before very long.

All these developments have diminished the reasons which led people to avoid divorce. As divorce becomes more frequent and more easy the family is still further weakened, since in effect it usually results in a child having only one parent.

For all these and other reasons set forth in Dr Watson's contribution,[1] it seems inevitable, for good or evil, that the family as a unit should more and more fade away, leaving no group to interpose its authority between the individual and the State. This does not apply so much to the well-to-do, who may continue to employ special nurseries, special schools, special doctors, and all the expensive mechanisms of private enterprise; but for wage earners the cost of such individualism is prohibitive. Where their children are concerned it is inevitable that any functions no longer performed by parents must come to be undertaken by the State. As regards the immense majority, therefore, the choice lies, not between parental care and the care of experts selected by parents, but between parents and the State.

This prospect entails upon all who understand the modern scientific attitude towards children a grave responsibility of propaganda. At present the State, except in Russia, is in the grip of moral and religious prejudices which make it totally incapable of dealing with children in a scientific manner. I would recommend readers to consider, for example, the contributions of Havelock Ellis[2] and Phyllis Blanchard[3] to the following pages. Every candid reader must realise that, so long as traditional ethics and theology cannot be flouted by politicians, the methods advocated in these contributions will not be employed in any institution over which the State has control. The State of New York, for example, still officially holds that masturbation causes insanity, and it is clear that no politician could controvert this opinion without bringing his career to an abrupt close. It cannot therefore be hoped that masturbation will be scientifically treated in any State institution other than a lunatic asylum or home for the feeble-minded. These institutions alone are allowed to adopt proper methods, because lunatics and idiots are not considered morally responsible. This state of affairs is absurd. One might as well have a law that only cheap cars could be repaired, while expensive cars were to be whipped or

---

[1] Russell here refers to Watson's article 'After the Family – What?' which was contained in *The New Generation*.

[2] Havelock Ellis: *Perversion in Childhood and Adolescence*.

[3] Phyllis Blanchard: *Obscenity in Children*.

treated by sermons from ministers of religion. Those who visualise a great extension of State institutions for children in the future generally imagine themselves or their friends at the head of such institutions. This, of course, is a fond delusion. Since a considerable salary would be attached to the control of any important institution of this kind, it is clear that the superintendent would usually be the maiden aunt of some prominent politician. Under her noble inspiration, the children would be taught to say their prayers, to revere the cross and the flag, to feel agonies of remorse when they masturbated and deep horror when they heard other children mentioning how babies are made. With institutions economically adapted to the machine age such mental slavery might be prolonged for countless ages, the more so as there would be plenty of renegade scientists willing to help in closing young people's minds against all the approaches of reason. It might even prove possible to eradicate the practice of birth control, in which case, in view of the efficiency of modern medicine, it would be necessary greatly to increase the frequency and ferocity of war in order to deal with the surplus population.

For such reasons, if the State is to acquire such immense powers it is imperative that the State should become enlightened. It will not do this of itself; it will do it only when the majority of the population has ceased to insist upon the preservation of ancient superstitions. Most enlightened people live in an unreal world, associating with their friends and imagining that only a few freaks are unenlightened nowadays. A little experience of practical politics, and still more of the administration of the law wherever so-called moral issues are involved, would be highly beneficial to all who have rational opinions whether on child-nuture or on any other topic. I am convinced that a widespread popular propaganda of rationalism is far more important than it is thought to be by most rationalists outside Russia.

Assuming the break-up of the family and the establishment of rationally conducted State institutions for children, it will probably be found necessary to go a step further in the substitution of regulation for instinct. Women accustomed to birth control and not allowed to keep their own children would have little motive for enduring the discomfort of gestation and the pain of childbirth. Consequently in order to keep up the population it would probably be necessary to make child-bearing a well-paid profession, not of course to be undertaken by all women or even by a majority, but only by a certain percentage who would have to pass tests as to their fitness from a stock-breeding point of view. What tests should be imposed upon sires and what proportion they should form of the male population are questions which we are not yet called upon to decide. But the question of securing an adequate number of births is likely to become acute very soon, since the diminution of the birth rate continues and must soon entail a diminution of the population, or at any rate of the able-bodied population – for if medicine were to succeed in keeping most people alive up to the age of a hundred the gain to the community would be problematical.

The gain to the human race to be expected from a rational psychology in the handling of children is almost unlimited. The most important sphere is of course that of sex. Children are taught a superstitious attitude about certain parts of the body, about certain words and thoughts, and about certain kinds of play to which nature prompts them. The result is that when they become adult they are stiff and awkward in all matters of love. Throughout the English-speaking world most people while still in the nursery are rendered incapable of satisfactory marriage. There is no other adult activity for which children are forbidden to prepare themselves by play, or in regard to which there is expected to be a sudden transition from absolute taboo to perfect competence.

The sense of sin which dominates many children and young people and often lasts on into later life is a misery and a source of distortion that serves no useful purpose of any sort or kind. It is produced almost entirely by conventional moral teaching in the sphere of sex. The feeling that sex is wicked makes happy love impossible, causing men to despise the women with whom they have relations and often to have impulses of cruelty towards them. Moreover, the indirection which is forced upon the sexual impulse when it is inhibited, leading it to take the form of sentimental friendship or religious ardour or whatnot, causes a lack of intellectual sincerity which is very inimical to intelligence and to the sense of reality. Cruelty, stupidity, incapacity for harmonious personal relations, and many other defects, have their source in most cases in the moral teaching endured during childhood. Let it be said with the utmost simplicity and directness: there is nothing bad in sex, and the conventional attitude in this matter is morbid. I believe that no other one evil in our society is so potent a source of human misery, since not only does it directly cause a long train of evils, but it inhibits that kindliness and human affection that might lead men to remedy the other remediable evils, economical, political, and racial, by which humanity is tortured.

For these reasons books which spread knowledge and a rational attitude on the subject of child psychology are much needed. There is in our day a kind of race between the increasing power of the State and the diminishing power of superstition. That the powers of the State should increase seems inevitable, as we have seen in relation to children. But if these powers increase beyond a point while superstitions still control the majority, the unsuperstitious minority will be squeezed out by State propaganda and further protests will become impossible in every democratic country. Our society is becoming so closely knit that reform in any one direction is bound up with reform in every other and no question can be adequately treated in isolation. But I think our age is more kindly disposed towards children than any earlier age has been, and if it comes to be understood that conventional moral teaching is a cause of suffering to the young we may hope for a demand that it shall be replaced by something at once more kindly and more scientific.

## Chapter 11

# Our Sexual Ethics[1]

I

Sex, more than any other element in human life, is still viewed by many, perhaps by most, in an irrational way. Homicide, pestilence, insanity, gold and precious stones – all the things, in fact, that are the objects of passionate hopes or fears – have been seen, in the past, through a mist of magic or mythology; but the sun of reason has now dispelled the mist, except here and there. The densest cloud that remains is in the territory of sex, as is perhaps natural since sex is concerned in the most passionate part of most people's lives.

It is becoming apparent, however, that conditions in the modern world are working to effect a change in the public attitude towards sex. As to what change, or changes, this will bring about, no one can speak with any certainty; but it is possible to note some of the forces now at work, and to discuss what their results are likely to be upon the structure of society.

Insofar as human nature is concerned, it cannot be said to be *impossible* to produce a society in which there is very little sexual intercourse outside of marriage. The conditions necessary for this result, however, are such as are made almost unattainable by modern life. Let us, then, consider what they are.

The greatest influence towards effecting monogamy is immobility in a region containing few inhabitants. If a man hardly ever has occasion to leave home, and seldom sees any woman but his wife, it is easy for him to be faithful; but if he travels without her, or lives in a crowded urban community, the problem is proportionately more difficult. The next greatest assistance to monogamy is superstition: those who genuinely believe that 'sin' leads to eternal punishment might be expected to avoid it, and to some extent they do so, although not to so great an extent as might be expected. The third support of virtue is public opinion. Where, as in agricultural societies, all that a man does is known to his neighbours, he has power-

[1] First published in 1936.

ful motives for avoiding whatever convention condemns. But all these causes of correct behaviour are much less potent than they used to be. Fewer people live in isolation; the belief in hell-fire is dying out; and in large towns no one knows what his neighbour does. It is, therefore, not surprising that both men and women are less monogamous than they were before the rise of modern industrialism.

Of course, it may be said that, while an increasing number of people fail to observe the moral law, that is no reason for altering our standards. Those who sin, we are sometimes told, should know and recognise that they sin, and an ethical code is none the worse for being difficult to live up to. But I should reply that the question whether a code is good or bad is the same as the question whether or not it promotes human happiness. Many adults, in their hearts, still believe all that they were taught in childhood, and feel wicked when their lives do not conform to the maxims of the Sunday school. The harm done is not merely to introduce a division between the conscious reasonable personality and the unconscious infantile personality; the harm lies also in the fact that the valid parts of conventional morality become discredited along with the invalid parts and it comes to be thought that, if adultery is excusable, so are laziness, dishonesty, and unkindness. This danger is inseparable from a system which teaches the young, *en bloc*, a number of beliefs that they are almost sure to discard when they become mature. In the process of social and economic revolt, they are likely to throw over the good along with the bad.

The difficulty of arriving at a workable sexual ethic arises from the conflict between the impulse to jealousy and the impulse to polygamy. There is no doubt that jealousy, while in part instinctive, is to a very large degree conventional. In societies in which a man is considered a fit object for ridicule if his wife is unfaithful, he will be jealous where she is concerned, even if he no longer has any affection for her. Thus jealousy is intimately connected with the sense of property, and is much less where this sense is absent. If faithfulness is no part of what is conventionally expected, jealousy is much diminished. But although there is more possibility of lessening jealousy than many people suppose, there are very definite limits so long as fathers have rights and duties. So long as this is the case, it is inevitable that men should desire some assurance that they are the fathers of their wives' children. If women are to have sexual freedom, fathers must fade out, and wives must no longer expect to be supported by their husbands. This may come about in time, but it will be a profound social change, and its effects, for good or ill, are incalculable.

In the meantime, if marriage and paternity are to survive as social institutions, some compromise is necessary between complete promiscuity and life-long monogamy. To decide on the best compromise at any given moment is not easy; and the decision should vary from time to time, according to the habits of the population and the reliability of birth-control methods. Some things, however, can be said with some definiteness.

In the first place, it is undesirable, both physiologically and educationally, that women should have children before the age of twenty. Our ethics should, therefore, be such as to make this a rare occurrence.

In the second place, it is unlikely that a person without previous sexual experience, whether man or woman, will be able to distinguish between mere physical attraction and the sort of congeniality that is necessary in order to make marriage a success. Moreover, economic causes compel men, as a rule, to postpone marriage, and it is neither likely that they will remain chaste in the years from twenty to thirty, nor desirable psychologically that they should do so; but it is much better that, if they have temporary relations, these should be not with professionals, but with girls of their own class, whose motive is affection rather than money. For both these reasons, young unmarried people should have considerable freedom as long as children are avoided.

In the third place, divorce should be possible without blame to either party, and should not be regarded as in any way disgraceful. A childless marriage should be terminable at the wish of one of the partners, and any marriage should be terminable by mutual consent — a year's notice being necessary in either case. Divorce should, of course, be possible on a number of other grounds — insanity, desertion, cruelty, and so on; but mutual consent should be the most usual ground.

In the fourth place, everything possible should be done to free sexual relations from the economic taint. At present, wives, just as much as prostitutes, live by the sale of their sexual charms; and even in temporary free relations the man is usually expected to bear all the joint expenses. The result is that there is a sordid entanglement of money with sex, and that women's motives not infrequently have a mercenary element. Sex, even when blessed by the Church, ought not to be a profession. It is right that a woman should be paid for housekeeping or cooking or the care of children, but not merely for having sexual relations with a man. Nor should a woman who has once loved and been loved by a man be able to live ever after on alimony when his love and hers have ceased. A woman, like a man, should work for her living, and an idle wife is no more intrinsically worthy of respect than a gigolo.

## II

Two very primitive impulses have contributed, though in very different degrees, to the rise of the currently accepted code of sexual behaviour. One of these is modesty, and the other, as mentioned above, is jealousy. Modesty, in some form and to some degree, is almost universal in the human race, and constitutes a taboo which must only be broken through in accordance with certain forms and ceremonies, or, at the least, in conformity with some recognised etiquette. Not everything may be seen, and not all facts may be mentioned. This is not, as some moderns suppose, an invention of the Victorian age; on the contrary, anthropologists have found the most elaborate forms of prudery among primitive savages. The conception of the obscene has its roots deep in human nature. We may go against it from a love of rebellion, or from loyalty to the scientific spirit, or from a wish to feel wicked, such as existed in Byron; but we do not thereby eradicate it from among our natural impulses. No doubt convention determines, in a given community, exactly what is to be considered indecent, but the universal existence of *some* convention of the kind is conclusive evidence of a source which is not merely conventional. In almost every human society, pornography and exhibitionism are reckoned as offences, except when, as not infrequently occurs, they form part of religious ceremonies.

Ascetism – which may or may not have a psychological connection with modesty – is an impulse which seems to arise only where a certain level of civilisation has been reached, but may then become powerful. It is not to be found in the earlier books of the Old Testament, but it appears in the later books, in the Apocrypha, and in the New Testament. Similarly among the Greeks there is little of it in early times, but more and more as time goes on. In India, it arose at a very early date, and acquired great intensity. I will not attempt to give a psychological analysis of its origin, but I cannot doubt that it is a spontaneous sentiment, existing, to some slight extent, in almost all civilised human beings. Its faintest form is reluctance to imagine a revered individual – especially a person possessed of religious sanctity – engaged in love-making, which is felt to be scarcely compatible with the highest degree of dignity. The wish to free the spirit from bondage to the flesh has inspired many of the great religions of the world, and is still powerful even among modern intellectuals.

But jealousy, I believe, has been the most potent single factor in the genesis of sexual morality. Jealousy instinctively rouses anger; and anger, rationalised, becomes moral disapproval. The purely instinctive motive must have been reinforced, at an early stage in the development of civilisation, by the desire of males to be certain of paternity. Without security in this respect the patriarchal family would have been impossible, and fatherhood, with all its economic implications, could not have become the basis of social institutions. It was, accordingly, wicked to have relations with another man's wife, but not even mildly reprehensible to have relations with an unmarried woman. There were excellent practical reasons for condemning the adulterer, since he caused confusion and very likely bloodshed. The siege of Troy was an extreme example of the upheavals due to disrespect for the rights of husbands, but something of the sort, though on a smaller scale, was to be expected even when the parties concerned were less exalted. There were, of course, in those days, no corresponding rights of wives; a husband had no duty to his wife, though he had the duty of respecting the property of other husbands.

The old system of the patriarchal family, with an ethic based on the feelings that we have been considering, was, in a sense, successful: men, who dominated, had considerable liberty, and women, who suffered, were in such complete subjection that their unhappiness seemed not important. It is the claim of women to equality with men that has done most to make a new system necessary in the world today. Equality can be secured in two ways: either by exacting from men the same strict monogamy as was, in the past, exacted from women; or by allowing women, equally with men, a certain relaxation of the traditional code. The first of these ways was preferred by most of the pioneers of women's rights, and is still preferred by the churches; but the second has many more adherents in practice, although most of them are in doubt as to the theoretical justifiability of their own behaviour. And those who recognise that *some* new ethic is required find it difficult to know just what its precepts should be.

There is another source of novelty, and that is the effect of the scientific outlook in weakening the taboo on sexual knowledge. It has come to be understood that various evils – for example, venereal disease – cannot be effectively combated unless they are spoken of much more openly than was formerly thought permissible; and it has also been found that reticence and ignorance are apt to have injurious effects upon the psychology of the individual. Both sociology and psychoanalysis have led serious students to deprecate the policy of silence in regard to sexual matters, and many practical educators, from experience with children, have adopted the same position. Those who have a scientific outlook on human behaviour, moreover, find it impossible to label any action as 'sin'; they realise that what we do has its origin in our heredity, our education, and our environment, and that it is by control of these causes, rather than by denunciation, that conduct injurious to society is to be prevented.

In seeking a new ethic of sexual behaviour, therefore, we must not ourselves be dominated by the ancient irrational passions which gave rise to the old ethic, though we should recognise that they may, by accident, have led to some sound maxims, and that, since they still exist, though perhaps in a weakened form, they are still among the data of our problem. What we have to do positively is to ask ourselves what moral rules are most likely to promote human happiness, remembering always that, whatever the rules may be, they are not likely to be universally observed. That is to say, we have to consider the effect which the rules will in fact have, not that which they would have if they were completely effective.

### III

Let us look next at the question of knowledge on sexual subjects, which arises at the earliest age and is the least difficult and doubtful of the various problems with which we are concerned. There is no sound reason, of any sort or kind, for concealing facts when talking to children. Their questions should be answered and their curiosity satisfied in exactly the same way in regard to sex as in regard to the habits of fishes, or any other subject that interests them. There should be no sentiment, because young children cannot feel as adults do, and see no occasion for high-flown talk. It is a mistake to begin with the loves of the bees and the flowers; there is no point in leading up to the facts of life by devious routes. The child who is told what he wants to know, and allowed to see his parents naked, will have no pruriency and no obsession of a sexual kind. Boys who are brought up in official ignorance think and talk much more about sex than boys who have always heard this topic treated on a level with any other. Official ignorance and actual knowledge teach them to be deceitful and hypocritical with their elders. On the other hand, real ignorance, when it is achieved, is likely to be a source of shock and anxiety, and to make adaptation to real life difficult. All ignorance is regrettable, but ignorance on so important a matter as sex is a serious danger.

When I say that children should be told about sex, I do not mean that they should be told only the bare physiological facts; they should be told whatever they wish to know. There should be no attempt to represent adults as more virtuous than they are, or sex as occurring only in marriage. There is no excuse for deceiving children. And when, as must happen in conventional families, they find that their parents have lied, they lose confidence in them, and feel justified in lying to them. There are facts which I should not obtrude upon a child, but I would tell him anything sooner than say what is not true. Virtue which is based upon a false view of the facts is not real virtue. Speaking not only from theory, but from practical experience, I am convinced that complete openness on sexual subjects is the best way to prevent children from thinking about them excessively, nastily, or unwholesomely, and also the almost indispensable preliminary to an enlightened sexual morality.

Where adult sexual behaviour is concerned, it is by no means easy to arrive at a rational compromise between the antagonistic considerations that have each their own validity. The fundamental difficulty is, of course, the conflict between the impulse to jealousy and the impulse to sexual variety. Neither impulse, it is true, is universal: there are those (though they are few) who are never jealous, and there are those (among men as well as among women) whose affections never wander from the chosen partner. If either of these types could be made universal, it would be easy to devise a satisfactory code. It must be admitted, however, that either type can be made more common by conventions designed to that end.

Much ground remains to be covered by a complete sexual ethic, but I do not think we can say anything very positive until we have more experience, both of the effects of various systems and of the changes resulting from a rational education in matters of sex. It is clear that marriage, as an institution, should only interest the State because of children, and should be viewed as a purely private matter so long as it is childless. It is clear, also, that, even where there are children, the State is only interested through the duties of fathers, which are chiefly financial. Where divorce is easy, as in Scandinavia, the children usually go with the mother, so that the patriarchal family tends to disappear. If, as is increasingly happening where wage-earners are concerned, the State takes over the duties that have hitherto fallen upon fathers, marriage will cease to have any *raison d'être*, and will probably be no longer customary except among the rich and the religious.

In the meantime, it would be well if men and women could remember, in sexual relations, in marriage, and in divorce, to practise the ordinary virtues of tolerance, kindness, truthfulness, and justice. Those who, by conventional standards, are sexually virtuous, too often consider themselves thereby absolved from behaving like decent human beings. Most moralists have been so obsessed by sex that they have laid much too little emphasis on other more socially useful kinds of ethically commendable conduct.

## Chapter 12

# Freedom and the Colleges

*This article was originally published in May 1940, very shortly after Judge McGeehan's finding that Russell was 'unfit' to be a professor at City College, New York.*

I

Before discussing the present status of academic freedom it may be as well to consider what we mean by the term. The essence of academic freedom is that teachers should be chosen for their expertness in the subject they are to teach, and that the judges of this expertness should be other experts. Whether a man is a good mathematician, or physicist, or chemist, can only be judged by other mathematicians, or physicists, or chemists. By them, however, it can be judged with a fair degree of unanimity.

The opponents of academic freedom hold that other conditions besides a man's skill in his own department should be taken into consideration. He should, they think, have never expressed any opinion which controverts those of the holders of power. This is a sharp issue, and one on which the totalitarian states have taken a vigorous line. Russia never enjoyed academic freedom except during the brief reign of Kerensky, but I think there is even less of it now than there was under the Tsars. Germany, before the war, while lacking many forms of liberty, recognised pretty fully the principle of freedom in university teaching. Now all this is changed, with the result that with few exceptions the ablest of the learned men of Germany are in exile. In Italy, though in a slightly milder form, there is a similar tyranny over universities. In Western democracies it is generally recognised that this state of affairs is deplorable. It cannot, however, be denied that there are tendencies which might lead to somewhat similar evils.

The danger is one which democracy by itself does not suffice to avert. A democracy in which the majority exercises its powers without restraint may be almost as tyrannical as a dictatorship. Toleration of minorities is an essential part of wise democracy, but a part which is not always sufficiently remembered.

In relation to university teachers, these general considerations are reinforced by some that are especially applicable to their case. University teachers are supposed to be men with special knowledge and special training such as should fit them to approach controversial questions in a manner peculiarly likely to throw light upon them. To decree that they are to be silent upon controversial issues is to deprive the community of the benefit which it might derive from their training in impartiality. The Chinese Empire, many centuries ago, recognised the need of licensed criticism, and therefore established a Board of Censors, consisting of men with a reputation for learning and wisdom, and endowed with the right to find fault with the Emperor and his government. Unfortunately, like everything else in traditional China, this institution became conventionalised. There were certain things that the censors were allowed to censure, notably the excessive power of eunuchs, but if they wandered into unconventional fields of criticism the Emperor was apt to forget their immunity. Much the same thing is happening among us. Over a wide field criticism is permitted, but where it is felt to be really dangerous, some form of punishment is apt to befall its author.

Academic freedom in this country is threatened from two sources: the plutocracy, and the churches, which endeavour between them to establish an economic and a theological censorship. The two are easily combined by the accusation of Communism, which is recklessly hurled against anyone whose opinions are disliked. For example, I have observed with interest that, although I have criticised the Soviet government severely ever since 1920, and although in recent years I have emphatically expressed the opinion that it is at least as bad as the government of the Nazis, my critics ignore all this and quote triumphantly the one or two sentences in which, in moments of hope, I have suggested the possibility of good ultimately coming out of Russia.

The technique for dealing with men whose opinions are disliked by certain groups of powerful individuals has been well perfected, and is a great danger to ordered progress. If the man concerned is still young and comparatively obscure, his official superiors may be induced to accuse him of professional incompetence, and he may be quietly dropped. With older men who are too well known for this method to be successful, public hostility is stirred up by means of misrepresentation. The majority of teachers naturally do not care to expose themselves to these risks, and avoid giving public expression to their less orthodox opinions. This is a dangerous state of affairs, by which disinterested intelligence is partially muzzled, and the forces of conservatism and obscurantism persuade themselves that they can remain triumphant.

## II

The principle of liberal democracy, which inspired the founders of the American Constitution, was that controversial questions should be decided by argument rather than by force. Liberals have always held that opinions should be formed by untrammelled debate, not by allowing only one side to be heard. Tyrannical governments, both ancient and modern, have taken the opposite view. For my part, I see no reason to abandon the liberal tradition in this matter. If I held power, I should not seek to prevent my opponents from being heard. I should seek to provide equal facilities for all opinions, and leave the outcome to the consequences of discussion and debate. Among the academic victims of German persecution in Poland there are, to my knowledge, some eminent logicians who are completely orthodox Catholics. I should do everything in my power to obtain academic positions for these men, in spite of the fact that their coreligionists do not return the compliment.

The fundamental difference between the liberal and the illiberal outlook is that the former regards all questions as open to discussion and all opinions as open to a greater or less measure of doubt, while the latter holds in advance that certain opinions are absolutely unquestionable, and that no argument against them must be allowed to be heard. What is curious about this position is the belief that if impartial investigation were permitted it would lead men to the wrong conclusion, and that ignorance is, therefore, the only safeguard against error. This point of view is one which cannot be accepted by any man who wishes reason rather than prejudice to govern human action.

The liberal outlook is one which arose in England and Holland during the late seventeenth century, as a reaction against the wars of religion. These wars had raged with great fury for 130 years without producing the victory of either party. Each party felt an absolute certainty that it was in the right and that its victory was of the utmost importance to mankind. At the end, sensible men grew weary of the indecisive struggle and decided that both sides were mistaken in their dogmatic certainty. John Locke, who expressed the new point of view both in philosophy and in politics, wrote at the beginning of an era of growing toleration. He emphasised the fallibility of human judgements, and ushered in an era of progress which lasted until 1914. It is owing to the influence of Locke and his school that Catholics enjoy toleration in Protestant countries, and Protestants in Catholic countries. Where the controversies of the seventeenth century are concerned, men have more or less learned the lesson of toleration, but in regard to the new controversies that have arisen since the end of the Great War the wise maxims of the philosophers of liberalism have been forgotten. We are no longer horrified by Quakers, as were the earnest Christians of Charles II's court, but we are horrified by the men who apply to present-day problems the same outlook and the same principles that seventeenth-century Quakers applied to the problems of their day. Opinions which we disagree with acquire a certain respectability by antiquity, but a new opinion which we do not share invariably strikes us as shocking.

There are two possible views as to the proper functioning of democracy. According to one view, the opinions of the majority should prevail absolutely in all fields. According to the other view, wherever a common decision is not necessary, different opinions should be represented, as nearly as possible, in proportion to their numerical frequency. The results of these two views in practice are very different. According to the former view, when the majority has decided in favour of some opinion, no other must be allowed to be expressed, or if expressed at all must be confined to obscure and uninfluential channels. According to the other view, minority opinions should be given the same opportunities for expression as are given to majority opinions, but only in a lesser degree.

This applies in particular to teaching. A man or woman who is to hold a teaching post under the state should not be required to express majority opinions, though naturally a majority of teachers will do so. Uniformity in the opinions expressed by teachers is not only not to be sought, but is, if possible, to be avoided, since diversity of opinion among preceptors is essential to any sound education. No man can pass as educated who has heard only one side on questions as to which the public is divided. One of the most important things to teach in the educational establishments of a democracy is the power of weighing arguments, and the open mind which is prepared in advance to accept whichever side appears the more reasonable. As soon as a censorship is imposed upon the opinions which teachers may avow, education ceases to serve this purpose and tends to produce, instead of a nation of men, a herd of fanatical bigots. Since the end of the Great War, fanatical bigotry has revived until it has become over a great part of the world as virulent as during the wars of religion. All those who oppose free discussion and who seek to impose a censorship upon the opinions to which the young are to be exposed are doing their share in increasing this bigotry and in plunging the world further into the abyss of strife and intolerance from which Locke and his coadjutors gradually rescued it.

There are two questions which are not sufficiently distinguished: the one as to the best form of government; the other as to the functions of government. I have no doubt in my mind that democracy is the best *form* of government, but it may go as much astray as any other form in regard to the *functions* of government. There are certain matters on which common action is necessary; as to these, the common action should be decided by the majority. There are other matters on which a common decision is neither necessary nor desirable. These matters include the sphere of opinion. Since there is a natural tendency for those who have power to exercise it to the utmost, it is a necessary safeguard against tyranny that there should be institutions and organised bodies which possess, either in practice or in theory, a certain limited independence of the State. Such freedom as exists in the countries which derive their civilisations from Europe is traceable historically to the conflict between Church and State in the Middle Ages. In the Byzantine Empire the Church was subdued by the State, and to this fact we may trace the total absence of any tradition of freedom in Russia, which derived its civilisation from Constantinople. In the West, first the Catholic Church and then the various Protestant sects gradually acquired certain liberties as against the State.

Academic freedom, in particular, was originally a part of the freedom of the Church, and accordingly suffered eclipse in England in the time of Henry VIII. In every state, I repeat, no matter what its form of government, the preservation of freedom demands the existence of bodies of men having a certain limited independence of the State, and among such bodies it is important that universities should be included. In America at the present day there is more academic freedom in private universities than in such as are nominally under a democratic authority, and this is due to a very widespread misconception as to the proper functions of government.

Taxpayers think that since they pay the salaries of university teachers they have a right to decide what these men shall teach. This principle, if logically carried out, would mean that all the advantages of superior education enjoyed by university professors are to be nullified, and that their teaching is to be the same as it would be if they had no special competence. 'Folly, doctor-like, controlling skill' is one of the things that made Shakespeare cry for restful death. Yet democracy, as understood by many Americans, requires that such control should exist in all state universities. The exercise of power is agreeable, especially when it is an obscure individual who exercises power over a prominent one. The Roman soldier who killed Archimedes, if in his youth he had been compelled to study geometry, must have enjoyed a quite special thrill in ending the life of so eminent a malefactor. An ignorant American bigot can enjoy the same thrill in pitting his democratic power against men whose views are obnoxious to the uneducated.

There is perhaps a special danger in democratic abuses of power, namely that being collective they are stimulated by mob hysteria. The man who has the art of arousing the witch-hunting instincts of the mob has a quite peculiar power for evil in a democracy where the habit of the exercise of power by the majority has produced that intoxication and impulse to tyranny which the exercise of authority almost invariably produces sooner or later. Against this danger the chief protection is a sound education, designed to combat the tendency to irrational eruptions of collective hate. Such an education the bulk of university teachers desire to give, but their masters in the plutocracy and the hierarchy make it as difficult as possible for them to carry out this task effectively. For it is to the irrational passions of the mass that these men owe their power, and they know that they would fall if the power of rational thinking became common. Thus the interlocking power of stupidity below and love of power above paralyses the efforts of rational men. Only through a greater measure of academic freedom than has yet been achieved in the public educational institutions of this country can this evil be averted. The persecution of unpopular forms of intelligence is a very grave danger to any country, and has not infrequently been the cause of national ruin. The stock example is Spain, where the expulsion of the Jews and Moors led to the decay of agriculture and the adoption of a completely mad finance. These two causes, though their effects were masked at first by the power of Charles V, were mainly responsible for the decline of Spain from its dominant position in Europe. It may safely be assumed that the same causes will produce the same effects in Germany, ultimately, if not in the near future. In Russia, where the same evils have been in operation for a longer time, the effects have become plainly visible, even in the incompetence of the military machine.

Russia is, for the moment, the most perfect example of a country where ignorant bigots have the degree of control that they are attempting to acquire in New York. Professor A. V. Hill quotes the following from the *Astronomical Journal of the Soviet Union* for December 1938:

1 Modern bourgeois cosmogony is in a state of deep ideological confusion resulting from its refusal to accept the only true dialectic-materialistic concept, namely the infinity of the universe with respect to space as well as time.
2 The hostile work of the agents of Fascism, who at one time managed to penetrate to leading positions in certain astronomical and other institutions as well as in the press, has led to revolting propaganda of counter-revolutionary bourgeois ideology in the literature.
3 The few existing Soviet materialistic works on problems of cosmology have remained in isolation and have been suppressed by the enemies of the people, until recently.
4 Wide circles interested in science have been taught, at best, only in the spirit of indifference towards the ideological aspect of the current bourgeois cosmologic theories . . .
5 The *exposé* of the enemies of the Soviet people makes necessary the development of a new Soviet materialistic cosmology . . .
6 It is deemed necessary that Soviet science should enter the international scientific arena carrying concrete achievements in cosmologic theories on the basis of our philosophic methodology.

For 'Soviet' substitute 'American', for 'Fascism' substitute 'Communism', for 'dialectic-materialism' substitute 'Catholic truth', and you will obtain a document to which the enemies of academic freedom in this country might almost subscribe.

## IV

There is one encouraging feature about the situation, which is that the tyranny of the majority in America, so far from being new, is probably less than it was a hundred years ago. Anybody may draw this conclusion from De Tocqueville's *Democracy in America.* Much of what he says is still applicable, but some of his observations are certainly no longer true. I cannot agree, for example, 'that in no country in the civilised world is less attention paid to philosophy than in the United States'. But I think there is still some justice, though less than in De Tocqueville's day, in the following passage:

'In America the majority raises very formidable barriers to the liberty of opinion: within these barriers an author may write whatever he pleases, but he will repent it if he ever steps beyond them. Not that he is exposed to the terrors of an *auto-da-fé*, but he is tormented by the slights and persecutions of daily obloquy. His political career is closed forever, since he has offended the only authority which is able to promote his success. Every sort of compensation, even that of celebrity, is refused to him. Before he published his opinions he imagined that he held them in common with many others; but no sooner has he declared them openly than he is loudly censured by his overbearing opponents, whilst those who think without having the courage to speak, like him, abandon him in silence. He yields at length, oppressed by the daily efforts he has been making, and he subsides into silence, as if he was tormented by remorse for having spoken the truth.'

I think it must also be admitted that De Tocqueville is right in what he says about the power of society over the individual in a democracy:

'When the inhabitant of a democratic country compares himself individually with all those about him, he feels with pride that he is the equal of any one of them; but when he comes to survey the totality of his fellows, and to place himself in contrast to so huge a body, he is instantly overwhelmed by the sense of his own insignificance and weakness. The same quality which renders him independent of each of his fellow-citizens taken severally, exposes him alone and unprotected to the influence of the greater number. The public has therefore among a democratic people a singular power, of which aristocratic nations could never so much as conceive an idea; for it does not persuade to certain opinions, but it enforces them, and infuses them into the faculties by a sort of enormous pressure of the minds of all upon the reason of each.'

The diminution in the stature of the individual through the hugeness of the Leviathan has, since De Tocqueville's day, taken enormous strides, not only, and not chiefly, in democratic countries. It is a most serious menace to the world of Western civilisation, and is likely, if unchecked, to bring intellectual progress to an end. For all serious intellectual progress depends upon a certain kind of independence of outside opinion, which cannot exist where the will of the majority is treated with that kind of religious respect which the orthodox give to the will of God. A respect for the will of the majority is more harmful than respect for the will of God, because the will of the majority can be ascertained. Some forty years ago, in the town of Durban, a member of the Flat Earth Society challenged the world to public debate. The challenge was taken up by a sea captain whose only argument in favour of the world's being round was that he had been round it. This argument, of course, was easily disposed of, and the Flat Earth propagandist obtained a two-thirds majority. The voice of the people having been thus declared, the true democrat must conclude that in Durban the earth is flat. I hope that from that time onward no one was allowed to teach in the public schools of Durban (there is, I believe, no university there) unless he subscribed to the declaration that the roundness of the earth is an infidel dogma designed to lead to communism and the destruction of the family. As to this, however, my information is deficient.

Collective wisdom, alas, is no adequate substitute for the intelligence of individuals. Individuals who opposed received opinions have been the source of all progress, both moral and intellectual. They have been unpopular, as was natural. Socrates, Christ, and Galileo all equally incurred the censure of the orthodox. But in former times the machinery of suppression was far less adequate than it is in our day, and the heretic, even if executed, still obtained adequate publicity. The blood of the martyrs was the seed of the Church, but this is no longer true in a country like modern Germany, where the martyrdom is secret and no means exists of spreading the martyr's doctrine.

The opponents of academic freedom, if they could have their way, would reduce this country to the level of Germany as regards the promulgation of doctrines of which they disapprove. They would substitute organised tyranny for individual thought; they would proscribe everything new; they would cause the community to ossify; and in the end they would produce a series of generations which would pass from birth to death without leaving any trace in the history of mankind. To some it may seem that what they are demanding at the moment is not a very grave matter. Of what importance, it may be said, is such a question as academic freedom in a world distracted by war, tormented by persecution, and abounding in concentration camps for those who will not be accomplices in iniquity? In comparison with such things, I admit, the issue of academic freedom is not in itself of the first magnitude. But it is part and parcel of the same battle. Let it be remembered that what is at stake, in the greatest issues as well as in those that seem smaller, is the freedom of the individual human spirit to express its beliefs and hopes for mankind, whether they be shared by many or by few or none. New hopes, new beliefs, and new thoughts are at all times necessary to mankind, and it is not out of a dead uniformity that they can be expected to arise.

*Chapter 13*

# The Existence
# of God

## A Debate Between Bertrand Russell and Father
## F. C. Copleston, SJ

*This debate was originally broadcast in 1948 on the Third Programme of the B.B.C. It was published in* Humanitas *for the autumn of 1948 and is here reprinted with the kind permission of Father Copleston.*

COPLESTON: As we are going to discuss the existence of God, it might perhaps be as well to come to some provisional agreement as to what we understand by the term 'God'. I presume that we mean a supreme personal being – distinct from the world and creator of the world. Would you agree – provisionally at least – to accept this statement as the meaning of the term 'God'?

RUSSELL: Yes, I accept this definition.

COPLESTON: Well, my position is the affirmative position that such a being actually exists, and that His existence can be proved philosophically. Perhaps you would tell me if your positon is that of agnosticism or of atheism. I mean, would you say that the non-existence of God can be proved?

RUSSELL: No, I should not say that: my position is agnostic.

COPLESTON: Would you agree with me that the problem of God is a problem of great importance? For example, would you agree that if God does not exist, human beings and human history can have no other purpose than the purpose they choose to give themselves, which – in practice – is likely to mean the purpose which those impose who have the power to impose it?

RUSSELL: Roughly speaking, yes, though I should have to place some limitation on your last clause.

COPLESTON: Would you agree that if there is no God – no absolute Being – there can be no absolute values? I mean, would you agree that if there is no absolute good the relativity of values results?

RUSSELL: No, I think these questions are logically distinct. Take, for instance, G. E. Moore's *Principia Ethica*, where he maintains that there is a distinction of good and evil, that both of these are definite concepts. But he does not bring in the idea of God to support that contention.

COPLESTON: Well, suppose we leave the question of good till later, till we come to the moral argument, and I give first a metaphysical argument. I'd like to put the main weight on the metaphysical argument based on Leibniz's argument from 'Contingency' and then later we might discuss the moral argument. Suppose I give a brief statement on the metaphysical argument and that then we go on to discuss it?

RUSSELL: That seems to me to be a very good plan.

## THE ARGUMENT FROM CONTINGENCY

COPLESTON: Well, for clarity's sake, I'll divide the argument in distinct stages. First of all, I should say, we know that there are at least some beings in the world which do not contain in themselves the reason for their existence. For example, I depend on my parents, and now on the air, and on food and so on. Now, secondly, the world is simply the real or imagined totality or aggregate of individual objects, none of which contain in themselves alone the reason for their existence. There isn't any world distinct from the objects which form it, any more than the human race is something apart from the members. Therefore, I should say, since objects or events exist, and since no object of experience contains within itself the reason of its existence, this reason, the totality of objects, must have a reason external to itself. That reason must be an existent being. Well, this being is either itself the reason for its own existence, or it is not. If it is, well and good. If it is not, then we must proceed farther. But if we proceed to infinity in that sense, then there's no explanation of existence at all. So, I should say, in order to explain existence, we must come to a being which contains within itself the reason for its own existence, that is to say, which cannot not-exist.

RUSSELL: This raises a great many points and it is not altogether easy to know where to begin, but I think that, perhaps, in answering your argument, the best point at which to begin is the question of necessary being. The word 'necessary' I should maintain, can only be applied significantly to propositions. And, in fact, only to such as are analytic – that is to say – such as it is self-contradictory to deny. I could only admit a necessary being if there were a being whose existence it is self-contradictory to deny. I should like to know whether you would accept Liebniz's division of propositions into truths of reason and truths of fact. The former – the truths of reason – being necessary.

COPLESTON: Well, I certainly should not subscribe to what seems to be Leibniz's idea of truths of reason and truths of fact, since it would appear that, for him, there are in the long run only analytic propositions. It would seem that for Leibniz truths of fact are ultimately reducible to truths of reason, that is to say, to analytic propositions, at least for an omniscient mind. Well, I couldn't agree with that. For one thing, it would fail to meet the requirements of the experience of freedom. I don't want to uphold the whole philosophy of Leibniz. I have made use of his argument from contingent to necessary being, basing the argument on the principle of sufficient reason, simply because it seems to me a brief and clear formulation of what is, in my opinion, the fundamental metaphysical argument for God's existence.

RUSSELL: But, to my mind, 'a necessary proposition' has got to be analytic. I don't see what else it can mean. And analytic propositions are always complex and logically somewhat late. 'Irrational animals are animals' is an analytic proposition; but a proposition such as 'This is an animal' can never be analytic. In fact, all the propositions that can be analytic are somewhat late in the build-up of propositions.

COPLESTON: Take the proposition 'If there is a contingent being then there is a necessary being.' I consider that the proposition hypothetically expressed is a necessary proposition. If you are going to call every necessary proposition an analytic proposition, then – in order to avoid a dispute in terminology – I would agree to call it analytic, though I don't consider it a tautological proposition. But the proposition is a necessary proposition only on the supposition that there is a contingent being. That there is a contingent being actually existing has to be discovered by experience, and the proposition that there is a contingent being is certainly not an analytic proposition, though once you know, I should maintain, that there is a contingent being, it follows of necessity that there is a necessary being.

RUSSELL: The difficulty of this argument is that I don't admit the idea of a necessary being and I don't admit that there is any particular meaning in calling other beings 'contingent'. These phrases don't for me have a significance except within a logic that I reject.

COPLESTON: Do you mean that you reject these terms because they won't fit in with what is called 'modern logic'?

RUSSELL: Well, I can't find anything that they could mean. The word 'necessary', it seems to me, is a useless word, except as applied to analytic propositions, not to things.

COPLESTON: In the first place, what do you mean by 'modern logic'? As far as I know, there are somewhat differing systems. In the second place, not all modern logicians surely would admit the meaninglessness of metaphysics. We both know, at any rate, one very eminent modern thinker whose knowledge of modern logic was profound, but who certainly did not think that metaphysics are meaningless or, in particular, that the problem of God is meaningless. Again, even if all modern logicians held that metaphysical terms are meaningless, it would not follow that they were right. The proposition that metaphysical terms are meaningless seems to me to be a proposition based on an assumed philosophy. The dogmatic position behind it seems to be this: What will not go into my machine is non-existent, or it is meaningless; it is the expression of emotion. I am simply trying to point out that anybody who says that a particular system of modern logic is the sole criterion of meaning is saying something that is over dogmatic; he is dogmatically insisting that a part of philosophy is the whole of philosophy. After all, a 'contingent' being is a being which has not in itself the complete reason for its existence, that's what I mean by a contingent being. You know, as well as I do, that the existence of neither of us can be explained without reference to something or somebody outside us, parents, for example. A 'necessary' being, on the other hand, means a being that must and cannot not-exist. You may say that there is no such being, but you will find it hard to convince me that you do not understand the terms I am using. If you do not understand them, then how can you be entitled to say that such a being does not exist, if that is what you do say?

RUSSELL: Well, there are points here that I don't propose to go into at length. I don't maintain the meaningless of metaphysics in general at all. I maintain the meaningless of certain particular terms – not on any general ground, but simply because I've not been able to see an interpretation of those particular terms. It's not a general dogma – it's a particular thing. But those points I will leave out for the moment. And I will say that what you have been saying brings us back, it seems to me, to the ontological argument that there is a being whose essence involves existence, so that his existence is analytic. That seems to me to be impossible, and it raises, of course, the question what one means by existence, and as to this, I think a subject named can never be significantly said to exist but only a subject described. And that existence, in fact, quite definitely is not a predicate.

COPLESTON: Well, you say, I believe, that it is bad grammar, or rather bad syntax to say for example 'T. S. Eliot exists'; one ought to say, for example, 'He, the author of *Murder in the Cathedral*, exists.' Are you going to say that the proposition, 'The cause of the world exists,' is without meaning? You may say that the world has no cause; but I fail to see how you can say that the proposition that 'the cause of the world exists' is meaningless. Put in the form of a question: 'Has the world a cause?' or 'Does a cause of the world exist?' Most people surely would understand the question, even if they don't agree about the answer.

RUSSELL: Well, certainly the question 'Does the cause of the world exist?' is a question that has meaning. But if you say 'Yes, God is the cause of the world' you're using God as a proper name; then 'God exists' will not be a statement that has meaning; that is the position that I'm maintaining. Because, therefore, it will follow that it cannot be an analytic proposition ever to say that this or that exists. For example, suppose you take as your subject 'the existent round-square', it would look like an analytic proposition that 'the existent round-square exists,' but it doesn't exist.

COPLESTON: No, it doesn't. Then surely you can't say it doesn't exist unless you have a conception of what existence is. As to the phrase 'existent round-square', I should say that it has no meaning at all.

RUSSELL: I quite agree. Then I should say the same thing in another context in reference to a 'necessary being'.

COPLESTON: Well, we seem to have arrived at an impasse. To say that a necessary being is a being that must exist and cannot not-exist has for me a definite meaning. For you it has no meaning.

RUSSELL: Well, we can press the point a little, I think. A being that must exist and cannot not-exist, would surely, according to you, be a being whose essence involved existence.

COPLESTON: Yes, a being the essence of which is to exist. But I should not be willing to argue the existence of God simply from the idea of His essence because I don't think we have any clear intuition of God's essence as yet. I think we have to argue from the world of experience to God.

RUSSELL: Yes, I quite see the distinction. But, at the same time, for a being with sufficient knowledge it would be true to say 'Here is this being whose essence involves existence!'

COPLESTON: Yes, certainly if anybody saw God, he would see that God must exist.

RUSSELL: So that I mean there is a being whose essence involves existence although we don't know that essence. We only know there is such a being.

COPLESTON: Yes, I should add we don't know the essence *a priori*. It is only *a posteriori* through our experience of the world that we come to a knowledge of the existence of that being. And then one argues, the essence and existence must be identical. Because if God's essence and God's existence was not identical, then some sufficient reason for this existence would have to be found beyond God.

RUSSELL: So it all turns on this question of sufficient reason, and I must say you haven't defined 'sufficient reason' in a way that I can understand – what do you mean by sufficient reason? You don't mean cause?

COPLESTON: Not necessarily. Cause is a kind of sufficient reason. Only contingent being can have a cause. God is His own sufficient reason; and He is not cause of Himself. By sufficient reason in the full sense I mean an explanation adequate for the existence of some particular being.

RUSSELL: But when is an explanation adequate? Suppose I am about to make a flame with a match. You may say that the adequate explanation of that is that I rub it on the box.

COPLESTON: Well, for practical purposes – but theoretically, that is only a partial explanation. An adequate explanation must ultimately be a total explanation, to which nothing further can be added.

RUSSELL: Then I can only say that you're looking for something which can't be got, and which one ought not to expect to get.

COPLESTON: To say that one has not found it is one thing; to say that one should not look for it seems to me rather dogmatic.

RUSSELL: Well, I don't know. I mean, the explanation of one thing is another thing which makes the other thing dependent on yet another, and you have to grasp this sorry scheme of things entire to do what you want, and that we can't do.

COPLESTON: But are you going to say that we can't, or we shouldn't even raise the question of the existence of the whole of this sorry scheme of things – of the whole universe?

RUSSELL: Yes. I don't think there's any meaning in it at all. I think the word 'universe' is a handy word in some connections, but I don't think it stands for anything that has a meaning.

COPLESTON: If the word is meaningless, it can't be so very handy. In any case, I don't say that the universe is something different from the objects which compose it (I indicated that in my brief summary of the proof), what I'm doing is to look for the reason, in this case the cause of the objects – the real or imagined totality of which constitute what we call the universe. You say, I think that the universe – or my existence if you prefer, or any other existence – is unintelligible?

RUSSELL: First may I take up the point that if a word is meaningless it can't be handy? That sounds well but isn't in fact correct. Take, say, such a word as 'the' or 'than'. You can't point to any object that those words mean, but they are very useful words; I should say the same of 'universe'. But leaving that point, you ask whether I consider that the universe is unintelligible. I shouldn't say unintelligible – I think it is without explanation. Intelligible, to my mind, is a different thing. Intelligible has to do with the thing itself intrinsically and not with its relations.

COPLESTON: Well, my point is that what we call the world is intrinsically unintelligible, apart from the existence of God. You see, I don't believe that the infinity of the series of events – I mean a horizontal series, so to speak – if such an infinity could be proved, would be in the slightest degree relevant to the situation. If you add up chocolates you get chocolates after all and not a sheep. If you add up chocolates to infinity, you presumably get an infinite number of chocolates. So if you add up contingent beings to infinity, you still get contingent beings, not a necessary being. An infinite series of contingent beings will be, to my way of thinking, as unable to cause itself as one contingent being. However, you say, I think, that it is illegitimate to raise the question of what will explain the existence of any particular object?

RUSSELL: It's quite all right if you mean by explaining it, simply finding a cause for it.

COPLESTON: Well, why stop at one particular object? Why shouldn't one raise the question of the cause of the existence of all particular objects?

RUSSELL: Because I see no reason to think there is any. The whole concept of cause is one we derive from our observation of particular things; I see no reason whatsoever to suppose that the total has any cause whatsoever.

COPLESTON: Well, to say that there isn't any cause is not the same thing as saying that we shouldn't look for a cause. The statement that there isn't any cause should come, if it comes at all, at the end of the inquiry, not the beginning. In any case, if the total has no cause, then to my way of thinking it must be its own cause, which seems to me impossible. Moreover, the statement that the world is simply there, if in answer to a question, presupposes that the question has meaning.

RUSSELL: No, it doesn't need to be its own cause, what I'm saying is that the concept of cause is not applicable to the total.

COPLESTON: Then you would agree with Sartre that the universe is what he calls 'gratuitous'?

RUSSELL: Well, the word 'gratuitous' suggests that it might be something else; I should say that the universe is just there, and that's all.

COPLESTON: Well, I can't see how you can rule out the legitimacy of asking the question how the total, or anything at all comes to be there. Why something rather than nothing, that is the question? The fact that we gain our knowledge of casuality empirically, from particular causes, does not rule out the possibility of asking what the cause of the series is. If the word 'cause' were meaningless or if it could be shown that Kant's view of the matter were correct, the question would be illegitimate I agree; but you don't seem to hold that the word 'cause' is meaningless, and I do not suppose you are a Kantian.

RUSSELL: I can illustrate what seems to me your fallacy. Every man who exists has a mother, and it seems to me your argument is that therefore the human race must have a mother, but obviously the human race hasn't a mother – that's a different logical sphere.

COPLESTON: Well, I can't really see any parity. If I were saying 'every object has a phenomenal cause, therefore, the whole series has a phenomenal cause,' there would be a parity; but I'm not saying that; I'm saying, every object has a phenomenal cause if you insist on the infinity of the series – but the series of phenomenal causes is an insufficient explanation of the series. Therefore, the series has not a phenomenal cause but a transcendent cause.

RUSSELL: That's always assuming that not only every particular thing in the world, but the world as a whole must have a cause. For that assumption I see no ground whatever. If you'll give me a ground I'll listen to it.

COPLESTON: Well, the series of events is either caused or it's not caused. If it is caused, there must obviously be a cause outside the series. If it's not caused then it's sufficient to itself, and if it's sufficient to itself it is what I call necessary. But it can't be necessary since each member is contingent, and we've agreed that the total is no reality apart from its members, therefore, it can't be necessary. Therefore, it can't be (caused) – uncaused – therefore it must have a cause. And I should like to observe in passing that the statement 'the world is simply there and is inexplicable' can't be got out of logical analysis.

RUSSELL: I don't want to seem arrogant, but it does seem to me that I can conceive things that you say the human mind can't conceive. As for things not having a cause, the physicists assure us that individual quantum transition in atoms have no cause.

COPLESTON: Well, I wonder now whether that isn't simply a temporary inference.

RUSSELL: It may be, but it does show that physicists' minds can conceive it.

COPLESTON: Yes, I agree, some scientists – physicists – are willing to allow for indetermination within a restricted field. But very many scientists are not so willing. I think that Professor Dingle, of London University, maintains that the Heisenberg uncertainty principle tells us something about the success (or lack of it) of the present atomic theory in correlating observations, but not about nature in itself, and many physicists would accept this view. In any case, I don't see how physicists can fail to accept the theory in practice, even if they don't do so in theory. I cannot see how science could be conducted on any other assumption than that of order and intelligibility in nature. The physicist presupposes, at least tacitly, that there is some sense in investigating nature and looking for the causes of events, just as the detective presupposes that there is some sense in looking for the cause of a murder. The metaphysician assumes that there is sense in looking for the reason or cause of phenomena, and, not being a Kantian, I consider that the metaphysician is as justified in his assumption as the physicist. When Sartre, for example, says that the world is gratuitous, I think that he has not sufficiently considered what is implied by 'gratuitous'.

RUSSELL: I think – there seems to me a certain unwarrantable extension here; a physicist looks for causes; that does not necessarily imply that there are causes everywhere. A man may look for gold without assuming that there is gold everywhere; if he finds gold, well and good, if he doesn't he's had bad luck. The same is true when the physicists look for causes. As for Sartre, I don't profess to know what he means, and I shouldn't like to be thought to interpret him, but for my part, I do think the notion of the world having an explanation is a mistake. I don't see why one should expect it to have, and I think what you say about what the scientist assumes is an over-statement.

COPLESTON: Well, it seems to me that the scientist does make some such assumption. When he experiments to find out some particular truth, behind that experiment lies the assumption that the universe is not simply discontinuous. There is the possibility of finding out a truth by experiment. The experiment may be a bad one, it may lead to no result, or not to the result that he wants, but that at any rate there is the possibility, through experiment, of finding out the truth that he assumes. And that seems to me to assume an ordered and intelligible universe.

RUSSELL: I think you're generalising more than is necessary. Undoubtedly the scientist assumes that this sort of thing is likely to be found and will often be found. He does not assume that it will be found, and that's a very important matter in modern physics.

COPLESTON: Well, I think he does assume or is bound to assume it tacitly in practice. It may be that, to quote Professor Haldane, 'when I light the gas under the kettle, some of the water molecules will fly off as vapour, and there is no way of finding out which will do so,' but it doesn't follow necessarily that the idea of chance must be introduced except in relation to our knowledge.

RUSSELL: No it doesn't – at least if I may believe what he says. He's finding out quite a lot of things – the scientist is finding out quite a lot of things that are happening in the world, which are, at first, beginnings of causal chains – first causes which haven't in themselves got causes. He does not assume that everything has a cause.

COPLESTON: Surely that's a first cause within a certain selected field. It's a relatively first cause.

RUSSELL: I don't think he'd say so. If there's a world in which most events, but not all, have causes, he will then be able to depict the probabilities and uncertainties by assuming that this particular event you're interested in probably has a cause. And since in any case you won't get more than probability that's good enough.

COPLESTON: It may be that the scientist doesn't hope to obtain more than probability, but in raising the question he assumes that the question of explanation has a meaning. But your general point then, Lord Russell, is that it's illegitimate even to ask the question of the cause of the world?

RUSSELL: Yes, that's my position.

COPLESTON: If it's a question that for you has no meaning, it's of course very difficult to discuss it, isn't it?

RUSSELL: Yes, it is very difficult. What do you say – shall we pass on to some other issue?

### RELIGIOUS EXPERIENCE

COPLESTON: Let's. Well, perhaps I might say a word about religious experience, and then we can go on to moral experience. I don't regard religious experience as a strict proof of the existence of God, so the character of the discussion changes some what, but I think it's true to say that the best explanation of it is the existence of God. By religious experience I don't mean simply feeling good. I mean a loving, but unclear, awareness of some object which irresistibly seems to the experiencer as something transcending the self, something transcending all the normal objects of experience, something which cannot be pictured or conceptualised, but of the reality of which doubt is impossible – at least during the experience. I should claim that cannot be explained adequately and without residue, simply subjectively. The actual basic experience at any rate is most easily explained on the hypotheses that there is actually some objective cause of that experience.

RUSSELL: I should reply to that line of argument that the whole argument from our own mental states to something outside us, is a very tricky affair. Even where we all admit its validity, we only feel justified in doing so, I think, because of the consensus of mankind. If there's a crowd in a room and there's a clock in a room, they can all see the clock. The fact that they can all see it tends to make them think that it's not an hallucination: whereas these religious experiences do tend to be very private.

COPLESTON: Yes, they do. I'm speaking strictly of mystical experience proper, and I certainly don't include, by the way, what are called visions. I mean simply the experience, and I quite admit it's indefinable, of the transcendent object or of what seems to be a transcendent object. I remember Julian Huxley in some lecture saying that religious experience, or mystical experience, is as much a real experience as falling in love or appreciating poetry and art. Well, I believe that when we appreciate poetry and art we appreciate definite poems or a definite work of art. If we fall in love, well, we fall in love with somebody and not with nobody.

RUSSELL: May I interrupt for a moment here. That is by no means always the case. Japanese novelists never consider that they have achieved a success unless large numbers of real people commit suicide for love of the imaginary heroine.

COPLESTON: Well, I must take your word for these goings on in Japan. I haven't committed suicide, I'm glad to say, but I have been strongly influenced in the taking of two important steps in my life by two biographies. However, I must say I see little resemblance between the real influence of those books on me and the mystic experience proper, so far, that is, as an outsider can obtain an idea of that experience.

RUSSELL: Well, I mean we wouldn't regard God as being on the same level as the characters in a work of fiction. You'll admit there's a distinction here?

COPLESTON: I certainly should. But what I'd say is that the best explanation seems to be the not purely subjectivist explanation. Of course, a subjectivist explanation is possible in the case of certain people in whom there is little relation between the experience and life, in the case of deluded people and hallucinated people, and so on. But when you get what one might call the pure type, say St Francis of Assisi, when you get an experience that results in an overflow of dynamic and creative love, the best explanation of that it seems to me is the actual existence of an objective cause of the experience.

RUSSELL: Well, I'm not contending in a dogmatic way that there is not a God. What I'm contending is that we don't know that there is. I can only take what is recorded as I should take other records and I do find that a very great many things are reported, and I am sure you would not accept things about demons and devils and what not – and they're reported in exactly the same tone of voice and with exactly the same conviction. And the mystic, if his vision is veridical, may be said to know that there are devils. But I don't know that there are.

COPLESTON: But surely in the case of the devils there have been people speaking mainly of visions, appearances, angels or demons and so on. I should rule out the visual appearances, because I think they can be explained apart from the existence of the object which is supposed to be seen.

RUSSELL: But don't you think there are abundant recorded cases of people who believe that they've heard Satan speaking to them in their hearts, in just the same way as the mystics assert God – and I'm not talking now of an external vision, I'm talking of a purely mental experience. That seems to be an experience of the same sort as mystics' experience of God, and I don't see that from what mystics tell us you can get any argument for God which is not equally an argument for Satan.

COPLESTON: I quite agree, of course, that people have imagined or thought they have heard or seen Satan. And I have no wish in passing to deny the existence of Satan. But I do not think that people have claimed to have experienced God. Take the case of a non-Christian, Plotinus. He admits the experience is something inexpressible, the object is an object of love, and therefore, not an object that causes horror and disgust. And the effect of that experience is, I should say, borne out, or I mean the validity of the experience is borne out in the records of the life of Plotinus. At any rate it is more reasonable to suppose that he had that experience if we're willing to accept Porphyry's account of Plotinus's kindness and benevolence.

RUSSELL: The fact that a belief has a good moral effect upon a man is no evidence whatsoever in favour of its truth.

COPLESTON: No, but if it could actually be proved that the belief was actually responsible for a good effect on a man's life, I should consider it a presumption in favour of some truth, at any rate of the positive part of the belief not of its entire validity. But in any case I am using the character of the life as evidence in favour of the mystic's veracity and sanity rather than as a proof of the truth of his beliefs.

RUSSELL: But even that I don't think is any evidence. I've had experiences myself that have altered my character profoundly. And I thought at the time at any rate that it was altered for the good. Those experiences were important but they did not involve the existence of something outside me, and I don't think that if I'd thought they did, the fact that they had a wholesome effect would have been any evidence that I was right.

COPLESTON: No, but I think that the good effect would attest your veracity in describing your experience. Please remember that I'm not saying that a mystic's mediation or interpretation of his experience should be immune from discussion or criticism.

RUSSELL: Obviously the character of a young man may be – and often is – immensely affected for good by reading about some great man in history, and it may happen that the great man is a myth and doesn't exist, but the boy is just as much affected for good as if he did. There have been such people. Plutarch's *Lives* take Lycurgus as an example, who certainly did not exist, but you might be very much influenced by reading Lycurgus under the impression that he had previously existed. You would then be influenced by an object that you'd loved, but it wouldn't be an existing object.

COPLESTON: I agree with you on that, of course, that a man may be influenced by a character in fiction. Without going into the question of what it is precisely that influences him (I should say a real value) I think that the situation of that man and of the mystic are different. After all the man who is influenced by Lycurgus hasn't got the irresistible impression that he's experienced in some way the ultimate reality.

RUSSELL: I don't think you've quite got my point about these historical characters – these unhistorical characters in history. I'm not assuming what you call an effect on the reason. I'm assuming that the young man reading about this person and believing him to be real loves him – which is quite easy to happen, and yet he's loving a phantom.

COPLESTON: In one sense he's loving a phantom that's perfectly true, in the sense, I mean, that he's loving X or Y who doesn't exist. But at the same time, it is not, I think, the phantom as such that the young man loves; he perceives a real value, an idea which he recognises as objectively valid, and that's what excites his love.

RUSSELL: Well, in the same sense we had before about the characters in fiction.

COPLESTON: Yes, in one sense the man's loving a phantom – perfectly true. But in another sense he's loving what he perceives to be a value.

### THE MORAL ARGUMENT

RUSSELL: But aren't you now saying in effect, I mean by God whatever is good or the sum total of what is good – the system of what is good, and, therefore, when a young man loves anything that is good he is loving God. Is that what you're saying, because if so, it wants a bit of arguing.

COPLESTON: I don't say, of course, that God is the sum total or system of what is good in the pantheistic sense; I'm not a pantheist, but I do think that all goodness reflects God in some way and proceeds from Him, so that in a sense the man who loves what is truly good, loves God even if he doesn't advert to God. But still I agree that the validity of such an interpretation of a man's conduct depends on the recognition of God's existence, obviously.

RUSSELL: Yes, but that's a point to be proved.

COPLESTON: Quite so, but I regard the metaphysical argument as probative, but there we differ.

RUSSELL: You see, I feel that some things are good and that other things are bad. I love the things that are good, that I think are good, and I hate the things that I think are bad. I don't say that these things are good because they participate in the Divine goodness.

COPLESTON: Yes, but what's your justification for distinguishing between good and bad or how do you view the distinction between them?

RUSSELL: I don't have any justification any more than I have when I distinguish between blue and yellow. What is my justification for distinguishing between blue and yellow? I can see they are different.

COPLESTON: Well, that is an excellent justification, I agree. You distinguish blue and yellow by seeing them, so you distinguish good and bad by what faculty?

RUSSELL: By my feelings.

COPLESTON: By your feelings. Well, that's what I was asking. You think that good and evil have reference simply to feeling?

RUSSELL: Well, why does one type of object look yellow and another blue? I can more or less give an answer to that thanks to the physicists, and as to why I think one sort of thing good and another evil, probably there is an answer of the same sort, but it hasn't been gone into in the same way and I couldn't give it you.

COPLESTON: Well, let's take the behaviour of the Commandant of Belsen. That appears to you as undesirable and evil and to me too. To Adolf Hitler we suppose it appeared as something good and desirable. I suppose you'd have to admit that for Hitler it was good and for you it is evil.

RUSSELL: No, I shouldn't quite go so far as that. I mean, I think people can make mistakes in that as they can in other things. If you have jaundice you see things yellow that are not yellow. You're making a mistake.

COPLESTON: Yes, one can make mistakes, but can you make a mistake if it's simply a question of reference to a feeling or emotion? Surely Hitler would be the only possible judge of what appealed to his emotions.

RUSSELL: It would be quite right to say that it appealed to his emotions, but you can say various things about that, among others that if that sort of thing makes that sort of appeal to Hitler's emotions, then Hitler makes quite a different appeal to my emotions.

COPLESTON: Granted. But there's no objective criterion outside feeling then for condemning the conduct of the Commandant of Belsen, in your view?

RUSSELL: No more than there is for the colour-blind person who's in exactly the same state. Why do we intellectually condemn the colour-blind man? Isn't it because he's in the minority?

COPLESTON: I would say because he is lacking in a thing which normally belongs to human nature.

RUSSELL: Yes, but if he were in the majority, we shouldn't say that.

COPLESTON: Then you'd say that there's no criterion outside feeling that will enable one to distinguish between the behaviour of the Commandant of Belsen and the behaviour, say, of Sir Stafford Cripps or the Archbishop of Canterbury.

RUSSELL: The feeling is a little too simplified. You've got to take account of the effects of actions and your feelings towards those effects. You see, you can have an argument about it if you say that certain sorts of occurrences are the sort you like and certain others the sort you don't like. Then you have to take account of the effects of actions. You can very well say that the effects of the actions of the Commandant of Belsen were painful and unpleasant.

COPLESTON: They certainly were, I agree, very painful and unpleasant to all the people in the camp.

RUSSELL: Yes, but not only to the people in the camp, but to outsiders contemplating them also.

COPLESTON: Yes, quite true in imagination. But that's my point. I don't approve of them, and I know you don't approve of them, but I don't see what ground you have for not approving of them, because after all, to the Commandant of Belsen himself, they're pleasant, those actions.

RUSSELL: Yes, but you see I don't need any more ground in that case than I do in the case of colour perception. There are some people who think everything is yellow, there are people suffering from jaundice, and I don't agree with these people. I can't prove that the things are not yellow, there isn't any proof, but most people agree with me that they're not yellow, and most people agree with me that the Commandant of Belsen was making mistakes.

COPLESTON: Well, do you accept any moral obligation?

RUSSELL: Well, I should have to answer at considerable length to answer that. Practically speaking – yes. Theoretically speaking I should have to define moral obligation rather carefully.

COPLESTON: Well, do you think that the word 'ought' simply has an emotional connotation?

RUSSELL: No, I don't think that, because you see, as I was saying a moment ago, one has to take account of the effects, and I think right conduct is that which would probably produce the greatest possible balance in intrinsic value of all the acts possible in the circumstances, and you've got to take account of the probable effects of your action in considering what is right.

COPLESTON: Well, I brought in moral obligation because I think that one can approach the question of God's existence in that way. The vast majority of the human race will make and always have made, some distinction between right and wrong. The vast majority I think has some consciousness of an obligation in the moral sphere. It's my opinion that the perception of values and the consciousness of moral law and obligation are best explained through the hypothesis of a transcendent ground of value and of an author of the moral law. I do mean by 'author of the moral law' an arbitrary author of the moral law. I think, in fact, that those modern atheists who have argued in the converse way 'there is no God; therefore, there are no absolute values and no absolute law', are quite logical.

RUSSELL: I don't like the word 'absolute'. I don't think there is anything absolute whatever. The moral law, for example, is always changing. At one period in the development of the human race, almost everybody thought cannibalism was a duty.

COPLESTON: Well, I don't see that differences in particular moral judgements are any conclusive argument against the universality of the moral law. Let's assume for the moment that there are absolute moral values. Even on that hypothesis it's only to be expected that different individuals and different groups should enjoy varying degrees of insight into those values.

RUSSELL: I'm inclined to think that 'ought', the feeling that one has about 'ought', is an echo of what has been told one by one's parents or one's nurses.

COPLESTON: Well, I wonder if you can explain away the idea of the 'ought' merely in terms of nurses and parents. I really don't see how it can be conveyed to anybody in other terms than itself. It seems to me that if there is a moral order bearing upon the human conscience, that that moral order is unintelligible apart from the existence of God.

RUSSELL: Then you have to say one or other of two things. Either God only speaks to a very small percentage of mankind – which happens to include yourself – or He deliberately says things that are not true in talking to the consciences of savages.

COPLESTON: Well, you see, I'm not suggesting that God actually dictates moral precepts to the conscience. The human being's ideas of the content of the moral law depends certainly to a large extent on education and environment, and a man has to use his reason in assessing the validity of the actual moral ideas of his social group. But the possibility of criticising the accepted moral code presupposes that there is an objective standard, that there is an ideal moral order, which imposes itself (I mean the obligatory character of which can be recognised). I think that the recognition of this ideal moral order is part of the recognition of contingency. It implies the existence of a real foundation of God.

RUSSELL: But the law-giver has always been, it seems to me, one's parents or someone like. There are plenty of terrestrial law-givers to account for it, and that would explain why people's consciences are so amazingly different in different times and places.

COPLESTON: It helps to explain differences in the perception of particular moral values, which otherwise are inexplicable. It will help to explain changes in the matter of the moral law in the content of the precepts as accepted by this or that nation, or this or that individual. But the form of it, what Kant calls the categorical imperative, the 'ought', I really don't see how that can possibly be conveyed to anybody by nurse or parent because there aren't any possible terms, so far as I can see, with which it can be explained. It can't be defined in other terms than itself, because once you've defined it in other terms than itself you've explained it away. It's no longer a moral 'ought'. It's something else. ·

RUSSELL: Well, I think the sense of 'ought' is the effect of somebody's imagined disapproval, it may be God's imagined disapproval, but it's somebody's imagined disapproval. And I think that is what is meant by 'ought'.

COPLESTON: It seems to me to be external customs and taboos and things of that sort which can most easily be explained simply through environment and education, but all that seems to me to belong to what I call the matter of the law, the content. The idea of the 'ought' as such can never be conveyed to a man by the tribal chief or by anybody else, because there are no other terms in which it could be conveyed. It seems to me entirely – [Russell breaks in].

RUSSELL: But I don't see any reason to say that – I mean we all know about conditioned reflexes. We know that an animal, if punished habitually for a certain sort of act, after a time will refrain. I don't think the animal refrains from arguing within himself 'Master will be angry if I do this.' He has a feeling that that's not the thing to do. That's what we can do with ourselves and nothing more.

COPLESTON: I see no reason to suppose that an animal has a consciousness of moral obligation; and we certainly don't regard an animal as morally responsible for his acts of disobedience. But a man has a consciousness of obligation and of moral values. I see no reason to suppose that one could condition all men as one can 'condition' an animal, and I don't suppose you'd really want to do so even if one could. If 'behaviourism' were true, there would be no objective moral distinction between the emperor Nero and St Francis of Assisi. I can't help feeling, Lord Russell, you know, that you regard the conduct of the Commandant at Belsen as morally reprehensible, and that you yourself would never under any circumstances act in that way, even if you thought, or had reason to think, that possibly the balance of the happiness of the human race might be increased through some people being treated in that abominable manner.

RUSSELL: No. I wouldn't imitate the conduct of a mad dog. The fact that I wouldn't do it doesn't really bear on this question.

COPLESTON: No, but if you were making a utilitarian explanation of right and wrong in terms of consequences, it might be held, and I suppose some of the Nazis of the better type would have held that although it's lamentable to have to act in this way, yet the balance in the long run leads to greater happiness. I don't think you'd say that, would you? I think you'd say that that sort of action is wrong – and in itself, quite apart from whether the general balance of happiness is increased or not. Then, if you're prepared to say that, then I think you must have some criterion of right and wrong, that is outside the criterion of feeling, at any rate. To me, that admission would ultimately result in the admission of an ultimate ground of value in God.

RUSSELL: I think we are perhaps getting into confusion. It is not direct feeling about the act by which I should judge, but rather a feeling as to the effects. And I can't admit any circumstances in which certain kinds of behaviour, such as you have been discussing, would do good. I can't imagine circumstances in which they would have a beneficial effect. I think the persons who think they do are deceiving themselves. But if there were circumstances in which they would have a beneficial effect, then I might be obliged, however reluctantly, to say – 'Well, I don't like these things, but I will acquiesce in them,' just as I acquiesce in the Criminal Law, although I profoundly dislike punishment.

COPLESTON: Well, perhaps it's time I summed up my position. I've argued two things. First, that the existence of God can be philosophically proved by a metaphysical argument; secondly, that it is only the existence of God that will make sense of man's moral experience and of religious experience. Personally, I think that your way of accounting for man's moral judgements leads inevitably to a contradiction between what your theory demands and your own spontaneous judgements. Moreover, your theory explains moral obligation away, and explaining away is not explanation. As regards the metaphysical argument, we are apparently in agreement that what we call the world consists simply of contingent beings. That is, of beings no one of which can account for its own existence. You say that the series of events needs no explanation: I say that if there were no necessary being, no being which must exist and cannot not-exist, nothing would exist. The infinity of the series of contingent beings, even if proved, would be irrelevant. Something does exist; therefore, there must be something which accounts for this fact, a being which is outside the series of contingent beings. If you had admitted this, we could then have discussed whether that being is personal, good, and so on. On the actual point discussed, whether there is or is not a necessary being, I find myself, I think, in agreement with the great majority of classical philosophers.

You maintain, I think, that existing beings are simply there, and that I have no justification for raising the question of the explanation of their existence. But I would like to point out that this position cannot be substantiated by logical analysis; it expresses a philosophy which itself stands in need of proof. I think we have reached an impasse because our ideas of philosophy are radically different; it seems to me that what I call a part of philosophy, that you call the whole, insofar at least as philosophy is rational. It seems to me, if you will pardon my saying so, that besides your own logical system – which you call 'modern' in opposition to antiquated logic (a tendentious adjective) – you maintain a philosophy which cannot be substantiated by logical analysis. After all, the problem of God's existence is an existential problem whereas logical analysis does not deal directly with problems of existence. So it seems to me, to declare that the terms involved in one set of problems are meaningless because they are not required in dealing with another set of problems, is to settle from the beginning the nature and extent of philosophy, and that is itself a philosophical act which stands in need of justification.

RUSSELL: Well, I should like to say just a few words by way of summary on my side. First, as to the metaphysical argument: I don't admit the connotations of such a term as 'contingent' or the possibility of explanation in Fr Copleston's sense. I think the word 'contingent' inevitably suggests the possibility of something that wouldn't have this what you might call accidental character of just being there, and I don't think is true except in the purely causal sense. You can sometimes give a causal explanation of one thing as being the effect of something else, but that is merely referring one thing to another thing and there's no – to my mind – explanation in Fr Copleston's sense of anything at all, nor is there any meaning in calling things 'contingent' because there isn't anything else they could be. That's what I should say about that, but I should like to say a few words about Fr Copleston's accusation that I regard logic as all philosophy – that is by no means the case. I don't by any means regard logic as all philosophy. I think logic is an essential part of philosophy and logic has to be used in philosophy, and in that I think he and I are at one. When the logic that he uses was new – namely, in the time of Aristotle, there had to be a great deal of fuss made about it; Aristotle made a lot of fuss about that logic. Nowadays it's become old and respectable, and you don't have to make so much fuss about it. The logic that I believe in is comparatively new, and therefore I have to imitate Aristotle in making a fuss about it; but it's not that I think it's all philosophy by any means – I don't think so. I think it's an important part of philosophy, and when I say that, I don't find a meaning for this or that word, that is a position of detail based upon what I've found out about that particular word, from thinking about it. It's not a general position that all words that are used in metaphysics are nonsense, or anything like that which I don't really hold.

As regards the moral argument, I do find that when one studies anthropology or history, there are people who think it their duty to perform acts which I think abominable, and I certainly can't, therefore, attribute Divine origin to the matter of moral obligation, which Fr Copleston doesn't ask me to; but I think even the form of moral obligation, when it takes the form of enjoining you to eat your father or what not, doesn't seem to me to be such a very beautiful and noble thing; and, therefore, I cannot attribute a Divine origin to this sense of moral obligation, which I think is quite easily accounted for in quite other ways.

*Chapter 14*

# Can Religion Cure
# Our Troubles?[1]

## I

Mankind is in mortal peril, and fear now, as in the past, is inclining men to seek refuge in God. Throughout the West there is a very general revival of religion. Nazis and Communists dismissed Christianity and did things which we deplore. It is easy to conclude that the repudiation of Christianity by Hitler and the Soviet Government is at least in part the cause of our troubles and that if the world returned to Christianity, our international problems would be solved. I believe this to be a complete delusion born of terror. And I think it is a dangerous delusion because it misleads men whose thinking might otherwise be fruitful and thus stands in the way of a valid solution.

The question involved is not concerned only with the present state of the world. It is a much more general question, and one which has been debated for many centuries. It is the question whether societies can practise a sufficient modicum of morality if they are not helped by dogmatic religion. I do not myself think that the dependence of morals upon religion is nearly as close as religious people believe it to be. I even think that some very important virtues are more likely to be found among those who reject religious dogmas than among those who accept them. I think this applies especially to the virtue of truthfulness or intellectual integrity. I mean by intellectual integrity the habit of deciding vexed questions in accordance with the evidence, or of leaving them undecided where the evidence is inconclusive. This virtue, though it is underestimated by almost all adherents of any system of dogma, is to my mind of the very greatest social importance and far more likely to benefit the world than Christianity or any other system of organised beliefs.

[1] The two parts of this essay originally appeared as articles in the Stockholm newspaper, *Dagens Nyheter*, on November 9 and 11, 1954.

Let us consider for a moment how moral rules have come to be accepted. Moral rules are broadly of two kinds: there are those which have no basis except in a religious creed; and there are those which have an obvious basis in social utility. In the Greek Orthodox Church, two godparents of the same child must not marry. For this rule, clearly, there is only a theological basis; and, if you think the rule important, you will be quite right in saying that the decay of religion is to be deprecated because it will lead to the rule being infringed. But it is not this kind of moral rule that is in question. The moral rules that are in question are those for which there is a social justification independently of theology.

Let us take theft, for example. A community in which everybody steals is inconvenient for everybody, and it is obvious that most people can get more of the sort of life they desire if they live in a community where theft is rare. But in the absence of laws and morals and religion a difficulty arises: for each individual, the ideal community would be one in which everybody else is honest and he alone is a thief. It follows that a social institution is necessary if the interest of the individual is to be reconciled with that of the community. This is effected more or less successfully by the criminal law and the police. But criminals are not always caught, and the police may be unduly lenient to the powerful. If people can be persuaded that there is a God who will punish theft, even when the police fail, it would seem likely that this belief would promote honesty. Given a population that already believes in God, it will readily believe that God has prohibited theft. The usefulness of religion in this respect is illustrated by the story of Naboth's vineyard where the thief is the king, who is above earthly justice.

I will not deny that among semi-civilised communities in the past such considerations may have helped to promote socially desirable conduct. But in the present day such good as may be done by imputing a theological origin to morals is inextricably bound up with such grave evils that the good becomes insignificant in comparison. As civilisation progresses, the earthly sanctions become more secure and the divine sanctions less so. People see more and more reason to think that if they steal they will be caught and less and less reason to think that if they are not caught God will nevertheless punish them. Even highly religious people in the present day hardly expect to go to Hell for stealing. They reflect that they can repent in time, and that in any case Hell is neither so certain nor so hot as it used to be. Most people in civilised communities do not steal, and I think the usual motive is the great likelihood of punishment here on earth. This is borne out by the fact that in a mining camp during a gold rush, or in any such disorderly community, almost everybody does steal.

But, you may say, although the theological prohibition of theft may no longer be very necessary, it at any rate does no harm since we all wish people not to steal. The trouble is, however, that as soon as men incline to doubt received theology it comes to be supported by odious and harmful means. If a theology is thought necessary to virtue and if candid inquirers see no reason to think the theology true, the authorities will set to work to discourage candid inquiry. In former centuries, they did so by burning the inquirers at the stake. In Russia they still have methods which are little better; but in Western countries the authorities have perfected somewhat milder forms of persuasion. Of these, schools are perhaps the most important: the young must be preserved from hearing the arguments in favour of the opinions which the authorities dislike, and those who nevertheless persist in showing an inquiring disposition will incur social displeasure and, if possible, be made to feel morally reprehensible. In this way, any system of morals which has a theological basis becomes one of the tools by which the holders of power preserve their authority and impair the intellectual vigour of the young.

I find among many people at the present day an indifference to truth which I cannot but think extremely dangerous. When people argue, for example, in defence of Christianity, they do not, like Thomas Aquinas, give reasons for supposing that there is a God and that He has expressed His will in the Scriptures. They argue instead that, if people think this, they will act better than if they do not. We ought not therefore – so these people contend – to permit ourselves to speculate as to whether God exists. If, in an unguarded moment, doubt rears its head, we must suppress it vigorously. If candid thought is a cause of doubt, we must eschew candid thought. If the official exponents of orthodoxy tell you that it is wicked to marry your deceased wife's sister, you must believe them lest morals collapse. If they tell you that birth control is sin, you must accept their dictum however obvious it may be to you that without birth control disaster is certain. As soon as it is held that any belief, no matter what, is important for some other reason than that it is true, a whole host of evils is ready to spring up. Discouragement of inquiry, which I spoke of before, is the first of these, but others are pretty sure to follow. Positions of authority will be open to the orthodox. Historical records must be falsified if they throw doubt on received opinions. Sooner or later unorthodoxy will come to be considered a crime to be dealt with by the stake, the purge, or the concentration camp. I can respect the men who argue that religion is true and therefore ought to be believed, but I can only feel profound moral reprobation for those who say that religion ought to be believed because it is useful, and that to ask whether it is true is a waste of time.

It is customary among Christian apologists to regard Communism as something very different from Christianity and to contrast its evils with the supposed blessings enjoyed by Christian nations. This seems to me a profound mistake. The evils of Communism are the same as those that existed in Christianity during the Ages of Faith. The Ogpu differs only quantitatively from the Inquisition. Its cruelties are of the same sort, and the damage that it does to the intellectual and moral life of Russians is of the same sort as that which was done by the Inquisitors whenever they prevailed. The Communists falsify history, and the Church did the same until the Renaissance. If the Church is not now as bad as the Soviet Government, that is due to the influence of those who attacked the Church: from the Council of Trent to the present day whatever improvements it has effected have been due to its enemies. There are many who object to the Soviet Government because they dislike the Communist economic doctrine, but this the Kremlin shares with the early Christians, the Franciscans, and the majority of mediaeval Christian heretics. Nor was the Communist doctrine confined to heretics: Sir Thomas More, an orthodox martyr, speaks of Christianity as Communistic and says that this was the only aspect of the Christian religion which commended it to the Utopians. It is not Soviet doctrine in itself that can be justly regarded as a danger. It is the way in which the doctrine is held. It is held as sacred and inviolable truth, to doubt which is sin and deserving of the severest punishment. The Communist, like the Christian, believes that his doctrine is essential to salvation, and it is this belief which makes salvation possible for him. It is the similarities between Christianity and Communism that makes them incompatible with each other. When two men of science disagree, they do not invoke the secular arm; they wait for further evidence to decide the issue, because, as men of science, they know that neither is infallible. But when two theologians differ, since there are no criteria to which either can appeal, there is nothing for it but mutual hatred and an open or covert appeal to force. Christianity, I will admit, does less harm than it used to do; but this is because it is less fervently believed. Perhaps, in time, the same change will come over Communism; and, if it does, that creed will lose much of what now makes it obnoxious. But if in the West the view prevails that Christianity is essential to virtue and social stability, Christianity will once again acquire the vices which it had in the Middle Ages; and, in becoming more and more like Communism, will become more and more difficult to reconcile with it. It is not along this road that the world can be saved from disaster.

II

In my first article I was concerned with the evils resulting from any system of dogmas presented for acceptance, not on the ground of truth, but on the ground of social utility. What I had to say applies equally to Christianity, Communism, Islam, Buddhism, Hinduism and all theological systems, except in so far as they rely upon grounds making a universal appeal of the sort that is made by men of science. There are, however, special arguments which are advanced in favour of Christianity on account of its supposed special merits. These have been set forth eloquently and with a show of erudition by Herbert Butterfield, Professor of Modern History in the University of Cambridge,[1] and I shall take him as spokesman of the large body of opinion to which he adheres.

Professor Butterfield seeks to secure certain controversial advantages by concessions that make him seem more open-minded than in fact he is. He admits that the Christian Church had relied upon persecution and that it is pressure from without that has led it to abandon this practice in so far as it has been abandoned. He admits that the present tension between Russia and the West is a result of power politics such as might have been expected even if the Government of Russia had continued to adhere to the Greek Orthodox Church. He admits that some of the virtues which he regards as distinctively Christian have been displayed by some Freethinkers and have been absent in the behaviour of many Christians. But, in spite of these concessions, he still holds that the evils from which the world is suffering are to be cured by adherence to Christian dogma, and he includes in the necessary minimum of Christian dogma, not only belief in God and immortality, but also belief in the Incarnation. He emphasises the connection of Christianity with certain historical events, and he accepts these events as historical on evidence which would certainly not convince him if it were not connected with his religion. I do not think the evidence for the Virgin Birth is such as would convince any impartial inquirer if it were presented outside the circle of theological beliefs he was accustomed to. There are innumerable such stories in Pagan mythology, but no

[1] *Christianity and History* (London, 1950).

one dreams of taking them seriously. Professor Butterfield, however, in spite of being an historian, appears to be quite uninterested in questions of historicity wherever the origins of Christianity are concerned. His argument, robbed of his urbanity and his deceptive air of broad-mindedness, may be stated crudely but accurately, as follows: 'It is not worth while to inquire whether Christ really was born of a Virgin and conceived of the Holy Ghost because, whether or not this was the case, the belief that it was the case offers the best hope of escape from the present troubles of the world.' Nowhere in Professor Butterfield's work is there the faintest attempt to prove the truth of any Christian dogma. There is only the pragmatic argument that belief in Christian dogma is useful. There are many steps in Professor Butterfield's contention which are not stated with as much clarity and precision as one could desire, and I fear the reason is that clarity and precision make them implausible. I think the contention, stripped of inessentials, is as follows: it would be a good thing if people loved their neighbours, but they do not show much inclination to do so; Christ said they ought to, and if they believe that Christ was God, they are more likely to pay attention to His teachings on this point than if they do not; therefore, men who wish people to love their neighbours will try to persuade them that Christ was God.

The objections to this kind of argumentation are so many that it is difficult to know where to begin. In the first place, Professor Butterfield and all who think as he does are persuaded that it is a good thing to love your neighbour, and their reasons for holding this view are not derived from Christ's teaching. On the contrary, it is because they already hold this view that they regard Christ's teaching as evidence of His divinity. They have, that is to say, not an ethic based on theology, but a theology based upon their ethic. They apparently hold, however, that the non-theological grounds which make them think it a good thing to love your neighbour are not likely to make a wide appeal, and they therefore proceed to invent other arguments which they hope will be more effective. This is a very dangerous procedure. Many Protestants used to think it as wicked to break the Sabbath as to commit murder. If you persuaded them it was not wicked to break the Sabbath, they might infer that it was not wicked to commit murder. Every theological ethic is in part such as can be defended rationally, and in part a mere embodiment of superstitious taboos. The part which can be defended rationally should be so defended, since otherwise those who discover the irrationality of the other part may rashly reject the whole.

But has Christianity, in fact, stood for a better morality than that of its rivals and opponents? I do not see how any honest student of history can maintain that this is the case. Christianity has been distinguished from other religions by its greater readiness for persecution. Buddhism has never been a persecuting religion. The Empire of the Caliphs was much kinder to Jews and Christians than Christian States were to Jews and Mohammedans. It left Jews and Christians unmolested, provided they paid tribute. Anti-Semitism was promoted by Christianity from the moment when the Roman Empire became Christian. The religious fervour of the Crusades led to pogroms in Western Europe. It was Christians who unjustly accused Dreyfus, and Freethinkers who secured his final rehabilitation. Abominations have in modern times been defended by Christians not only when Jews were the victims, but also in other connections. The abominations of King Leopold's government of the Congo were concealed or minimised by the Church and were ended only by an agitation conducted mainly by Freethinkers. The whole contention that Christianity has had an elevating moral influence can only be maintained by whosesale ignoring or falsification of the historical evidence.

The habitual answer is that the Christians who did things which we deplore were not *true* Christians in the sense that they did not follow the teachings of Christ. One might of course equally well argue that the Soviet Government does not consist of true Marxists, for Marx taught that Slavs are inferior to Germans and this doctrine is not accepted in the Kremlin. The followers of a teacher always depart in some respects from the doctrine of the master. Those who aim at founding a Church ought to remember this. Every Church develops an instinct of self-preservation and minimises those parts of the founder's doctrine which do not minister to that end. But in any case what modern apologists call 'true' Christianity is something depending upon a very selective process. It ignores much that is to be found in the Gospels: for example, the parable of the sheep and the goats, and the doctrine that the wicked will suffer eternal torment in Hell fire. It picks out certain parts of the Sermon on the Mount, though even these it often rejects in practice. It leaves the doctrine of non-resistance, for example, to be practised only by non-Christians such as Gandhi. The precepts that it particularly favours are held to embody such a lofty morality that they must have had a divine origin. And yet Professor Butterfield must know that these precepts were uttered by Jews before the time of Christ. They are to be found, for example, in the teaching of Hillel and in the 'Testaments of the Twelve Patriarchs', concerning which the

Rev. Dr R. H. Charles, a leading authority in this matter, says: 'The Sermon on the Mount reflects in several instances the spirit and even reproduces the very phrases of our text: many passages in the Gospels exhibit traces of the same, and St Paul seems to have used the book as a *vade mecum.*' Dr Charles is of the opinion that Christ must have been acquainted with this work. If, as we are sometimes told, the loftiness of the ethical teaching proves the divinity of its author, it is the unknown writer of these Testaments who must have been divine.

That the world is in a bad shape is undeniable, but there is not the faintest reason in history to suppose that Christianity offers a way out. Our troubles have sprung, with the inexorability of Greek tragedy, from the First World War, of which the Communists and the Nazis were products. The First World War was wholly Christian in origin. The three Emperors were devout, and so were the more warlike of the British Cabinet. Opposition to the war came, in Germany and Russia, from the Socialists, who were anti-Christian; in France, from Jaurès, whose assassin was applauded by earnest Christians; in England, from John Morley, a noted atheist. The most dangerous features of Communism are reminiscent of the mediaeval Church. They consist of fanatical acceptance of doctrines embodied in a Sacred Book, unwillingness to examine these doctrines critically, and savage persecution of those who reject them. It is not to a revival of fanaticism and bigotry in the West that we must look for a happy issue. Such a revival, if it occurs, will only mean that the hateful features of the Communist regime have become universal. What the world needs is reasonableness, tolerance, and a realisation of the interdependence of the parts of the human family. This interdependence has been enormously increased by modern inventions, and the purely mundane arguments for a kindly attitude to one's neighbour are very much stronger than they were at any earlier time. It is to such considerations that we must look, and not to a return to obscurantist myths. Intelligence, it might be said, has caused our troubles; but it is not unintelligence that will cure them. Only more and wiser intelligence can make a happier world.

*Chapter 15*

# Religion and Morals[1]

Many people tell us that without belief in God a man can be neither happy nor virtuous. As to virtue, I can speak only from observation, not from personal experience. As to happiness, neither experience nor observation has led me to think that believers are either happier or unhappier, on the average, than unbelievers. It is customary to find 'grand' reasons for unhappiness, because it is easier to be proud if one can attribute one's misery to lack of faith than if one has to put it down to the liver. As to morality, a great deal depends upon how one understands that term. For my part, I think the important virtues are kindness and intelligence. Intelligence is impeded by any creed, no matter what; and kindness is inhibited by the belief in sin and punishment (this belief, by the way, is the only one that the Soviet Government has taken over from orthodox Christianity).

There are various practical ways in which traditional morality interferes with what is socially desirable. One of these is the prevention of venereal disease. More important is the limitation of population. Improvements in medicine have made this matter far more important than it ever was before. If the nations and races which are still as prolific as the British were a hundred years ago do not change their habits in this respect, there is no prospect for mankind except war and destitution. This is known to every intelligent student, but it is not acknowledged by theological dogmatists.

I do not believe that a decay of dogmatic belief can do anything but good. I admit at once that new systems of dogma, such as those of the Nazis and the Communists, are even worse than the old systems, but they could never have acquired a hold over men's minds if orthodox dogmatic habits had not been instilled in youth. Stalin's language is full of reminiscences of the theological seminary

[1] Written in 1952.

in which he received his training. What the world needs is not dogma, but an attitude of scientific inquiry, combined with a belief that the torture of millions is not desirable, whether inflicted by Stalin or by a Deity imagined in the likeness of the believer.

## Appendix

## How Bertrand Russell was Prevented from Teaching at the College of the City of New York[1]

### I

After the retirement of the two full professors of philosophy, Morris Raphael Cohen and Harry Overstreet, the members of the Philosophy Department at the College of the City of New York, as well as the administration of the College, agreed to approach an eminent philosopher to fill one of the vacant positions. The department recommended that an invitation be sent to Bertrand Russell, who was at the time teaching at the University of California. This recommendation was enthusiastically approved by the faculty of the College, the Acting President, the administrative committee of the Board of Higher Education, and finally by the Board itself, which passes on appointments at this level. Nobody comparable in fame and distinction had ever before been a professor at City College. Nineteen of the twenty-two Board members attended the meeting at which the appointment was discussed, and all nineteen voted in favour of it. When Bertrand Russell accepted the invitation, Ordway Tead, the chairman of the Board, sent him the following letter:

'My dear Professor Russell:

'It is with a deep sense of privilege that I take this opportunity of notifying you of your appointment as Professor of Philosophy at the City College for the period February 1, 1941, to June 30, 1942, pursuant to action taken by the Board of Higher Education at its meeting of February 26, 1940.

'I know that your acceptance of this appointment will add luster

[1] In writing this account I have been greatly helped by the excellent book, *The Bertrand Russell Case*, edited by Professor Horace M. Kallen and the late John Dewey (The Viking Press, 1941). I am particularly indebted to the essays by Kallen, Dewey and Cohen.

to the name and achievements of the Department and College and that it will deepen and extend the interest of the College in the philosophic bases of human living.'

At the same time Acting President Mead issued a statement to the press to the effect that the College was singularly fortunate in securing the services of such a world-renowned scholar as Lord Russell. The date of this was February 24, 1940.

In view of later developments it is necessary to emphasise two facts. Bertrand Russell was to teach the following three courses and no others:

Philosophy 13: A study of modern concepts of logic and of its relation to science, mathematics, and philosophy.

Philosophy 24B: A study of the problems in the foundations of mathematics.

Philosophy 27: The relations of pure to applied sciences and the reciprocal influence of metaphysics and scientific theories.

Furthermore, at the time when Bertrand Russell was appointed only men could attend day session courses in liberal arts subjects at City College.

II

When Russell's appointment was made public, Bishop Manning of the Protestant Episcopal Church wrote a letter to all New York newspapers in which he denounced the Board's action. 'What is to be said of colleges and universities,' he wrote, 'which hold up before our youth as a responsible teacher of philosophy . . . a man who is a recognised propagandist against both religion and morality, and who specifically defends adultery. . . . Can anyone who cares for the welfare of our country be willing to see such teaching disseminated with the countenance of our colleges and universities?' Returning to the offensive a few days later, the bishop said: 'There are those who are so confused morally and mentally that they see nothing wrong in the appointment . . . of one who in his published writings said "outside of human desires there is no moral standard".' It should be remarked in passing that if it were a requirement for teachers of philosophy to reject ethical relativism in its various forms, as Bishop Manning implied, half or more of them would have to be summarily dismissed.

The bishop's letter was the signal for a campaign of vilification and intimidation unequalled in American history since the days of Jefferson and Thomas Paine. The ecclesiastical journals, the Hearst press, and just about every Democratic politician joined the chorus of defamation. Russell's appointment, said *The Tablet*, came as a 'brutal, insulting shock to old New Yorkers and all real Americans'. Demanding that the appointment be revoked, it editorially described Russell as a 'professor of paganism', as 'the philosophical anarchist and moral nihilist of Great Britain ... whose defense of adultery became so obnoxious that one of his "friends" is reported to have thrashed him'. The Jesuit weekly, *America,* was even more polite. It referred to Russell as 'a desiccated, divorced and decadent advocate of sexual promiscuity ... who is now indoctrinating the students at the University of California ... in his libertarian rules for loose living in matters of sex and promiscuous love and vagrant marriage ... This corrupting individual ... who has betrayed his "mind" and "conscience" ... This professor of immorality and irreligion ... who is ostracized by decent Englishmen.' The letters to the editor in these periodicals, were even more frenzied. If the Board of Higher Education did not rescind its action, said one correspondent in *The Tablet*, then 'Quicksands threaten! The snake is in the grass! The worm is busy in the mind! Were Bertrand Russell honest even with himself, he would declare, as did Rousseau: "I cannot look at any of my books without shuddering; instead of instructing, I corrupt; instead of nourishing, I poison. But passion blinds me, and with all my fine discourses, I am nothing but a scoundrel".' The letter was a copy of a telegram which had been sent to Mayor LaGuardia. 'I beg Your Honour,' it continued, 'to protect our youth from the baneful influence of him of the poisoned pen – an ape of genius, the devil's minister of men.'

Meanwhile, Charles H. Tuttle, a member of the Board and a leading layman of the Protestant Episcopal Church, announced that at the next Board meeting on March 18 he would move to reconsider the appointment. Tuttle explained that he had not been familiar with Russell's views at the time of the appointment. He would have voted against it if he had known about them at the time. With the meeting only a few days away, the fanatics now did all they could to frighten members of the Board and to expand the catalogue of Russell's sins. 'Our group,' said Winfield Demarest of the American Youth League, 'does not favor the Russell idea of coeducational dormitories.' Demanding an investigation of the Board of Higher Education, Hearst's *Journal & American* (now the *Journal-American*) maintained that Russell favoured 'nationalization of women ... child-bearing out of wedlock ... and children reared as pawns of a godless State'. By the device of quoting out of context from a book written many years previously, it also branded

Russell as an exponent of Communism. In spite of Russell's well-known opposition to Soviet Communism, he was from then on constantly referred to as 'pro-Communist' by the zealots. Of all the features of this campaign of hate none perhaps was uglier than this deliberate travesty.

Motions demanding Russell's ouster, and also as a rule the ousting of Board members who had voted for his appointment, were passed daily by numerous organisations well known for their interest in education, such as the Sons of Xavier, the New York branch of the Catholic Central Verein of America, The Ancient Order of Hibernians, the Knights of Columbus, the Guild of Catholic Lawyers, the St Joan of Arc Holy Name Society, the Metropolitan Baptist Ministers' Conference, the Midwest Conference of the Society of New England Women, and the Empire State Sons of the American Revolution. These were reported in the press together with profound orations on the part of clerical luminaries whose attacks centred more and more around two charges – that Russell was an alien and therefore legally barred from teaching at the College, and that his views on sex were somehow really incitements to crime. 'Why not get the G-men after your Board of Higher Education?' demanded the Reverend John Schultz, Professor of Sacred Eloquence at the Redemptorist Seminary at Esopus, N.Y. 'Young people in this city,' the noted scholar proceeded, 'are taught that there is no such thing as a lie. They are taught that stealing is justified and so is robbery and plunder. They are taught, as Loeb and Leopold were taught at Chicago University, that inhumanly cruel crimes are justified.' Needless to say, all these dreadful things were closely connected with the appointment of Bertrand Russell – 'the master mind of Free Love, of sex promiscuity for the young, of hatred for parents'. As if that were not bad enough, Russell was also linked by another orator with 'pools of blood'. Speaking at the annual communion breakfast of the Holy Name Society of the New York Police Department, Monsignor Francis W. Walsh recalled to the assembled policemen that they had, on occasion, learned the full meaning of the so-called 'matrimonial triangle' by finding one corner of the triangle in a pool of blood. 'I dare say, therefore,' he continued, 'that you will join me in demanding that any professor guilty of teaching or writing ideas which will multiply the stages upon which these tragedies are set shall not be countenanced in this city and shall receive no support from its taxpayers . . .'

While Mayor LaGuardia remained studiously silent, numerous Tammany politicians went into action. Their conception of academic freedom was well revealed by John F. X. McGohey, first

Deputy District Attorney of New York State and president of the Sons of Xavier (now Judge McGohey), who protested against the use of taxpayers' money 'to pay for teaching a philosophy of life which denies God, defies decency and completely contradicts the fundamental religious character of our country, government, and people'. On March 15, three days before the Board was to reconvene, Borough President of the Bronx, James J. Lyons, one of the inquisitors' big guns, introduced a motion in the City Council calling upon the Board to cancel Russell's appointment. The motion was carried by a vote of 16 to 5. It must be recorded, as a permanent testimony to his courage and indifference to mob sentiment, that Republican Stanley Issacs spoke out vigorously in defence of Bertrand Russell and the Board of Higher Education. In addition to introducing his resolution, Lyons announced that at the next budget discussion he would move to 'strike out the line which provides for compensation for this dangerous appointment'. Borough President Lyons, however, was meek and mild compared to Borough President George V. Harvey of Queens, who declared at a mass meeting that if Russell were not ousted, he would move to strike out the entire 1941 appropriation of $7,500,000 for the upkeep of the municipal colleges. If he had it his way, he said, 'the colleges would either be godly colleges, American colleges, or they would be closed'. At the same protest meeting other eminent and dignified speakers were heard. Referring to Russell as a 'dog', Councilman Charles E. Keegan remarked that 'if we had an adequate system of immigration, that bum could not land within a thousand miles'. But now that he had landed, Miss Martha Byrnes, the Registrar of New York county, told the audience what to do with the 'dog'. Russell, she shouted, should be 'tarred and feathered and driven out of the country'. This, I take it, is what the speakers meant by the 'godly' and the 'American' way.

### III

If the zealots were powerful in local politics, the supporters of independent scholarship were powerful in all the major colleges and universities throughout the nation. To Russell's defence came numerous college presidents, including Gideonse of Brooklyn, Hutchins of Chicago (where Russell had taught the previous year), Graham of North Carolina, who later became a U.S. Senator, Neilson of Smith, Alexander of Antioch, and Sproule of the University of California, where Russell was at the time 'indoctrinating the students in his libertarian rules for loose living in matters of sex and promiscuous love'. To Russell's defence also rallied the current and past presidents of the learned societies – Nicholson of the Phi Beta Kappa, Curry of the American Mathematical Association, Hankins of the American Sociological Association, Beard of the American Historical Association, Ducasse of the American Philosophical Association, Himstead of the American Association of University Professors, and many others. Seventeen of the country's most distinguished scholars (including Becker of Cornell, Lovejoy of Johns Hopkins, and Cannon, Kemble, Perry, and Schlesinger of Harvard) sent a letter to Mayor LaGuardia protesting the 'organised attack upon the appointment of the world-renowned philosopher, Bertrand Russell . . .' If the attack proved successful, the letter went on, 'no American college or university is safe from inquisitional control by the enemies of free inquiry . . . To receive instruction from a man of Bertrand Russell's intellectual caliber is a rare privilege for students anywhere . . . His critics should meet him in the open and fair field of intellectual discussion and scientific analysis. They have no right to silence him by preventing him from teaching . . . The issue is so fundamental that it cannot be compromised without imperilling the whole structure of intellectual freedom upon which American university life rests.' Whitehead, Dewey, Shapley, Kasner, Einstein – all the nation's foremost philosophers and scientists went on record in support of Russell's appointment. 'Great spirits,' Einstein remarked, 'have always found violent opposition from mediocrities. The latter cannot understand it when a man does not thoughtlessly submit to hereditary prejudices but honestly and courageously uses his intelligence.'

Support for Russell was by no means confined to the academic community. Russell's appointment and the independence of the appointing authority were of course endorsed by the American Civil Liberties Union and the Committee for Cultural Freedom, whose president at that time was Sidney Hook. Russell's side was also taken by all the leading spokesmen of the more liberal religious groups, including Rabbi Jonah B. Wise, Professor J. S. Bixler of Harvard Divinity School, Professor E. S. Brightman, the Director of the National Council on Religion and Education, the Reverend Robert G. Andrus, counsellor to Protestant students at Columbia University, the Reverend John Haynes Holmes, and the Reverend Guy Emery Shipler, who disputed Bishop Manning's right to speak for the Episcopal Church. Nine major publishers, including Bennett Cerf of Random House, Cass Canfield of Harper's, Alfred A. Knopf, and Donald Brace of Harcourt Brace, issued a statement commending Russell's selection 'as one which reflects only the greatest credit on the Board of Higher Education'. Speaking of Russell's 'brilliant achievements in philosophy' and his 'high qualities as an educator', the publishers declared that it would be 'a pity for students in New York City not to benefit from his appointment'. As publishers, they continued, 'we do not necessarily subscribe personally to all the views expressed by those whose books we publish, but we welcome great minds to our lists, particularly now at a time when brute force and ignorance have gained such ascendancy over reason and intellect in many parts of the world. We think it more important than ever to honor intellectual superiority whenever the opportunity presents itself.' Similar sentiments were expressed by the *Publishers' Weekly* and the *New York Herald Tribune*, both editorially and by Dorothy Thompson in her column 'On the Record'. 'Lord Russell is not immoral,' she wrote. 'Anyone who knows him is aware that he is a man of the most exquisite intellectual and personal integrity.'

At City College itself there was great resentment, among students and faculty alike, over ecclesiastical and political interference in college affairs. At a mass meeting in the Great Hall, Professor Morris Raphael Cohen compared Russell's situation to that of Socrates. If Russell's appointment were revoked, he said, 'the fair name of our city will suffer as did Athens for condemning Socrates as a corrupter of its youth, or Tennessee for finding Scopes guilty of teaching evolution'. At the same meeting Professor Herman Randall, Jr, the distinguished historian of philosophy and himself a religious man, denounced the opposition of churchmen to Russell's appointment as 'sheer effrontery' and 'a gross impertinence'. Three hundred members of the City College faculty signed a letter felicitating the Board of Higher Education upon the splendid appointment. Nor were the parents of City College students alarmed over the prospect of having their children exposed to the corroding influence of 'the master mind of Free Love'. Although most of Russell's opponents paraded as spokesmen of 'offended parents', the Parent Association of City College voted unanimously in favour of the Board's action.

IV

Amid the shouts and threats of the zealots, some members of the Board lost their nerve. Nevertheless, at the meeting on March 18, the majority remained true to their convictions, and the controversial appointment was confirmed by a vote of 11 to 7. The opposition had expected this defeat and was ready to move on all

fronts. Having failed so far to get an annulment of Russell's appointment to City College, they tried to prevent him from teaching
at Harvard. Russell had been invited to give the William James
Lectures there in the fall semester of 1940. On March 24 Thomas
Dorgan, 'legislative agent' for the city of Boston, wrote to President
James B. Conant: 'You know that Russell advocates companionate
marriage and the loosening of the bonds that restrain moral conduct. To hire this man, please note, is an insult to every American
citizen in Massachusetts.'

At the same time, the New York State Legislature was asked to
call on the Board of Higher Education to rescind Russell's appointment. Senator Phelps Phelps, Manhattan Democrat, introduced a resolution which would put the Legislature on record as
holding that 'an advocate of barnyard morality is an unfit person to
hold an important post in the educational system of our State at the
expense of the tax-payers'. This resolution was adopted, and as far
as I know not a single voice was raised in opposition.

The resolution was the prelude to more drastic action. Eleven
members of the Board of Higher Education had been so headstrong
as to defy the orders of the hierarchy. The heretics had to be punished. They had to be shown who wields the real power in the State
of New York. Basing his opinion on the statements of Bishop Manning and President Gannon of Fordham University, Senator John
F. Dunigan, the minority leader, told the Senate that Russell's philosophy 'debauches religion, the State and the family relationship'.
He complained about 'the godless, materialistic theories of those
now governing the New York City school system'. The attitude of
the Board which 'insisted on Russell's appointment despite great
public opposition', the Senator argued, 'is a matter of concern for
this Legislature'. He demanded a sweeping investigation of the educational system in New York City and made it clear that such an
investigation would be aimed principally at the college facilities
under the Board of Higher Education. Senator Dunigan's resolution was also adopted with only a minor modification.

But these were only minor skirmishes. The main manoeuvre was
carried out in New York itself. A Mrs Jean Kay of Brooklyn, not
previously noted for her interest in public questions, filed a taxpayer's suit in the New York Supreme Court to void Russell's appointment on the ground that he was an alien and an advocate of
sexual immorality. She declared herself concerned over what might
happen to her daughter, Gloria, if she were to become a student of
Bertrand Russell's. The fact that Gloria Kay could not have become
one of Russell's students at City College was apparently not con-

sidered relevant. Later Mrs Kay's attorneys presented two further grounds for barring Bertrand Russell. For one thing, he had not been given a competitive examination, and for another, 'it was contrary to public policy to appoint as a teacher anyone believing in atheism'.

Mrs Kay was represented by a lawyer named Joseph Goldstein who, under the Tammany administration preceding LaGuardia, had been a city magistrate. In his brief Goldstein described Russell's works as 'lecherous, libidinous, lustful, venerous, erotomaniac, aphrodisiac, irreverent, narrow-minded, untruthful, and bereft of moral fiber'. But this was not all. According to Goldstein, 'Russell conducted a nudist colony in England. His children paraded nude. He and his wife have paraded nude in public. This man, who is now about seventy, has gone in for salacious poetry. Russell winks at homosexuality. I'd go further and say he approves of it.' But even this was not all. Goldstein, who presumably spends his spare time studying philosophy, concluded with a verdict on the quality of Russell's work. This ruinous verdict read as follows:

'He is not a philosopher in the accepted meaning of the word; not a lover of wisdom; not a searcher after wisdom; not an explorer of that universal science which aims at the explanation of all phenomena of the universe by ultimate causes; that in the opinion of your deponent and multitudes of other persons he is a sophist; practices sophism; that by cunning contrivances, tricks and devices and by mere quibbling, he puts forth fallacious arguments and arguments that are not supported by sound reasoning; and he draws inferences which are not justly deduced from a sound premise; that all his alleged doctrines which he calls philosophy are just cheap, tawdry, worn out, patched up fetishes and propositions, devised for the purpose of misleading the people.'

According to the *Daily News* neither Mrs Kay nor her husband nor Goldstein would say who was paying the cost of the suit.

Russell up to this point had refrained from any comments except for a brief statement at the very beginning of the campaign, in which he had said: 'I have no wish to answer Bishop Manning's attack ... Anyone who decides in youth both to think and to speak honestly, regardless of hostility and misrepresentation, expects such attacks and soon learns that it is best to ignore them.' Now, however, that the assault had been carried into a court of law, Russell felt obliged to publish a reply. 'I have hitherto kept an almost unbroken silence in the controversy concerning my appointment to the City College,' he remarked, 'as I could not admit that my opinions were relevant. But when grossly untrue statements as to my actions are made in court, I feel that I must give them the lie. I never conducted a nudist colony in England. Neither my wife nor I ever paraded in nude in public. I never went in for salacious poetry. Such assertions are deliberate falsehoods which must be known to those who make them to have no foundation in fact. I shall be glad of an opportunity to deny them on oath.' It should be added that Russell also never 'approved' of homosexuality. But this is a point which I shall discuss in detail later on.

Mrs Kay's suit was heard before Justice McGeehan, who had been associated with the Bronx Democratic machine. McGeehan had already, before this case, distinguished himself by trying to have a portrait of Martin Luther removed from a courthouse mural illustrating legal history. Nicholas Bucci, Assistant Corporation Counsel, represented the Board of Higher Education. He very properly refused to be drawn into a discussion of Russell's wicked opinions and incompetence as a philosopher. He confined himself to the only legally relevant point in the brief – that an alien could not be appointed to a post in a city college. Bucci denied that this was the case and accordingly asked for a dismissal. McGeehan ominously replied: 'If I find that these books sustain the allegations of the petition I will give the Appellate Division and the Court of Appeals something to think about.' The books here referred to were those introduced by Goldstein to back up his charges. They were *Education and the Good Life, Marriage and Morals, Education and the Modern World,* and *What I Believe.*

## v

Two days later, on March 30, the judge revealed his meditations. Basing himself on 'norms and criteria ... which are the laws of nature and nature's God', he revoked Russell's appointment and described it, like the clerical orators before him, as 'an insult to the people of the City of New York'. The Board's action, he concluded, was 'in effect establishing a chair of indecency', and in so doing it had 'acted arbitrarily, capriciously, and in direct violation of the public health, safety, and the morals of the people and of the petitioner's rights herein, and the petitioner is entitled to an order revoking the appointment of the said Bertrand Russell'. According to the *Sunday Mirror*, the judge admitted that his verdict was 'dynamite'. That his mind was not on the law alone, if it was there at all, is also evident from his further statement that 'this decision has laid the groundwork for the legislative investigating committee and

I dare say they will be interested in finding out how Bertrand Russell's appointment was brought about'.

The *New Republic* pointed out that McGeehan's judgement 'must have been produced at superhuman speed'. John Dewey voiced the suspicion that the judge never read the books which were introduced as evidence by Mr Goldstein. What is certain is that judgement was pronounced in unbecoming haste. It is impossible that in the course of two days McGeehan should have given careful study to four books in addition to writing his lengthy opinion. That the judge made no attempt whatever to guard the rights of all parties, as any conscientious judge should, is also evident from several other features of the case. Thus, he made no attempt to allow Russell to deny Goldstein's charges, but accepted them apparently without further ado. McGeehan gave Russell no opportunity to say whether his interpretation of Russell's views was correct. Nor did he try to ascertain whether Russell still held the views expressed in books which had been written between eight and fifteen years previously. All this would seem to be required by elementary canons of common decency, if not judicial fairness as well.

As we saw, Mr Bucci, who represented the Board of Higher Education, had confined himself in his answer to the charge that, as an alien, Russell could not be lawfully appointed to the faculty of City College. McGeehan, however, based his voiding of the appointment chiefly on other charges in Mrs Kay's petition. He published his decision without giving Mr Bucci an opportunity to respond to the other charges. The respondent, McGeehan said, had 'informed the Court that he would not serve an answer'. This Mr Bucci categorically denied in a sworn affidavit which was never challenged. He had been given to understand by the judge, Mr Bucci swore, that he would be permitted to set forth the Board's answer after a denial of his motion to dismiss the suit.

These procedural outrages, however, were nothing as compared with the distortions, libels, and non-sequiturs contained in the judgement itself, which deserves the most careful study. It shows what apparently can be done in broad daylight, even in a democratic state, if an ardent partisan has achieved a position of judicial power and feels himself supported by influential politicians. It is necessary to quote extensively from this amazing document, since otherwise the reader will not believe that this sort of thing actually took place. Moreover, I have no wish to emulate the judge's practice of distortion by culling quotations from their context. Judge McGeehan, as we shall see, showed himself to be an accomplished practitioner of this ignoble art, and frequently succeeded in making

Russell appear to be advocating the opposite of what he actually stood for.

The appointment was revoked on three grounds. Firstly, Russell was an alien:

'Petitioner contends, in the first place, the Section 550 of the Education Law requires that "No person shall be employed or authorized to teach in the public schools of the state who is . . . 3. Not a citizen; the provisions of this subdivision shall not apply, however, to an alien teacher now or hereafter employed, provided such teacher shall make due application to become a citizen and thereafter within the time prescribed by law shall become a citizen." It is conceded that Bertrand Russell is not a citizen and that he has not applied to become a citizen. The corporation counsel contends that he has a reasonable time after appointment to make the application. He further contends that the section does not apply to teachers in the colleges of the City of New York, contending that if Section 550 did apply, most of the teachers in the colleges of the City of New York would be holding their appointments illegally because they are neither graduates of a state normal school nor have they licences from the Commissioner of Education . . . It does not seem logical that the section was ever intended to cover a case similar to the case of Bertrand Russell who has been in this country for some time and who has never made any application for citizenship and who apparently, as shall hereafter appear, would be denied citizenship. The section applies generally to "teachers and pupils" and is not limited to elementary and secondary schools, and the court therefore holds that Bertrand Russell is not qualified to teach by reason of the provisions of this section, but the decision herein made is not based solely upon this ground.'

One does not need to be an expert to detect the legal howlers in the judge's reasoning. The statute invoked refers quite clearly to public schools and not to colleges. It contains a great many other provisions which are never applied to college professors. But even in the public schools the law allows an alien to teach if he declares his intention to become a citizen. Russell had nearly a year in which to do so. McGeehan had no right to assume that Russell would not apply for citizenship. Nor had he any right to speak for the authorities of the Immigration and Naturalization Bureau.

Because of this usurpation of powers alone, a higher court could not conceivably have upheld McGeehan's judgement. The flimsiness, furthermore, of his constant implications that Russell was a person of 'bad character' and guilty of moral turpitude may be gauged from the fact that the immigration authorities did not, either before or after the verdict, make any attempt to deport Russell.

Secondly, Russell's appointment was declared null and void on the ground that he had not been given a competitive examination:

'The second contention of the petitioner is that no examination of any kind was given to Bertrand Russell at the time of his appointment, and this is borne out by the minutes of the Administrative Committee of the City College of the City of New York and of the Board of Higher Education at the time of his appointment.'

This law contains a provision recognising the possibility that a competitive examination may not be practicable and that in any given case it is up to the Board of Higher Education to decide whether this is so. McGeehan could not entirely ignore this provision. But Russell had to be found unfit at all costs. Hence this provision was circumvented by the following ingenious argument:

'While it is not necessary for this court to adjudicate the action of the Board of Higher Education in proceeding by assuming that a competitive examination for the position of Professor of Philosophy in City College was impracticable, such assumption on the part of the Board of Higher Education is held to be unwarranted, arbitrary and capricious and in direct violation of the plain mandate of the Constitution of the State of New York. If there were only one person in the world who knew anything about philosophy and mathematics and that person was Mr Russell, the taxpayers might be asked to employ him without examination, but it is hard to believe, considering the vast sums of money that have been spent on American education, that there is no one available, even in America, who is a credit both to learning and to public life. Other universities and colleges, both public and private, seem to be able to find American citizens to employ, and to say that the College of the City of New York could not employ a professor of philosophy by an examination of some sort is an assumption by the Board of Higher Education of the power which was denied to them by the people of the State of New York in the Constitution and no Legislature and no board can violate this mandate.'

It is difficult to take seriously McGeehan's contention that the Board was acting 'unwarrantably, arbitrarily and capriciously' in not subjecting Russell to a competitive examination. It is even more difficult to suppose that the judge was maintaining this in good faith. If a competitive examination were really a legal requirement for college teachers, then every professor in every state-supported college would have to be dismissed. Every member of the Board of Trustees of Higher Education would have to be charged with making illegal appointments. The New York State Commissioner of Education would have to be punished for allowing so many professors to teach illegally. But in any event a competitive examination is not a legal requirement, and there is nothing in the law which prevents the Board from judging circumstances to render an examination impracticable in the case of aliens any more than in the case of citizens.[1]

By McGeehan's logic, distinguished foreign teachers could hardly ever be engaged, since presumably in most cases there are Americans who could also fill the posts competently. Everyone knows that all major institutions of higher learning in the United States regularly employ foreigners. Prior to the McCarran immigration law, this was officially recognised by exempting foreign teachers from the usual immigration quotas. I note that recently the distinguished Catholic philosopher, Jacques Maritain, was appointed to the faculty of one of the municipal colleges. Every sensible person must welcome this appointment, but as far as I know Martitain is an alien who has never applied for naturalisation. Nor was he given a competitive examination. There has been no taxpayer's suit to void the appointment. I also wonder how seriously Judge McGeehan would treat these grounds if they were made the basis of a petition in Maritain's case.

The third ground of his opinion the judge approached with great relish. In the first two a certain apologetic tone was still noticeable. Not so in the third, when 'morality' had to be defended against the corrupter of youth and his suspicious promoters on the Board of Higher Education. Now McGeehan became a ferocious crusader. As Russell later commented, 'the judge let himself go'. The opinion at this stage became rather muddled and rational argument, whatever there was of it in the earlier portions, petered out. Fury and holy wrath took undisputed possession. It was not always easy to determine on what ground the judge based his order to bar Russell, since he himself curiously admitted that a great many of his obser-

[1] This aspect of McGeehan's judgement is discussed at greater length in three articles in legal journals: Walter H. Hamilton's 'Trial by Ordeal, New Style,' *Yale Law Journal*, March, 1941; Comment, 'The Bertrand Russell Litigation' (1941), 8 *University of Chicago Law Review* 316; Comment, 'The Bertrand Russell Case: The History of a Litigation' (1940), 53 *Harvard Law Review*, 1192. I am indebted to these articles for several other points concerning the illegalities and irregularities of McGeehan's procedure.

vations were irrelevant to the decision. Clear beyond the faintest doubt, however, were Russell's 'immoral character' and the 'salacious' nature of his teachings:

'The foregoing reasons would be sufficient to sustain the petition and to grant the relief prayed for but there is a third ground on which the petitioner rests and which, to the court, seems most compelling. The petitioner contends that the appointment of Bertrand Russell has violated the public policy of the state and of the nation because of the notorious immoral and salacious teachings of Bertrand Russell and because the petitioner contends he is a man not of good moral character.

It has been argued that the private life and writings of Mr Russell have nothing whatsoever to do with his appointment as a teacher of philosophy. It has also been argued that he is going to teach mathematics. His appointment, however, is to the department of philosophy in City College.'

In this consideration, the judge proceeded, he was 'completely dismissing any question of Mr Russell's attack upon religion.' This, one is constrained to admit, was very generous of the judge. Perhaps now and then it is worth pointing out that, in spite of the power of such dignitaries as Councilman Charles Keegan and Senator Phelps Phelps, New York City is in the United States of America, a secular nation, and not part of Franco Spain or the Holy Roman Empire. In any event, the judge was prepared to exercise all possible leniency on the question of Russell's criticism of religious theories. On other matters, however, it was necessary to speak in sterner language:

... 'but there are certain basic principles upon which this government is founded. If a teacher, who is a person not of good moral character, is appointed by any authority the appointment violates these essential prerequisites. One of the prerequisites of a teacher is a good moral character. In fact, this is a prerequisite for appointment in civil service in the city and state, or political subdivisions, or in the United States. It needs no argument here to defend this statement. It need not be found in the Education Law. It is found in the nature of the teaching profession. Teachers are supposed not only to impart instruction in the classroom but by their example to teach the students. The taxpayers of the City of New York spend millions to maintain the colleges of the City of New York. They are not spending that money nor was the money appropriated for the purpose of employing teachers who are not of good moral character. However, there is ample authority in the Education Law to support this contention.'

It should be noted that in spite of his numerous assertions throughout his judgement that Russell was a person of 'immoral character', McGeehan nowhere condescended to list Russell's real or alleged conduct which supposedly supported such a conclusion. It is impossible to be sure, for instance, whether he accepted Goldstein's charge that Russell and his wife had 'paraded nude in public' or that Russell had 'gone in for salacious poetry'. It is equally impossible to know whether the judge based his conclusion on Russell's imprisonment over his pacifism during the First World War about which Goldstein as well as numerous Irishmen, not heretofore known as champions of British Imperial interests, became so excited. I do not know how such a procedure of making derogatory statements without offering a shred of evidence appears to people blessed with insight into 'God's *normae*'. To people like myself who are less fortunate, it appears highly unethical; and if it comes from a judge, in the course of his official duties, it seems a serious abuse of his position.

Russell's character was pretty bad, but his doctrines were even worse:

'The contention of the petitioner that Mr Russell has taught in his books immoral and salacious doctrines is amply sustained by the books conceded to be the writings of Bertrand Russell, which were offered in evidence. It is not necessary to detail here the *filth*[1] which is contained in the books. It is sufficient to record the following. From *Education and the Modern World*, pages 119 and 120: "I am sure that university life would be better, both intellectually and morally, if most university students had temporary childless marriages. This would afford a solution to the sexual urge neither restless nor surreptitious, neither mercenary nor casual, and of such a nature that it need not take up time which ought to be given to work."[1] From *Marriage and Morals*, pages 165 and 166: "For my part, while I am quite convinced that companionate marriage would be a step in the right direction, and would do a great deal of good, I do not think that it goes far enough. I think that all sex-relations which do not involve children should be regarded as a purely private affair, and that if a man and a woman choose to live together without having children, that should be no one's business but their own. I should not hold it desirable that either a man or a woman should enter upon the serious business of a marriage intended to lead to

[1] My italics.

children without having had previous sexual experience." "The peculiar importance attached, at the present, to adultery, is quite irrational." (From *What I Believe*, page 50.)

Perhaps the judge did not detail any 'filth' contained in Russell's books for the simple reason that none is to be found there. As John Dewey put it in an article in *The Nation*: 'The persons, if there be such, who go to Mr Russell's writings in search of filth and obscenity will be disappointed. These things are so lacking that the intemperate and morally irresponsible way in which they are charged against Mr Russell is good reason for believing that those who put them forth hold such an authoritarian view of morals that they would, if they had power, suppress all critical discussion of beliefs and practices they want to impose on others.' As for the judge's language – 'filth', 'chair of indecency', and other expressions of a like order – it was pointed out by several writers that if he had repeated these remarks outside his court, he would have been open to libel action.

McGeehan appeared to realise that what had so far been demonstrated about Russell and his teaching was not quite enough. Russell's doctrines had been shown to be 'salacious', it is true; but this fact itself did not give the court the right to intervene. Something more was needed. Something more drastic or, shall we say, more dramatic. The situation called for a display of creative imagination and the judge rose to the challenge brilliantly. Like the Rev. Professor Schultz and other specialists in sacred eloquence, he hit upon the idea of linking Russell with incitements to violate the Penal Law.

'The Penal Law of the State of New York is a most important factor in the lives of our people. As citizens and residents of our city we come within its protective scope. In dealing with human behaviour the provisions of the Penal Law and such conduct as are therein condemned must not be lightly treated or completely ignored. Even assuming that the Board of Higher Education possesses the maximum power which the Legislature could possibly confer upon it in the appointment of its teachers, it must act so as not to violate the Penal Law or to encourage the violation of it. Where it so acts as to sponsor or encourage violations of the Penal Law, and its actions adversely affect the public health, safety, and morals, its acts are void and of no legal effect. A court of equity, with the powers inherent in that court, has ample jurisdiction to protect the taxpayers of the City of New York from such acts as this of the Board of Higher Education.'

After this high-minded defence of the Penal Law, the judge proceeded with evident gusto to cite a number of its provisions:

'The Penal Law of the State of New York defines the crime of abduction and provides that a person who uses, or procures to be taken or used, a female under eighteen years of age, when not her husband, for the purpose of sexual intercourse, or a person who entices an unmarried female of any age of previous chaste character to any place for the purpose of sexual intercourse, is guilty of abduction and punishable by imprisonment for not more than ten years (S. 70). Furthermore, the Penal Law provides that even a parent or guardian having legal charge of a female under eighteen years of age and who consents to her being taken by any person for the purpose of sexual intercourse violates the law and is punishable by imprisonment for not more than ten years (S. 70).

'As to the crime of rape the Penal Law provides that a person who perpetrates an act of sexual intercourse with a female not his wife under the age of eighteen years, under the circumstances not amounting to rape in the first degree is guilty of rape in the second degree and punishable by imprisonment for not more than ten years (S. 2010).

'S. 100 of the Penal Law makes adultery a criminal offence.

'S. 2460 of the Penal Law, among other things, provides that any person who shall induce or attempt to induce any female to reside with him for immoral purposes shall be guilty of a felony and on conviction punishable by imprisonment for not less than two years, nor more than twenty years, and by a fine not exceeding $5,000.'

Of these provisions only that relating to adultery has even any superficial relevance. Russell nowhere advocated 'rape' or 'abduction' and he never urged anybody to 'induce any female to reside with him for immoral purposes'. Not even McGeehan, with all his skill in quoting out of context, could subsequently produce any passages that might be construed as incitement to these crimes. Why then quote these provisions? Why quote them unless it was the judge's intention to establish in the public mind, especially among people unacquainted with Russell's books, an association between these crimes and Russell's name? I doubt if this sort of demagogic device has ever before been employed by the judge of an American court.

I shall reproduce the remainder of the judgement without interruption so as not to disturb the train of the judge's thoughts. His profound reflections on the academic freedom 'to do good' and his remarkable doctrine of 'indirect influence' by means of which a teacher, lecturing on the philosophy of mathematics or physics, can cause 'sexual intercourse between students, where the female is under the age of eighteen years' deserves the attention of serious students. The latter of these theories which might perhaps be called the doctrine of 'extraordinary influence' should surely interest psychologists and those concerned with extra-sensory perception.

'When we consider the vast amount of money that the taxpayers are assessed each year to enforce these provisions of the law, how repugnant to the common welfare must be any expenditure that seeks to encourage the violation of the provisions of the Penal Law. Conceding *arguendo* that the Board of Higher Education has sole and exclusive power to select the faculty of City College and that its discretion cannot be reviewed or curtailed by this court or any other agency, nevertheless such sole and exclusive power may not be used to aid, abet, or encourage any course of conduct tending to a violation of the Penal Law. Assuming that Mr Russell could teach for two years in City College without promulgating the doctrines which he seems to find necessary to spread on the printed pages at frequent intervals, his appointment violates a perfectly obvious canon of pedagogy, namely, that the personality of the teacher has more to do with forming a student's opinion than many syllogisms. A person we despise and who is lacking in ability cannot argue us into imitating him. A person whom we like and who is of outstanding ability does not have to try. It is contended that Bertrand Russell is extraordinary. That makes him the more dangerous. The philosophy of Mr Russell and his conduct in the past is in direct conflict and in violation of the Penal Law of the State of New York. When we consider how susceptible the human mind is to the ideas and philosophy of teaching professors, it is apparent that the Board of Higher Education either disregarded the probable consequences of their acts or were more concerned with advocating a cause that appeared to them to present a challenge to so-called "academic freedom" without according suitable consideration of the other aspects of the problem before them. While this court could not interfere with any action of the board insofar as a pure question of "valid" academic freedom is concerned, it will not tolerate academic freedom being used as a cloak to promote the popularization in the minds of adolescents of acts forbidden by the Penal Law. This appointment affects the public health, safety and morals of the community and it is the duty of the court to act. Academic freedom does not mean academic licence. It is the freedom to do good and not to teach evil. Academic freedom cannot authorise a teacher to teach that murder or treason are good. Nor can it permit a teacher to teach directly or indirectly that sexual intercourse between students, where the female is under the age of eighteen years, is proper. This court can take judicial notice of the fact that students in the colleges of the City of New York are under the age of eighteen years, although some of them may be older.

'Academic freedom cannot teach that abduction is lawful nor that adultery is attractive and good for the community. There are norms and criteria of truth which have been recognised by the founding fathers. We find a recognition of them in the opening words of the Declaration of Independence, where they refer to the laws of Nature and of Nature's God. The doctrines therein set forth, which have been held sacred by all Americans from that day to this, preserved by the Constitution of the United States and of the several states and defended by the blood of its citizens, recognising the inalienable rights with which men are endowed by their Creator must be preserved, and a man whose life and teachings run counter to these doctrines, who teaches and practises immorality and who encourages and avows violations of the Penal Law of the State of New York, is not fit to teach in any of the schools of this land. The judicial branch of our government, under our democratic institutions, has not been so emasculated by the opponents of our institutions to an extent to render it impotent to act to protect the rights of the people. Where public health, safety, and morals are so directly involved, no board, administrative or otherwise, may act in a dictatorial capacity, shielding their actions behind a claim of complete and absolute immunity from judicial review. The Board of Higher Education of the City of New York has deliberately and completely disregarded the essential principles upon which the selection of any teacher must rest. The contention that Mr Russell will teach mathematics and not his philosophy does not in any way detract from the fact that his very presence as a teacher will cause the students to look up to him, seek to know more about him, and the more he is able to charm them and impress them with his personal presence, the more potent will grow his influence in all spheres of their lives, causing the students in many instances to strive to emulate him in every respect.

'In considering the power of this court to review the determination and appointment of Dr Russell by the Board of Higher Education this court has divided the exhibits in this proceeding into two classes, namely, those exhibits which dealt with controversial measures not *malum in se* as far as the law is concerned, even though abhorrently repulsive to many people, and those considered *malum in se* by the court. Dr Russell's views on masturbation such as expressed in his book entitled *Education and the Good Life*, at page 211, in which he goes on to state: "Left to itself, infantile masturbation has, apparently, no bad effect upon health, and no discoverable bad effect upon character; the bad effects which have been observed in both respects are it.seems wholly attributable to attempts to stop it ... Therefore, difficult as it may be, the child should be let alone in this respect"; his views on nudity as expressed in the same book, on page 212, in which he goes on to state: "A child should, from the first, be allowed to see parents and brothers and sisters without their clothes whenever it so happens naturally. No fuss should be made either way; he should simply not know that people have feelings about nudity"; his views on religion and politics; his own personal life and conduct, with the incidental convictions and libels, are all matters that this court hold to be proper subjects to be considered by the Board of Higher Education in appraising the moral character of Dr Russell as a professor, and on these subjects the determination of the Board of Higher Education is final. If the standards of the Board of Higher Education in these respects are lower than common decency requires, the remedy is with the appointing power who may be held responsible for appointing individuals with moral standards below that required for the public good. But as to such conduct this court is powerless to act because of the power conferred by law on the Board of Higher Education. But where the matter transcends the field of controversial issues and enters the field of criminal law then this court has the power and is under a duty to act. While in encouraging adultery in the language used in the book *Education and the Good Life*, at page 221, "I shall not teach that faithfulness to our partner through life is in any way desirable, or that a permanent marriage should be regarded as excluding temporary episodes," it might be urged that he is only encouraging the commission of a misdemeanor rather than a felony, yet that mitigating argument must fall when we are confronted with Dr Russell's utterances as to the damnable felony of homosexualism, which warrants imprisonment for not more than twenty years in New York State, and concerning which degenerate practice Dr Russell has this to say in his book entitled *Education and the Modern World* at page 119: "It is possible that homosexual relations with other boys would not be very harmful if they were tolerated, but even there is danger lest they should interfere with the growth of normal sexual life later on."

'Considering Dr Russell's principles, with reference to the Penal Law of the State of New York, it appears that not only would the morals of the students be undermined, but his doctrines would tend to bring them, and in some cases their parents and guardians, in conflict with the Penal Law, and accordingly this court intervenes.'

The judge obviously implied that Russell was *encouraging* 'the damnable felony of homosexualism'; and this was the worst charge against him where all 'mitigating argument must fall'. As far as I know there are only two passages in Russell's many books in which homosexuality is discussed. One is that quoted by the judge. The other occurs in *Marriage and Morals* (p. 90) and reads as follows: 'Homosexuality between men, though not between women, is illegal in England, and it would be very difficult to present any argument for a change of the law in this respect which would not itself be illegal on the ground of obscenity. And yet every person who has taken the trouble to study the subject knows that this law is the effect of a barbarous and ignorant superstition, in favour of which no rational argument of any sort or kind can be advanced.' It is clear from this that Russell is opposed to existing laws against homosexuality. I note in a recent dispatch from London that influential Roman Catholics have lately, it seems, become converts to Russell's position and now also support abolition of these laws.[1] It is just as clear that Russell is not inciting anybody to break the law he opposes. In the passage quoted by the judge Russell is not even criticising laws. So far from encouraging homosexuality, he is stating a possibility and then pointing out some of the *harmful* effects of homosexual relations. This is the logic of *1984*: black is white and peace is war and freedom is slavery. How true it is that all fanatics are fundamentally alike, on this or the other side of the Iron Curtain.

It is also not true that Russell, either in the passages quoted by the judge or anywhere else, *encouraged* adultery. What Russell maintains is firstly that sexual relations between unmarried people are not morally wrong if they have sufficient affection for one another

---

[1] 'A Roman Catholic Commission of laymen and clergymen has recommended to the Home Office that "consentual acts done in private" by adult male homosexuals be considered no crime,' it was reported today. ... On the problem of homosexuality, the Commission said: 'Imprisonment is largely ineffectual to reorientate persons with homosexual tendencies and usually has a deleterious effect upon them. A satisfactory solution to the problem is not to be found in places of confinement usually reserved for homosexuals,' *The New York Post*, October 4, 1956. It is to be hoped that these humane and sensible members of the Church will never have to appear in a court presided over by Judge McGeehan to answer for encouraging the commission of a 'damnable felony.'

and that this is a purely private matter in which the state should take no interest. Secondly, he maintains that occasional extra-marital relations are not necessarily a ground for dissolving a marriage. This, as he insisted in public statements which McGeehan carefully ignored, is not at all the same thing as 'encouraging' adultery. If anything, Russell's advocacy of legalised companionate marriages may be regarded as an argument against adultery. But in any event the section of the New York Penal Law which makes adultery a criminal offence is not and has not been acted on for a long time. Everybody knows this. Perhaps the best evidence that it is a dead law comes from McGeehan's own record when he was District Attorney of Bronx County. During this period a large number of divorces were granted on the legally sufficient ground of adultery. Yet McGeehan, like all other District Attorneys, never prosecuted a single one of the parties whose guilt had thus been officially registered.

Russell's views on nudity, though not *malum in se,* were condemned as 'abhorrently repulsive' by the judge. He quoted from Russell's early book *Education and the Good Life,* in which Russell had written that 'a child should, from the first, be allowed to see his parents and brothers and sisters without their clothes whenever it so happens naturally. No fuss should be made either way; he should simply not know that people have feelings about nudity.' This was presented as evidence that the chair of philosophy at City College would become one of 'indecency' if the appointment were allowed to stand. McGeehan apparently hoped to make Russell appear a 'lustful, venerous, lecherous, erotomaniac' (to use Mr Goldstein's colourful language) who was advocating a kind of intra-family strip-tease. The judge carefully refrained from quoting the other parts of Russell's discussion in which the reasons for his view were explained. In these other passages, which McGeehan suppressed, Russell made it clear that he offered his recommendation and condemned the opposite practice of hiding the human body at all costs because the latter evoked 'the sense that there is a mystery, and having that sense, children will become prurient and indecent'.

The judge also carefully refrained from quoting the discussion of the same subject in *Marriage and Morals,* one of the books submitted by Goldstein and allegedly read by McGeehan. Goldstein's charge that Russell had 'conducted a nudist colony' were presumably derived from some statements in this passage. It reads as follows:

'The taboo against nakedness is an obstacle to a decent attitude on the subject of sex. Where young children are concerned, this is now recognised by many people. It is good for children to see each other and their parents naked whenever it so happens naturally. There will be a short period, probably at about three years old, when the child is interested in the differences between his father and his mother, and compares them with the differences between himself and his sister, but this period is soon over, and after this he takes no more interest in nudity than in clothes. So long as parents are un-willing to be seen naked by their children, the children will nec-essarily have a sense that there is a mystery, and having that sense they will become prurient and indecent. There is only one way to avoid indecency, and that is to avoid mystery. There are also many important grounds of health in favour of nudity in suitable circum-stances, such as out-of-doors in sunny weather. Sunshine on the bare skin has an exceedingly health-giving effect. Moreover anyone who has watched children running about in the open air without clothes must have been struck by the fact that they hold themselves much better and move more freely and more gracefully than when they are dressed. The same thing is true of grown-up people. The proper place for nudity is out-of-doors in the sunshine and in the water. If our conventions allowed of this, it would soon cease to make any sexual appeal; we should all hold ourselves better, we should be healthier from the contact of air and sun with the skin, and our standards of beauty would more nearly coincide with stan-dards of health, since they would concern themselves with the body and its carriage, not only with the face. In this respect the practice of the Greeks was to be commended.'

I must confess that I cannot conceive of any more wholesome atti-tude on this subject than that expressed in these remarks. McGeehan's reaction reminds one of a cartoon which became famous in the early years of this century when Anthony Comstock, one of the judge's spiritual ancestors, was campaigning against pictures and statues depicting the undraped human form. It showed Comstock dragging a woman into a courtroom and saying to the judge, 'Your Honor, this woman gave birth to a naked child.'

On the subject of masturbation, the judge was as usual guilty of a two-fold misrepresentation of Russell's views. He first quoted Rus-sell out of context in such a way as to misrepresent the real intention of his discussion. On top of that, McGeehan misinterpreted the pass-age he reproduced in his judgement. The judge tried to represent Russell as advising or sponsoring the practice of masturbation. In the passage quoted by the judge Russell did no such thing. He merely claimed that it was better to leave a child alone than to suppress masturbation by dire threats. The passage, furthermore, occurred in a context in which Russell, so far from promoting masturbation, recommended methods, other than direct prohibition, to *prevent* masturbation. As for Russell's actual views, they are and have for a long time been medical commonplaces. In this connection the *New Republic* aptly remarked that the judge merely showed himself ignorant 'of a whole generation of scientific thought in the medical and psychological field'. Perhaps rather than subject college professors to competitive examinations one should make a certain minimum acquaintance with medical psychology a requirement for prospective judges.

McGeehan not only distorted Russell's views on specific topics. The worst feature of his opinion was probably the distortion of Russell's over-all purpose in his criticism of conventional morality. Nobody would have gathered from the judge's opinion that Russell approached the whole subject of sexual morality in a spirit of high seriousness and that his intention was not to abandon moral restraints but to formulate a kindlier and more humane code. 'Sex,' Russell wrote in a passage which the judge probably never read, 'cannot dispense with an ethic, any more than business or sport or scientific research or any other branch of human activity. But it can dispense with an ethic based solely upon ancient prohibitions propounded by uneducated people in a society wholly unlike our own. In sex, as in economics and politics, our ethic is still dominated by fears which modern discoveries have made irrational ... It is true that the transition from the old system to the new has its own difficulties, as all transitions have ... The morality which I should advocate does not consist simply of saying to grown-up people or adolescents: "Follow your impulses and do as you like." There has to be consistency in life; there has to be continuous effort directed to ends that are not immediately beneficial and not at every moment attractive; there has to be consideration for others; and there should be certain standards of rectitude.' 'Sex morality,' he said elsewhere in *Marriage and Morals*, 'has to be derived from certain general principles, as to which there is perhaps a fairly wide measure of agreement, in spite of the wide disagreement as to the consequence to be drawn from them. The first thing to be secured is that there should be as much as possible of that deep, serious love between man and woman which embraces the whole personality of both and leads to a fusion by which each is enriched and enhanced ... The second thing of importance is that there should be adequate care of children, physical and psychological.' Russell is neither an advocate of 'wild living' nor is he an enemy of the institution of marriage. Marriage, in his view, is 'the best and most important relation that can exist between two human beings,' and he is most insistent that it 'is something more serious than the pleasure of two people in each other's company; it is an institution which, through the fact that it gives rise to children, forms part of the intimate texture of society and has an importance extending far beyond the personal feelings of the husband and wife.'

It may be doubted if these views are really so dangerous. But in any event it does not seem likely that McGeehan and the assorted champions of 'morality' had any fears for the innocence and purity of the students at City College, whether older or younger than eighteen. It should not have been difficult to ascertain whether Russell's presence at City College was likely to lead to 'loose living', 'abduction' and other dreadful practices. Russell had been a teacher most of his life – in England, in China, and in the United States. It would surely have been very simple to ask for reports about his influence from the presidents of the universities where he had taught, his colleagues there, and the students who had attended his classes. Such reports were indeed available, but the judge showed no interest in them. He showed no interest in them because all, without exception, spoke of Russell in terms of the highest praise. President Hutchins of the University of Chicago, where Russell had been the previous year, assured the Board of Higher Education of his 'important contribution' and vigorously supported the appointment. President Sproule of the University of California took a similar stand and spoke of Russell as 'a most valuable colleague'. Richard Payne, the editor of the student newspaper at U.C.L.A., sent a telegram to a protest meeting at City College saying 'You have the complete support of the U.C.L.A. students who know this great man. Good luck!' Dean Marjorié Nicolson of Smith College and President of the National Association of the United Chapters of Phi Beta Kappa also volunteered a statement. She had attended two of Russell's courses at the British Institute of Philosophical Studies. According to Dean Nicolson, 'Mr Russell never introduced into his discussions of philosophy any of the controversial questions which his opponents have raised ... Mr Russell is first and foremost a philosopher, and in his teaching he always remembers that. I should have had no way of knowing Mr Russell's opinions on marriage, divorce, theism, or atheism, had they not been given an exaggerated form in the newspapers.' Testimony of the same kind came from many other quarters. I have said above that Judge McGeehan's eyes were not on the law. I think it is fair to add that they were not upon the facts, either.

VI

The reactions to the verdict were as one might have expected. Russell's supporters were dismayed, while the opposition was jubilant. Russell's supporters were fearful lest heavy political pressure would prevent the Board from making an effective appeal in the higher courts. These fears, as we shall see, proved only too justified. The National Council of the American Association of University Professors, meeting in Chicago, unanimously adopted a resolution urging both Mayor LaGuardia and the Board to fight McGeehan's judgement. So did numerous other bodies, including the American Association of Scientific Workers and the Public Education Association. A special Academic Freedom – Bertrand Russell Committee was formed with Professor Montague of Columbia as chairman and Professor John Herman Randall, Jr, as secretary. It numbered among its sponsors Dr William A. Neilson, President Emeritus of Smith College; Presidents Sproule and Hutchins; Dr J. S. Bryn, President of William and Mary College; Dean Nicolson; Dr Frank Kingdon, and numerous other distinguished personalities from the academic world. Sixty members of the faculty of North-western University immediately sent financial contributions to the Committee, praising Bertrand Russell's highminded and courageous approach to moral questions. The Committee for Cultural Freedom sent a telegram to Mayor LaGuardia in which it pointed out that McGeehan had made Russell appear to be a 'profligate and a scoundrel'. This, the Committee added, was 'at crying variance with the known and easily verifiable facts, attested to by the presidents of American universities at which Mr Russell has taught'.

A protest meeting was organised by the American Committee for Democracy and Intellectual Freedom at which the speakers included Professor Walter Rautenstrauch of Columbia, Professor Franz Boas, the anthropologist, Dean N. H. Dearborn of New York University, and the Rev. H. N. Sibley. At City College itself, where the students were apparently pretty corrupt even before Russell had a chance further to undermine their health and morals, a mass meeting was held in the Great Hall. A message of support came from one of the most illustrious graduates of the college, Upton Sinclair, who declared that the judge and the bishop had 'publicised the fact that England has loaned us one of the most learned and generous men of our time.' The advocates of sex dogmas, he concluded, 'should not be allowed to rob us of Bertrand Russell's services.' The main speakers at the meeting were Professors Bridge of the Department of Classical Languages, Wiener of the Philosophy Department, Morris of the History Department, and Lyman Bryson of Teachers College, Columbia. 'If publicly supported colleges are not to be as free as others,' Professor Bryson remarked, 'they have no hope whatever of playing an important part in the intellectual progress of our lives.' This last consideration would perhaps not weigh too heavily with Judge McGeehan, Bishop Manning and the Tammany scholars who supported their valiant efforts.

Corruption must have been rampant at the City College for many years prior to this whole affair. For the board of directors of the Associate Alumni of City College voted unanimously to urge the Board to take an appeal. This motion was introduced by Dr Samuel Schulman, rabbi emeritus of Temple Emanu-El, an organisation well known for its subversive activities. One of the eighteen directors supporting the resolution was Supreme Court Justice Bernhard Shientag, who perhaps had not been properly instructed in the doctrine of 'indirect' influence.

The fact that not all judges were as well versed in the Penal Law and had as profound a conception of academic freedom as McGeehan was also evident from certain events in California. On April 30, the removal of Bertrand Russell from his position at the University of California was demanded by Mr I. R. Wall, a former minister, who filed a writ of prohibition in the District Court of Appeals in Los Angeles. Mr Wall charged that Bertrand Russell's doctrines were 'subversive'. In California, unlike New York, the writ was immediately thrown out by the court.

## VII

It goes without saying that McGeehan's judgement was considered a deed of great heroism by Russell's enemies. The judge now became the object of lyrical hymns of praise in the journals of the inquisitors. 'He is an American, a virile and staunch American,' wrote the Jesuit weekly *America.* More than this, 'He is a pure and honorable jurist and ... rates among the best as an authority on law.' He also 'lives his religion, in mind and soul,' and 'well over six feet in height, he is brimming with wit and kindliness.' Nor were these his only virtues. Russell's charge that the judge was a 'very ignorant fellow' was quite untrue. A classical scholar, a man 'keen in mind and brilliant in scholarship ... he reads Homer in the original

Greek and enjoys Horace and Cicero in the original Latin.' Many other voices joined the Jesuit periodical in a chorus of adulation. One of these was Francis S. Moseley, president of a Catholic teachers' association, who called McGeehan's decision 'an epic chapter in the history of jurisprudence' and 'a great victory for the forces of decency and morality as well as a triumph for true academic freedom'. The *Tablet*, after demanding an investigation of Ordway Tead, Acting President Mead, and other revolutionaries responsible for Russell's appointment, editorially declared that 'the decision of Justice McGeehan ... carries a note of simplicity and sincerity that immediately wins acclaim.'

It must have become obvious by now that Russell was not the only malefactor who had to be punished. The majority of the Board of Higher Education were almost equally blameworthy, and suitable action against them had to be taken. At a meeting of the New York State Education Council, which I believe is generally considered part of the 'lunatic fringe' of right-wing politics in the United States, Professor John Dewey and Mrs Franklin D. Roosevelt were denounced for preaching tolerance ('a sickly anaemic thing') in the place of 'common decency' and 'fair play,' as exemplified, I assume, in McGeehan's procedure. At the same meeting, Lambert Fairchild, Chairman of the National Committee for Religious Recovery, denounced the majority of the Board of Higher Education who had favoured Russell's appointment as 'renegade Jews and renegade Christians', and urged their replacement by persons 'who still believe in their country and in religion'. Charles E. Keegan, the polite gentleman whom we met before when he referred to Russell as a 'dog' and a 'bum', raised the matter in the City Council. Comparing Russell with the 'fifth columns' that aided in Nazi victories and calling him an 'avowed Communist', he urged that the Board members who had persisted in their attempts to 'place Russell on the City College faculty' should be dismissed. He introduced a resolution calling on the Mayor to reorganise the Board and to appoint members who would serve the city 'more creditably'. This resolution was adopted by a vote of 14 to 5. It should be added, however, that the Mayor cannot simply dismiss the members of the Board, and Councilman Keegan's motion amounted to no more than a noble gesture.

In addition to preventing Russell's appointment and castigating the Board members who had favoured it, there remained the task of enlightening the public on the true nature of freedom – a subject on which many Americans had serious misconceptions, probably through the influence of such deluded heretics as Jefferson and

Paine. The McGeehan–Moseley conception had to be made known more widely. In this campaign of enlightenment Monsignor Francis W. Walsh, the 'pools of blood' orator, played a prominent part. Taking the rostrum once again at the Hotel Astor, this time at the annual communion breakfast of the New York Post Office Holy Name Society, he first alluded briefly to the epic court decision. The last time he stood on this platform, he said, 'I discussed a problem known to professors of mathematics as the matrimonial triangle. But since Q.E.D. has been written to that by the Hon. Justice John E. McGeehan, we will pass on to a related subject.' Msgr Walsh went on to discuss 'a very much abused word,' namely, 'liberty'. Since human beings, he said, 'can continue to exist only by obedience to the law of God – the law of nature, the law of the Ten Commandments – then in this America of ours no one shall be permitted in the name of liberty to scoff at the law of God. No one shall be permitted to stand on the platform of liberty in order to stab liberty in the back. And this applies to all Communists and their fellow-travellers, to all Nazis and Fascists who put the law of the State above the law of God, to college professors, publishers of books or anyone else within the territorial limits of the United States.' That Msgr Walsh had a right to be considered an expert on the abuse of the word 'liberty' can hardly be denied.

## VIII

This account would not be complete without a few words about the role of the *New York Times* in this affair. When religious pressure groups are not involved, the *Times* is usually quick to protest against abuses of power. In the Russell case the news coverage was, as always, fair and comprehensive. However, throughout the entire month of March, when Russell and the members of the Board of Higher Education were daily maligned in the most outrageous terms, the *Times* kept completely silent. For three weeks after the McGeehan judgement there was not a word of editorial comment. Finally, on April 20, the *Times* published a letter by Chancellor Chase of New York University, which pointed out some of the implications of McGeehan's action. 'The real question,' Mr Chase wrote, 'is now one which, so far as I know, has never before been raised in the history of higher education in America. It is whether, in an institution supported in whole or in part by public funds, a court, given a taxpayer's suit, has the power to void a faculty appointment on account of an individual's opinion ... If the jurisdiction of the court is upheld, a blow has been struck at the security and intellectual independence of every faculty member in every public college and university in the United States. Its potential consequences are incalculable.'

The *Times* now felt obliged to take a stand in an editorial on the subject. It opened with some general comments deploring the unfortunate effects of the controversy which had been aroused. The dispute over the appointment of Bertrand Russell, the *Times* wrote, 'has done great harm in this community. It has created a bitterness of feeling which we can ill afford when the democracy of which we are all a part is threatened on so many sides.' Mistakes of judgement, the editorial proceeded with an appearance of neutrality, had been made 'by all the principals involved. The original appointment of Bertrand Russell was impolitic and unwise; for wholly aside from the question of Bertrand Russell's scholarship and his merits as a teacher, it was certain from the outset that the sentiments of a substantial part of this community would be outraged by the opinions he had expressed on various moral questions.' Whether an appointment is 'politic' or 'impolitic' should apparently count more than the question of the teacher's competence and scholarship. This, surely, is a remarkable doctrine for a liberal newspaper to advocate.

As for McGeehan's decision, the *Times* could only say that it was 'dangerously broad'. The main indignation of the liberal newspaper was reserved neither for the judge who had abused his position nor for the mayor whose cowardly conduct I shall describe in a moment, but for the victim of the malicious assault, Bertrand Russell. Mr Russell himself, the *Times* stated, 'should have had the wisdom to withdraw from the appointment as soon as its harmful results became evident.' To this Russell replied in a letter published on April 26:

'I hope you will allow me to comment on your references to the controversy originating in my appointment to the College of the City of New York, and particularly on your judgement that I "should have had the wisdom to withdraw . . . as soon as the harmful results became evident."

'In one sense this would have been the wisest course; it would certainly have been more prudent as far as my personal interests are concerned, and a great deal pleasanter. If I had considered only my own interests and inclinations I should have retired at once. But however wise such action might have been from a personal point of view, it would also, in my judgement, have been cowardly and selfish. A great many people who realise that their own interests and the principles of toleration and free speech were at stake were anxious from the first to continue the controversy. If I had retired I should have robbed them of their *casus belli* and tacitly assented to the proposition of opposition that substantial groups shall be allowed to drive out of public office individuals whose opinions, race or nationality they find repugnant. This to me would appear immoral.

'It was my grandfather who brought about the repeal of the English Test and Corporation Acts, which barred from public office anyone not a member of the Church of England, of which he himself was a member, and one of my earliest and most important memories is of a deputation of Methodists and Wesleyans coming to cheer outside his window on the 50th anniversary of this repeal, although the largest single group affected was Catholic.

'I do not believe that controversy is harmful on general grounds. It is not controversy and open differences that endanger democracy. On the contrary, these are its greatest safeguards. It is an essential part of democracy that substantial groups, even majorities, should extend toleration to dissentient groups, however small and however much their sentiments may be outraged.

'In a democracy it is necessary that people should learn to endure having their sentiments outraged . . .'

At the conclusion of its editorial on April 20, the *Times* made a special point of supporting Chancellor Chase in the hope that McGeehan's judgement would be reviewed by the higher courts. Later, when such a review was artfully prevented by the joint efforts of the judge and Mayor LaGuardia, it did not utter a word of protest. So much for the record of the 'world's greatest newspaper' in this case.

### IX

When the McGeehan decision was made public, some of Russell's enemies were frightened that the courts would overrule it. Thus Alderman Lambert, after rejoicing in 'the great victory for the forces of decency', pointed out that the fight was not yet won. Showing his great respect for the independence of the judiciary, he added that 'decent citizens must show such a front that no court will dare reverse this decision.'

The Alderman's fears were quite unnecessary. Mayor LaGuardia and several members of the City Council went to work to make certain that even if the courts upheld an appeal against the McGeehan judgement, Russell could not be restored to his original post. The Mayor simply struck from the budget the appropriation for the lectureship to which Russell had been appointed. This he did in a particularly sneaky fashion. He published his executive budget without saying a word about this matter. A few days later reporters noted the elimination of the line in the budget. When asked about it, the Mayor gave the hypocritical answer that his action was 'in keeping with the policy to eliminate vacant positions.' Roger Baldwin, the director of the American Civil Liberties Union, thereupon sent the mayor a telegram in which he expressed what was in the minds of many observers. 'This action of negating the action of your Board of Higher Education,' he wrote, 'seems to us even more objectionable than the decision of Justice McGeehan upon his own prejudices.' The mayor's move was unprecedented and, in the opinion of experts, had no legal force, since school boards alone control any expenditure within their budgets.

It was not enough, however, to strike the appropriation for Russell's lectureship from the budget. Every avenue had to be closed. To make sure that Russell could not be appointed to some other position, Borough President Lyons introduced a resolution at the meeting of the Board of Estimate which was made part of the terms and conditions of the next budget. 'No funds herein appropriated,' the resolution said, 'shall be used for the employment of Bertrand Russell.'

These measures made it most unlikely that any appeal in the courts would result in Russell's actual reinstatement. Nevertheless, as a matter of principle, the majority of the Board of Higher Education decided to take the matter to the higher courts. At this stage Mr W. C. Chandler, the Corporation Counsel, informed the Board that he would not take an appeal. He shared the Board's opinion that the McGeehan decision was 'not legally sound' and even advised the Board that it could ignore the decision in making future appointments. In spite of this, he recommended that the case should not be pursued any further. Because of the 'religious and moral controversies' involved, the higher courts, he said, might confirm the decision. At the same time the Mayor announced that he fully 'supported' Mr Chandler's refusal to appeal. Perhaps 'inspired' would have been a more accurate term to use.

The majority of the Board now turned to private counsel, and the firm of Root, Clark, Buckner & Ballantine volunteered its services without fee. Mr Buckner was a former United States Attorney for the Southern District of New York, and he was assisted by Mr John H. Harlan. Basing himself on a number of precedents, Mr Harlan applied to Judge McGeehan to have his law firm substituted for the Corporation Counsel as legal representative of the Board. He also emphasised that the Board had not interposed a formal answer before McGeehan's ruling, and contended that it was entitled to have the decree vacated in order to do so. It will come as no surprise to the reader that the crusader found no merit in Mr Harlan's submission. He decided that the Corporation Counsel could not be replaced without his consent, and contemptuously referred to the majority of the Board as a 'disgruntled faction' which 'cannot now re-litigate what has already been adjudicated.' All appeals from *this* ruling were rejected by the higher courts, and since the Corporation Counsel refused to act, the Board was powerless to appeal against McGeehan's judgement revoking Russell's appointment.

After McGeehan's judgement had been published with its slanders on his character, Russell was advised to be represented by independent counsel. He retained Mr Osmond K. Fraenkel, who was suggested to him by the American Civil Liberties Union. Fraenkel on Russell's behalf, immediately applied to have Russell made a part to the proceeding. He also applied for permission to file an answer to Goldstein's scandalous charges. McGeehan denied the application on the ground that Russell had no 'legal interest' in the matter. This decision was taken by Mr Fraenkel to the Appellate Division of the Supreme Court, which unanimously upheld McGeehan without giving any reason for its action. Permission was then asked of the Appellate Division for carrying an appeal to the Court of Appeals, and this was denied. The few remaining legal moves open to Mr Fraenkel were similarly fruitless. It is astounding indeed that Mrs Kay, whose daughter could not have become a student of Bertand Russell's, had a legal interest in the case while Russell, whose reputation and livelihood were at stake, had none. Professor Cohen aptly remarked that 'if this is law, then surely in the language of Dickens "the law is an ass".'

In this way both the Board of Higher Education and Bertrand Russell himself were prevented from making an effective appeal, and the McGeehan judgement became final. 'As Americans,' said John Dewey, 'we can only blush with shame for this scar on our repute for fair play.'

x

From California Russell went to Harvard, whose President and Fellows had perhaps insufficiently taken to heart Judge McGeehan's pronouncement that Russell was 'not fit to teach in any of the schools of this land'. In reply to Thomas Dorgan they issued a statement saying that they had 'taken cognizance of the criticism of this appointment' but had concluded, after reviewing all the circumstances, that it was 'for the best interests of the University to reaffirm their decision and they had done so.' Russell's lectures at Harvard proceeded without any incidents, though I suppose that the statistics for rape and abduction were somewhat higher than usual. Russell then taught for several years at the Barnes Foundation in Merion, Pennsylvania. In 1944 he returned to England, where a few years later King George VI bestowed upon him the Order of Merit. This, I must say, showed regrettable indifference on the part of the British monarchy to the importance of the Penal Law.

In 1950 Russell delivered the Machette Lectures at Columbia University. He was given a rousing reception which those who were present are not likely to forget. It was compared with the acclaim received by Voltaire in 1784, on his return to Paris, the place where he had been imprisoned and from which he had later been banished. In 1950 also, a Swedish committee, whose standards were presumably 'lower than common decency requires', awarded Bertrand Russell the Nobel Prize for Literature. There were no comments from Mrs Kay, Mr Goldstein, or Judge McGeehan. At any rate, none have been published.

# Index

## THE AUTOBIOGRAPHY OF
## BERTRAND RUSSELL

'*Three passions, simple but overwhelmingly strong, have governed my life: the longing for love, the search for knowledge, and unbearable pity for the suffering of mankind. These passions, like great winds, have blown me hither and thither . . . over a deep ocean of anguish, reaching to the very verge of despair.*'

Thinker, philosopher, mathematician, educational innovator and experimenter, champion of intellectual, social and sexual freedom, campaigner for peace and for civil and human rights, Bertrand Russell led a life of incredible variety and richness. In keeping with his character and beliefs, his life-story is told with vigour, disarming charm and total frankness. His childhood was bitterly lonely but unusually rich in experience. His adult-life was spent grappling both with his own beliefs and the problems of the universe and mankind, and the pursuit of love and permanent happiness which resulted in no less than five marriages. The many storms and episodes of his life are recalled with the vivid freshness and clarity which characterised all Russell's writing and which make this perhaps the most moving literary self-portrait of the twentieth century.

'Among the most glittering literary products of the decade'
Bernard Levin

'These pages are by turns hilarious and deeply moving, sharp and beautiful . . . something better than a book in a million.'
Michael Foot